THE COMPLETE IDIOT'S GUIDE TO

Walt Disney World

2013 EDITION

by Doug Ingersoll

ALPHA

A member of Penguin Group (USA) Inc.

ALPHA BOOKS

Published by Penguin Group (USA) Inc.

Penguin Group (USA) Inc., 375 Hudson Street, New York, New York 10014, USA • Penguin Group (Canada), 90 Eglinton Avenue East, Suite 700, Toronto, Ontario M4P 2Y3, Canada (a division of Pearson Penguin Canada Inc.) • Penguin Books Ltd., 80 Strand, London WC2R 0RL, England • Penguin Ireland, 25 St. Stephen's Green, Dublin 2, Ireland (a division of Penguin Books Ltd.) • Penguin Group (Australia), 250 Camberwell Road, Camberwell, Victoria 3124, Australia (a division of Pearson Australia Group Pty. Ltd.) • Penguin Books India Pvt. Ltd., 11 Community Centre, Panchsheel Park, New Delhi—110 017, India • Penguin Group (NZ), 67 Apollo Drive, Rosedale, North Shore, Auckland 1311, New Zealand (a division of Pearson New Zealand Ltd.) • Penguin Books (South Africa) (Pty.) Ltd., 24 Sturdee Avenue, Rosebank, Johannesburg 2196, South Africa • Penguin Books Ltd., Registered Offices: 80 Strand, London WC2R 0RL, England

International Standard Book Number: 978-1-61564-251-9
Library of Congress Catalog Card Number: 2012944786

14 13 12   8 7 6 5 4 3 2 1

Interpretation of the printing code: The rightmost number of the first series of numbers is the year of the book's printing; the rightmost number of the second series of numbers is the number of the book's printing. For example, a printing code of 12-1 shows that the first printing occurred in 2012.

Printed in the United States of America

Note: This publication contains the opinions and ideas of its author. It is intended to provide helpful and informative material on the subject matter covered. It is sold with the understanding that the author and publisher are not engaged in rendering professional services in the book. If the reader requires personal assistance or advice, a competent professional should be consulted.

The author and publisher specifically disclaim any responsibility for any liability, loss, or risk, personal or otherwise, which is incurred as a consequence, directly or indirectly, of the use and application of any of the contents of this book.

Most Alpha books are available at special quantity discounts for bulk purchases for sales promotions, premiums, fund-raising, or educational use. Special books, or book excerpts, can also be created to fit specific needs.

For details, write: Special Markets, Alpha Books, 375 Hudson Street, New York, NY 10014.

Publisher: *Mike Sanders*

Executive Managing Editor: *Billy Fields*

Executive Editor: *Lori Cates Hand*

Development/Production/Copy Editor:
  Janette Lynn

Cover Designer: *Kurt Owens*

Book Designers: *William Thomas, Rebecca Batchelor*

Indexer: *Angie Bess Martin*

Layout: *Brian Massey*

Senior Proofreader: *Laura Caddell*

This book is dedicated to the Moms (and Dads) on the Walt Disney World Moms Panel. You continually impress and amaze me with your giving, thoughtful spirits and your joy of life. You make me proud to call myself a Mom. And to Dannée, our sunflower, you will be missed, but never forgotten.

Table of Maps

Contents

Appendixes

Introduction

So you're finally ready to take the plunge and plan a Walt Disney World vacation. You've probably known friends or family who have gone, and you may have heard the stories and thought that planning a vacation to the Magic Kingdom sounded like a daunting task.

First you start with the four theme parks, with more than 150 attractions. What do you visit, and what do you choose to skip? Then there are the hotels. Disney has dozens, and Orlando has hundreds more. Where do you stay? Restaurants cloud your thoughts next. With almost 100 Disney restaurants, which ones are best for feeding your crew? Then just when you think you might be able to figure it all out, there are the ticket systems, the vacation packages, transportation headaches, and so much more to consider. How will you ever get this done?

Easily, that's how. And I'm here to help. You can navigate the seeming madness of Walt Disney World with ease if you just have someone steering you on the right course. We tackle all those challenges together, and when you're done, you'll have a simple-to-follow plan for getting your party there, having a great time, keeping within a sensible budget, and then getting home with great memories.

So remember, the most enjoyable part of the vacation is in the planning. Let's have fun planning your Walt Disney World vacation!

How to Use This Book

The Complete Idiot's Guide to Walt Disney World is a quick, concise guide to planning and enjoying a vacation to Walt Disney World. You probably already have a day job, and it's not vacation planning! This book takes a different approach than most other Walt Disney World travel books. *The Complete Idiot's Guide to Walt Disney World* gives you the basic facts about your entertainment, accommodation, and dining choices. It gives you the essential information to decide whether they're right for you, without offering excessive details or other information that you don't need. The book then gives you a way to record your planning notes with Trip Cards and, in an exercise in ultimate portability, to carry them into the parks without having to take the book along.

The Complete Idiot's Guide to Walt Disney World is all about real people vacationing at Walt Disney World. The book is designed for total newcomers who have never been here before, for those who may have not visited the park since they were little kids, and also for more regular visitors who want to keep track of their visit plans without having to drag a guidebook along for the ride. But most important, it is for those who know they're sinking a lot of money into their vacation and want to ensure they get the most out of it, but don't want to dedicate all their free time to trip preparation.

Now comes the planning. In a few easy steps, you'll be ready to enjoy the wide range of fun that is Walt Disney World and leave knowing that you made the most of your time.

So what are these magical steps? The first is planning the broader details of your vacation, such as when you'll visit, what your budget is, and how you'll get to central Florida. This is covered in Part 1 of the book. The second step is to plan your vacation so that you know everyone in your group will have a great time and that you won't leave regretting the things you missed. This step is supported by Parts 2 through 5.

But the unique part of this book involves the cards and itineraries found in the back of the book. I have never liked lugging a book on vacation, and Walt Disney World is no exception. Guidebooks for Walt Disney World can run to more than 700 pages, and that kind of cement block is not one that I want to lug around. So I devised a system that lets you easily and quickly record your plans onto small cards you can keep in your wallet, purse, or pocket. Leave the book back in the room, knowing that you have all the answers that matter to you already in hand.

As you move through the book, you can easily record on these cards the attractions, restaurants, and activities that are a *Must Do!* experience, as well as those that just aren't a good stop for your group. You can keep track of important information like meal reservation confirmation numbers, flight plans, and hotel phone numbers. You even have itineraries for each theme park that help you navigate through them in a quick, enjoyable, and logical manner. All in your pocket!

HIDDEN MAGIC!

Have a trivia buff in your group? Buy them either of Lou Mongello's trivia books for a great array of information and secrets about Walt Disney World. Volumes I and II of *The Walt Disney World Trivia Book* are available at major resellers or his website, www.disneyworldtrivia.com.

How This Book Is Organized

The book is organized into five parts, along with three important appendixes. Let's look at these parts to see what they'll do for you.

Part 1: Plan Your Walt Disney World Trip

Chapters 1 through 5 set you to the task of planning the big details of your vacation. You start with a planning overview and then set your budget, arrange your transportation to Orlando, buy park tickets, and review some Walt Disney World–specific vacation strategies.

Part 2: Choose Your Castle: Picking Your Resort Hotel

Now that you have your big picture set, Part 2 helps you determine where you'll stay. With a focus on the Disney resort hotels, Chapters 6 through 11 help you figure out what hotel has the right room rates, theme, location, and amenities to make your stay the best one possible.

Part 3: Feast Like Royalty: Dining at Walt Disney World

Eating at Walt Disney World is more than just filling your stomach. Bringing a new definition to entertainment dining, Disney has made your meal plans about more than cost and cuisine. Chapters 12 through 15 offer reviews of the dining and snack choices found in and around Walt Disney World.

Part 4: Bring on the Entertainment: The Theme Parks

Part 4 is what your whole vacation is all about: the Disney theme parks. Chapters 16 through 20 walk you through the four theme parks, complete with attraction ratings that will tell you what rides are appropriate for different age groups.

Part 5: The Rest of the Kingdom and Beyond

Disney has a lot more to offer than just the four parks, and here is where I explore those diversions. In Chapters 21 through 24, I cover the Disney nightlife, water parks, and other facilities, as well as some of the major non-Disney Orlando-area attractions, including competitive theme parks.

Appendixes

In the first two appendixes are the tools that bring it all together. The Itineraries and Trip Cards are the portable cards that you will take with you, providing a record of your preferences and reminding you what you want to do. The third appendix gives you a picture preview of some of the wonderful accommodations found at Walt Disney World.

Trip Planning

So how do you use the book to plan your vacation? Here are the basics.

Step 1: Plan the big details. Use Chapter 1 to figure out some of the big-picture details of your trip—namely, pick the time of year that you plan on visiting, and figure out how you plan to get there.

Step 2: Set your budget. Chapter 2 guides you through this. Set your budget for transportation, accommodations, dining, tickets and other entertainment, and incidentals. As you continue to go through the book, you can go back and adjust the budget so that you keep your wallet happy!

Step 3: Pick your hotel. With your budget now in mind, you can move to the task of selecting your accommodations. Start by deciding whether you want to stay at a Disney resort and then select the price class of hotel. From that class, you can pick the resort that you think best matches your group's needs.

Step 4: Plan your daily details. Decide what you'll do on each day of your trip, select restaurants for your meals, and work out your overall plan.

Step 5: Fill out your Trip Cards and Itineraries. Keep the cards in the back of the book handy as you read through the four theme park chapters. As you read those chapters, simply put a check in the box next to attractions that you're sure you want to try. If you decide that you don't want to try an attraction, place an X in that box. Leave the other boxes clear so you know that these rides are "maybes."

When it's time to go to the park, take the cards with you. You now know what rides you want to try and those you want to avoid—and when you have some free time, you can try one of the "maybes."

A theme park Trip Card.

Appendix A offers you a series of one-day and a few half-day theme park itineraries. These itineraries basically walk you through the park, showing you a sensible route that takes you through efficiently. You can use these with or in place of the cards. Check the rides on the itinerary that you intend to visit, and cross off those that are undesirable. Then when you enter the park, you have a blueprint for how to navigate the park to maximize your fun.

Hollywood Studios with Children Itinerary

☐ Pick up FASTPASS vouchers for any attraction that most appeals to you. Redeem them whenever they become valid, then seek out your next FASTPASS.

MICKEY AVENUE/ PIXAR PLACE

☐ (1) Toy Story Mania! AC FP

☐ (2) *Voyage of the Little Mermaid* FP AC

☐ (3) *Disney Junior—Live on Stage* AC

☐ (4) The Magic of Disney Imagination AC

Other Choices

☐ Hollywood Studios Backlot Tour

☐ The American Film Institute Showcase AC

☐ Walt Disney: One Man's Dream AC

STREETS OF AMERICA

☐ (5) *Lights, Motors, Action! Extreme Stunt Show* FP

☐ (6) *Jim Henson's Muppet Vision 3-D* AC

☐ (7) *Honey, I Shrunk the Kids* Movie Set Adventure

ECHO LAKE

☐ (8) *The American Idol Experience* AC

VINE STREET

☐ (9) *Indiana Jones Epic Stunt Spectacular* FP

Other Choices

☐ Star Tours FP AC fi -40"

☐ *Sounds Dangerous—Starring Drew Carey* AC OO

HOLLYWOOD BOULEVARD

☐ (10) The Great Movie Ride AC

Other Choices

☐ *Pixar Pals Countdown to Fun*

SUNSET BOULEVARD

☐ (11) *Beauty and the Beast—Live on Stage*

Other Choices

☐ Rock 'n' Roller Coaster Starring Aerosmith FP AC OO fi -48"

☐ The Twilight Zone Tower of Terror FP AC OO fi -40"

☐ *Fantasmic!*

A theme park Itinerary.

Understanding the Reviews

As we go through the book, we review attractions, restaurants, and hotels. Each review has different information that will help you decide what is the best hotel, meal, or ride for your group. Here's how you can easily use those to find out your best choices.

Hotel Reviews

It's time to look at your accommodation options. Part 2 reviews a variety of resort options. For the Disney resorts, I have provided some standardized information, including the following:

Overall Rating

The star ratings are intended to give you a general gauge of the resorts and how they compare. The overall score rates a resort for the hotel's features, amenities, appeal, and atmosphere. Although cost is taken somewhat into account, it is pretty secondary because you can always judge that element of the resort by looking at the price range. Star ratings range from 0 (worst) to 5 (best).

★ = Full star   ☆ = Half star

Location

The general location of the resort is identified. The areas within Walt Disney World are as follows:

- Animal Kingdom area
- Downtown Disney area
- Epcot area
- Magic Kingdom area

Price Range

General prices shown are for one night in a standard room, ranging from the least expensive to the most expensive resort seasons from 2012. With villas and campgrounds, multiple room type categories are compared.

Transportation

This is a review of the on-property transportation provided.

Special Features

This section provides an overview of some of the special amenities or resort features that distinguish it from other resorts at Walt Disney World.

Room Types

The standard room is described, with attention to bed types and arrangements. Of course, most resorts have special suites, so check with them if you're looking for something different.

Best Room Locations

This section identifies the more preferential room locations in a resort for you to request. Although the best room locations in most resorts will cost you a premium, some may not cost you extra, so try to get your room located accordingly, to improve your vacation stay.

Dining

An overview of the dining options in the resort is provided.

Atmosphere

This final section provides a more broad description of the ambiance, quality, and general appeal of the resort. The theme is explained, and some of the special features are elaborated on.

Restaurant Reviews

Part 3 reviews the restaurants in the parks, in the resorts, and elsewhere in Walt Disney World. The reviews include the following elements.

Cuisine Type

Restaurants are identified for cuisine types. Be aware that some establishments with otherwise exotic-sounding names may still just be serving standard American fare, so read carefully.

Serving Style

Restaurants in the Magic Kingdom all have different serving styles, so these describe the formats for ordering and service:

- **À la carte**—This is the standard restaurant ordering format, with you selecting items from a menu. Prix fixe menus are listed as à la carte as well, although that distinction is made later in the review.

- **Family style**—Food is served to the entire table as a group, even if there's more than one family/group there. This is a very good way to meet people and is used often at dinner show establishments.

- **Buffet**—The buffets here are pretty darn good, so don't let the designation turn you off.

Meal Listings

The next review elements list the key meals of the day, providing unique information for each. Breakfast, lunch, dinner, and, where appropriate, high tea are each rated for cost and other features. The ♛ icon means that, for that meal, the restaurant is hosting a character meal. The price range represents the per-adult cost for a buffet, or for an appetizer and an entrée.

$ = $10 to $20
$ $ = $21 to $30
$ $ $ = $31 to $40
$ $ $ $ = $41 or more

Finally, if a menu has a prix fixe menu, that is listed here.

D This indicates whether a restaurant participates in the Disney Dining Plan. If the meal will cost you two table-service credits for one meal, the symbol is followed by the number 2. For more information on the Disney Dining Plan, see Chapter 12.

Rating

The restaurant then is rated for its cuisine, appeal, and atmosphere. The star ratings range from 0 (worst) to 5 (best) and take into account food quality, general experience, entertainment, and atmosphere.

Description

The description gives you some idea of the nature of the restaurant, including the theme and atmosphere. If the menu includes a real "wow" item, it's listed here. Finally, this area can give you an idea of whether a restaurant is the right place for your romantic soiree, big family gathering, quiet night out, or other kind of dining experience.

Attraction Reviews

So what rides should you go on? That's what the ride ratings are for! All the attraction reviews in *The Complete Idiot's Guide to Walt Disney World* start with a few symbols that tell you some important information, including any height requirements, whether it has the FASTPASS advance-ticket system, and whether it is one of my *Must Do!* recommendations. I also identify those attractions that are mostly air-conditioned so that you can get out of the hot Florida sun, if needed.

Next, the ride type is identified so that you can get an idea of what kind of attraction it is. This lets you know, for example, whether it's a thrill ride, like a roller coaster, or a stage show.

After this, I provide a ride description and what you can expect. This is intended to paint you a picture of the attraction but does not spoil any of the surprises.

Finally, the review ends with an age-appropriate ratings system that shows what other guests, from a variety of age perspectives, thought about the rides. Ratings are listed for typical tots, young children, teens, adults, and seniors, with each group having a rating score of 0 to 5.

Symbols

The symbols next to the attraction name tell you some important information:

- 🔲 This is a *Must Do!* attraction—a ride that I think everyone visiting Walt Disney World *must* try. Now of course, some rides may not be suited for your particular group for one reason or another, so by all means, in that case feel free to pass. But for most guests, I liken it to the Eiffel Tower: you wouldn't consider taking a vacation to Paris without seeing it. It's just something everyone has to do!

- **FP** This symbol means that the attraction uses the FASTPASS advance-ticket system. This system is explained in greater detail later in the book, but basically it allows you to gain faster access to the ride later in the day, saving time in line so you can do something else in the park.

- **AC** The symbol tells you that the attraction is air conditioned.

- 🈺 Some rides have height requirements for safety. Some even have height restrictions that work in reverse, allowing only someone under a certain height in, to keep play areas reserved for smaller children. This symbol is paired with a number in inches for that height restriction.

- 👀 Some children are afraid of the dark, and rather than traumatize them, you can know ahead of time to avoid that attraction. Many rides have brief moments of darkness, but I put this only on attractions with a significant period of darkness.

Ride Types

You'll want to know what an attraction is all about, including what category it falls under. Here are the types:

- **Experience Area/Playground**—This includes playgrounds, exhibits, and any area where simply exploring the buildings is an attraction unto itself. Examples like the wildlife trails at the Animal Kingdom, the Epcot World Showcase pavilions, and Cinderella Castle at the Magic Kingdom show you that hopping on a ride car is not the only way to have fun.

- **Theater/Movie/Show**—Disney has developed numerous types of shows. This catchall category covers live theater, movies, 3-D movies, interactive cartoons, and other shows.

- **Parade/Fireworks**—This category is pretty self-explanatory, but know that these shows sometimes include theater seating.

- **Character Experience**—This category includes meeting the Disney characters, getting their autographs, and taking pictures that you'll cherish forever.

- **Theme Ride**—This category includes rides that might offer some suspense but are not the roller-coaster rides that some might choose to avoid. They're not all necessarily for guests of all ages, but they carry a central theme and can be fun, scenic, educational, and, in some cases, exciting.

- **Thrill Ride**—This category includes thrill rides. Not all of the attractions in this category are roller coasters. Some are simulation rides, others are multimedia presentations, and almost all are top draws—plan accordingly.

- **Carnival Attraction**—This category includes rides much like the ones you'd find on the state fair midway back home. However, at Disney World, they're clean and well maintained, and have a professional staff operating them.

Ratings

After the general ride description, you can view the age ratings. These ratings range from 0 (worst) to 5 (best) and are divided roughly into age groups. Remember that some 50-year-olds are far more daring than some 20-somethings, and there are 30-year-olds who grow excited over thrills a 7-year-old wouldn't even blink at. So take no offense at the age generalizations—pick the group that best symbolizes your attraction interest, and choose your rides! The age groups are listed here:

- Tots, up to 6 years old
- Young children, age 7 to 12 years old
- Teens, age 13 to 19 years old
- Young adults, age 20 to 50 years old
- Mature adults, age 50 and older

Tots	Young Children	Teens	Young Adults	Mature Adults

Things to Help You Along the Way

These special sections give you some information that can help you avoid vacation woes; find some special, little-known experiences; or explain some cryptic Disney lingo you may not understand.

HIDDEN MAGIC!

Discover a less traveled secret of Walt Disney World that can make your visit more special.

MICKEY-SPEAK

Master the Disney lingo so you can better understand what everyone is talking about!

DID YOU KNOW?

Absorb these seldom-known facts that can make the trip more interesting.

DISNEY DON'T

Follow these simple warnings to avoid a vacation headache.

Summary

Well, that should do it. The book is supposed to be simple, so if you follow the simple steps to planning listed within, you should be able to have an enjoyable, relaxing, and memorable vacation!

Acknowledgments

The only constant at Walt Disney World is change. Every time I think that the yearly updates will be a few price changes and little more, I get amazed by all the wonderful new dining and entertainment options being added to this magical place.

I would not be able to keep up with it all if not surrounded by a wonderful world of Disney enthusiasts that, like me, love this place. I always start with my sisters (and brothers) on the Walt Disney World Moms Panel (www.disneyworldmoms.com), to whom this book is dedicated. Thank you for letting me be the "ugly mom" and making me feel like one of the gals.

To others in the community, like Sara Varney (my travel agent!), Lou Mongello, Deb Wills, the podcast teams at the DIS Unplugged (SPOOKTACULAR!) and WDW Today, thanks for keeping love of Walt alive.

Thanks also go to the team at Disney that make me feel like a superstar, even though I am not. Thanks to Bebee Frost, Leanne Jakubowski, Laura Spencer, Jennifer Wilkes, Joyce Hogan, Karen Prince, and Gary Buchanan (Gary/Jerry?).

I love my publishers at Alpha, especially my new editor Lori Hand. She, along with Mike, Jill, Kurt (perge!), Jan (YAN!), and Dawn make this book happen.

Thanks as always to family and friends who indulge me by letting me help plan their trips, and report back on their experiences. You are in here, even if you don't see your names.

And to the constant that makes me live: the wonderful women in my life. Mom, who inspired my love of Disney, Abby and Annie who feed that love, and Tracy who supports it, even when it gets expensive and extreme.

T, you know I adore you.

Plan Your Walt Disney World Trip

A Walt Disney World vacation is not just a significant expense. It also requires an unusually higher level of planning than most trips. You still have all the usual travel plans to make: airfare, hotel, etc. However, in addition you have new challenges: character meals to schedule, theme park tickets to select, vacation plans to compare, and more. In Part 1, I help you part the fog and see the trip planning as a series of easy, manageable steps, from setting a budget to selecting ticket packages and planning out your stay. Ready?

How to Plan Your Trip

In This Chapter

- Figure out when you should go to Walt Disney World
- Learn how crowded, expensive, and hot it will be during your visit
- Plan your vacation

Planning is a required element to a Walt Disney World vacation. But it doesn't have to be a long-term headache, and it can even be fun if you let it. In this chapter, I walk you through a basic overview of the planning that you should do for your trip. I start with information about how weather, costs, and crowd sizes differ throughout the year, and then review the simple steps needed to plan out your adventure. After reading this chapter, you should have a good idea of your trip particulars.

When Should You Go?

I always start my planning for a trip to Walt Disney World by determining when I'll be going. With most groups, determining the time of year is the necessary first step because so many schedules have to be coordinated. You may not have much of a choice about when you are going, but if you have some flexibility, it's worth considering a few different scenarios to see what works best for you. Naturally, the time of year has an impact on the crowd size, weather, and overall cost of your vacation. So let's look at what different times of year will mean for your vacation.

Fireworks at the Magic Kingdom.
Photo © Disney.

Weather Throughout the Year

The good news is that the weather in Orlando is pretty good year round, averaging 73°F. It may not be shorts–and–T-shirt weather all 12 months long, though; it can get pretty hot and humid at times. For the most part, however, it's very pleasant. Let's look at the climate more closely, starting with the temperature and rainfall. Consider the high temps as your guide to what to wear during the day, and the lows as an indicator to what kind of jacket you might need in the evening.

What you can't read from the numbers is that summers get more than just hot—they get humid, too. From May to September, the humidity reaches a peak that you should prepare for. Ensure that you pace yourself during the midday heat and that you drink plenty of water.

On the other end of the spectrum, you need to be sure to bring a light jacket or sweater during the cooler months because the nights get colder than you might anticipate.

HIDDEN MAGIC!

In the listings in this book and on the Trip Cards in back, the air-conditioned attractions have an **AC** symbol next to them so you can retreat from the heat.

Rain is another issue. Rainfall levels start to pick up in June and average 5 to 7 inches through September. Even so, the rain comes during the warmer months, when Mother Nature will help you dry off, so it shouldn't totally ruin your fun. You may want to consider bringing some ponchos with you if you're coming during the monsoon season; otherwise, you'll have to buy them here for upward of $10. You will probably need them for one of the water rides, so plan ahead and save some money.

Temperatures and Rainfall in Orlando, Florida[1]

Month	High	Average	Low	Rain (in inches)
January	71.8	60.9	49.9	2.43
February	73.9	62.6	51.3	2.35
March	78.8	67.4	55.9	3.54
April	83.0	71.5	59.9	2.42
May	88.2	77.1	65.9	3.74
June	91.0	81.2	71.3	7.35
July	92.2	82.4	72.6	7.15
August	92.0	82.5	73.0	6.25
September	90.3	81.1	71.9	5.76
October	85.0	75.3	66.5	2.73
November	78.9	68.8	58.7	2.32
December	73.3	63.0	52.6	2.31

[1]*Temperature and rainfall data comes from the National Oceanic and Atmospheric Administration's National Weather Service website (www.nws.noaa.gov).*

Crowds Throughout the Year

When Walt Disney World is busy, it's packed. The very busiest times have crowds that can ruin your time. Long lines, high-stress levels, missed attractions and parades, long transportation waits—all of these can happen, making for a less than magical time.

You can avoid crowds, and it's not always a packed house, so don't worry that you'll have to face such hardships. So when *is* it most crowded?

The basic rule of thumb for why one time is busier than another revolves largely around school vacations. If kids are out of school, Walt Disney World is busy. If they're in session, the parks get lighter. Another gauge for when the parks are busiest is the Disney resort room rate seasons.

You can see these rate seasons in more detail in the Walt Disney World Resorts chapter.

HIDDEN MAGIC!

Are you a podcast enthusiast? These popular new downloadable audio programs from iTunes are a great way to get information on recent changes at the parks. Several podcasts are dedicated to Walt Disney World. Here are four of my favorites:

WDW Today—This panel is fun to listen to, offering shorter broadcasts focused on single topics.

The DIS Unplugged—A panel that actually meets in person in Orlando for a great family vibe, they pick topics from their popular DIS Forums to make their shows more relevant.

Be Our Guest Podcast—Another fun panel with an enthusiastic energy, this panel discusses how to stretch your dollars at Walt Disney World with a more realistic eye to what most of us can really afford.

The WDW Radio Show—Host Lou Mongello reviews all that is important regarding Walt Disney World and Disney in this longer, more in-depth show.

Bringing It All Together

Let's look at all these factors together. In the following chart, you will see the rate seasons, the high and low temperatures you can expect, when the rainy season hits, and what kind of general crowd sizes you can plan to contend with. The crowd size graph and the resort rate line are charted to four weeks per month, but be aware that the dates that holidays like Christmas and President's Day fall on will affect these slightly.

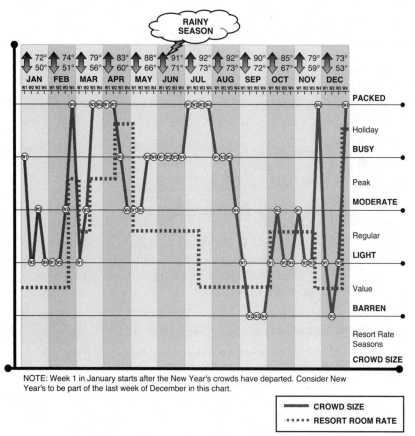

NOTE: Week 1 in January starts after the New Year's crowds have departed. Consider New Year's to be part of the last week of December in this chart.

Annual chart of crowd sizes, resort rates, and weather.

Special Events Throughout the Year

Walt Disney World hosts numerous special events throughout the year. Here I list just a few of the bigger ones. Once you know when you're planning to attend, be sure to check the Walt Disney World website to get exact dates and see what else might be going on when you are there. Although these events can get mobbed, they also offer some great activities, food, and entertainment that make it well worth dealing with the crowds.

- January: Walt Disney World Marathon
- March: Atlanta Braves Spring Training
- April/May/June: Epcot International Flower and Garden Festival
- May/June: *Star Wars* Weekends
- September: Night of Joy
- October: Mickey's Not-So-Scary Halloween Party
- October/November: International Food and Wine Festival
- November/December/January: Osborne Family Spectacle of Lights
- December: Mickey's Very Merry Christmas Party, Holidays Around the World

Time of Year: The Bottom Line

So now you know when Walt Disney World is at its busiest and when it's slow. You know how hot, cool, or wet it might get. You even have an eye to what major events might be going on while you're there. But when should you actually go?

DID YOU KNOW?

Another large gathering to be aware of at Walt Disney World is the annual Gay Days. This event is not affiliated with Disney World, but it certainly packs the Orlando parks and hotels, with more than 130,000 mostly gay and lesbian attendees. This weeklong get-together is usually held in early June, always taking place the first Saturday of the month. You can pinpoint the dates by going to www.gaydays.com.

Obviously, you might have your travel time of year chosen for you by work considerations, school vacation schedules, or other personal life issues. But if you have some flexibility, here are my personal suggestions:

- September is my favorite time to visit. Why? The weather is still of the summer variety that I expect when I think of a Florida vacation. The crowds are lighter, and the resort rates are at their lowest. Free dining packages have made it even more attractive, but also a bit more crowded.

- My second choice is anytime in October. It's only a bit cooler than September, and has a mild Halloween vibe that kids love later in the month. Plus I love the Food & Wine Festival!

- My next choice is the first three weeks of May. The weather is good, the rates are higher than in September but still pretty decent, and the crowds are still manageable.

- If your schedule places you at Walt Disney World during a packed crowd time, that doesn't mean you won't enjoy yourself. It just means that you might not get to ride as many attractions and that you have to do more advance meal planning. Besides, there's a reason why so many people visit at that time. Some of those reasons, like holiday decorations, could be the element that makes your trip extra special.

- When the parks are barren, it's a ride enthusiast's dream, but the atmosphere is not as fun as I prefer it. Also, Disney closes many attractions for repairs, so you may not get to see everything you hoped.

- Disney has really worked on getting crowd sizes up during the slower times of the year, with discount vacation packages and special events. Don't be surprised by large crowds at any time of the year.

Making the Big Decisions

I always suggest making a plan well in advance. Because there's more advance reservation planning in a Disney vacation than for most other vacations, the sooner you make your trip reservations, the sooner you can get to the other important steps of making meal reservations, planning special activities, and doing other last-minute trip adjustments. You have to plan for a few important considerations before calling your travel agent or logging on to the internet to make your reservation. Later chapters in this book help with those decisions, but to summarize, here they are:

- Establish your budget (see Chapter 2). Disney trips are rarely cheap, so you'll want to determine how much you can afford so that you can pick the right transportation to Florida, a hotel in your price range, tickets, and more. Use the guide in Chapter 2 as you go along to make sure you don't have to take out a second mortgage just to visit Mickey Mouse.

- Plan your transportation (see Chapter 3). Determine how you'll get to the Orlando area and then how you'll move around, whether it is by cab, rental car, bus, or other kind of transportation solution.

- Decide on tickets (see Chapter 4). Figure out what kind of theme park ticket package is right for your group and how best to buy it.

- Select your accommodations (see Chapters 6–11). Pick your temporary home at Walt Disney World, selecting that perfect place that fits your budget as well as your group's resort stay needs.

When you have all of these items planned out, it's time to make those reservations. Book your flights or plan your driving route to Orlando. Reserve your room and order your tickets. After that, you can get into the real fun of Walt Disney World vacation planning, as you delve into the daily details of what you'll see, where you'll eat, and how you'll experience the greatest vacation destination in the world!

Making Your Reservations

With whom should you make your reservations? There are numerous avenues to do this, and no single one is the right solution for all parties. Should you buy everything separately? Should you buy a package?

Where to Buy

If you're making your trip reservation directly with Disney, make sure you call them. It may be convenient to make the reservation on the website, but it doesn't pick up on all the specials that might be available. If you call them (407-939-7675), you can ask about any specials they may offer. On one trip they saved me $300 over the online price.

What about travel agents? There's no reason not to consider this option; a knowledgeable agent can be of great help. Keep an eye out for offers in your local newspaper, and see if any of your neighborhood agents are specialists in Disney trips. Or you could go with a national agent, like Mouse Fan Travel or Dreams Unlimited, who are specialists in Disney trips. They, like select others, are Authorized Disney Vacation Planners. There are also good deals to be had from AAA, AARP, and other similar organizations.

Bottom line: The most important thing is to look at a few offers and compare them to see which package best meets your needs for the least amount of money. I have found some great deals by dealing with Disney directly, but I know exactly what I need and how to get it. Lately, I have begun to see the light about working with agencies which are Authorized Disney Vacation Planners. Don't skip the important step of looking at good offers from travel service companies; they may have something good to offer.

Why work with an Authorized Disney Vacation Planner? Well, it's a good idea if you want to save time and money. Interested? Beci Mahnken of Mouse Fan Travel, an Authorized Disney Vacation Planner, is well known in the world of Walt Disney World enthusiasts. When you work with one of her agents, you get some great benefits, including:

- **No Fees.** They are a fee-free agency that makes their money from Disney, and that adds nothing to the cost of the vacation to you. This is *extremely* important, as many travel agents charge a fee, and you don't always know about it up front.

- **Discounts.** Obviously, Mouse Fan Travel applies any discounts available when you book your trip. But even after you have booked your trip through them, if a better discount comes along, they apply it to your trip and you save even more money. And because they are dialed in to all things Disney, they know of pretty much every promotion.

- **Dining and activity reservations.** Tell them your dining or activity wishes and they will work to get those reservations for you. When you get to the dining chapters in Part 3 and read about the Advance Dining Reservations system at Walt Disney World, you will know that this will take a huge amount of work off of your trip planning load.

- **Special events.** Mouse Fan Travel gets access to select special events, and can get you into some fun activities that you may never have found on your own.

- **Disney Cruise Line.** They are experts here, too, so you can look to them to help with these plans as well!

- **Advice.** They can provide specific advice particular to your group—it's like having a guidebook, but isn't reading my book more fun?

To give you an idea of how much I feel these agents can be of good value to you, I plan on using an agency for my next trip. Safe to say, I know what I am doing when it comes to traveling to Walt Disney World, and I know that using them is my best option. They can be found at www.mousefantravel.com.

What to Buy

As you read this book, you'll find out what elements you will need to buy and what other costs you may incur. From theme park tickets (see Chapter 4) to food costs (see Chapters 12–15) and more, you'll need to spend some of your hard-earned money in plenty of places. Chapter 2 helps you figure out just what all that is and how much you should spend.

Daily Planning

Now that you have your general vacation dates planned, let's get into the daily details. Take out your Weekly Schedule Card from Appendix B and start to fill in the blanks as you develop your plan.

Step 1: What Park on What Day?

You will find in the Vacations Strategy chapter a section on how to plan which park you visit on which day. It also speaks to what to do on your arrival and departure days as well, if parks are not going to be involved. However, there are a few things to remember:

- Make sure you plan enough relaxation afternoons for children in your group. Naps or pool time can help kids stay well rested and energized for the rest of the trip.

- Just because there are four parks doesn't mean you *have* to visit each one. If you have a three- and a five-year-old, you probably will want to visit the Magic Kingdom more than once, even if at the expense of seeing one of the other parks.

- If you have a dinner show planned in the evening, make sure that you give yourself enough time to get back to your resort to change or freshen up, and then enough time to get there early.

DID YOU KNOW?

Several websites are dedicated to Walt Disney World. If you're looking to get even more in-depth trip information, you should visit these:

www.disneyworld.com—Get the official word on what times parks are open, what rides will be closed for repairs, and just about anything else.

www.disneyworldmoms.com—Part of the Walt Disney World website, you will find a panel of real moms, dads, and grandparents who can answer any of your vacation planning questions. They are not Disney employees, but impartial lovers of Disney World who can answer your specific questions as based on their own real experiences.

www.allears.net—This is a great place to view resort photos, look up restaurant menus, and get reviews on just about everything. Of special note is that you can view photos of the attraction seating available for special-needs guests. This website is run by Deb Wills, who is also the author of *PassPorter's Walt Disney World for Your Special Needs.*

Step 2: What Meals?

Now that you know where you'll be each day, it's time to figure out your dining schedule. Review the chapters in Part 3 to find out where you want to eat. Then call the Walt Disney World dining reservation line to make your advance reservations (407-WDW-DINE, or 407-939-3463). You can make reservations up to 180 days ahead of time, and certain reservations will get filled up on that very first day, so make sure you plan to call on that first day! Jot down your reservation information on the Meal Reservation Card from Appendix B, and put the restaurant name in your Weekly Schedule Card as well.

Step 3: Plan Your Evenings

If you're not planning to be at a theme park in the evening, you might also consider your nighttime plans. Here are some thoughts:

- If you're at a dinner show, plan on letting that carry your evening plans.

- Consider a night each at Downtown Disney and the BoardWalk.

- Don't plan every evening if you have kids. Let a few nights be calmer experiences back at your hotel, with early nights in.

DID YOU KNOW?

If you have special plans, such as wedding-vow renewals, a fishing excursion, or a round of golf, consider making those reservations as soon as possible. Remember, this is the busiest vacation destination in the world. If you thought of doing something, so did a lot of other people!

Selecting Day-by-Day Activities

What are you going to do at each park? Obviously, you have the park cards in Appendix B to remind you of what rides you want to try and those you want to skip. But if you're still looking for a bit more guidance, you can look to the itineraries in Appendix A.

These itineraries are divided into ones for groups with children and groups without children. You have one-day itineraries for each of the parks, which give you a general recommended route through the park that should help you miss the bigger crowds somewhat.

Summary

When you're done with Part 1, you'll have your entire big-picture planning done and you can start dreaming about all the food, accommodations, and entertainment fun that Walt Disney World has to offer.

Establishing Your Budget

In This Chapter

- Plan your vacation's travel budget
- Figure out what the key elements will cost
- Get an idea of the hidden costs and savings for each budget line item

Ugh, nobody wants to talk about money. But if you spend just a few minutes planning out what you can afford up front, you can spend the rest of the trip enjoying yourself without worrying about what you're going to owe on your credit card when you get home.

On the budget spreadsheet later in this chapter, there's room for you to plan your costs. I have also put in the costs for a fictional family so that you have a framework for comparison. Be aware that I used fairly conservative costs for this model, showing you the high-end cost. However, there are certainly special vacation offers to be had, so know that this is not the basement price. It simply is an example to help you envision typical expenses and identify areas where you might work to find lower costs. So who is this mythical family?

Example Family

Here are the fictional family stats:

- Two adults, two children ages 6 and 8
- Flying to Orlando for six nights and seven days
- Going to the parks for six days, with no options
- Staying at a Disney Value resort

- Using the Standard Disney Dining Plan
- Planning a stay during September (a Value season)
- Assuming no special promotions (though plenty are out there!)

Disney has three age classifications:

- Infants under the age of 3
- Children from 3 to 9 years old
- Adults age 10 and over

For our example we have two adults and two children, but remember that if you had an 11 year old with you, the prices would be like having 3 adults and 1 child.

Also know that kids under 3 get to do many, if not most, things for free. This is the first way you may find your overall costs lowering from the one that we have in our fictional budget.

Remember that you can go for a shorter stay, so don't let the total at the bottom scare you off. Plenty of vacation deals can drop the price. The budget helps you gauge whether the offers you hear are worth your time. Where appropriate, I've also outlined some hidden costs and hidden savings that can influence the bottom line.

Transportation

In a recent survey of airfare from four U.S. cities (New York City, Charlotte, Indianapolis, and Des Moines), the price ranged from $650 to $850 for our family of four, with an average of $740. Considering price changes due to time of year and city of origin, at these rates, you can assume that airfare will cost approximately $200 per person, with West Coast departures adding another $100 per person or more to the total. We have assumed for our planning that the family will use the *Disney Magical Express* system. We also assume $10 per day for parking at the family's home airport.

MICKEY-SPEAK

Disney Magical Express is a free bus service from Orlando International Airport to Disney resorts exclusively for guests at those resorts. It is explained in greater detail in Chapter 3.

If you will drive instead, insert the estimated gas usage, as well as any overnight stays on the way that you may take. Don't underestimate the advantage of driving to Disney and having the freedom that your own car provides.

> **Bottom Line:** $740 (airfare) + $70 (airport parking) = $810

> **Hidden Cost:** Airport parking at your home city, airline bag check fees. Most travelers forget to take these into account.

> **Hidden Savings:** A little price shopping can get you a lower airfare bill.

Accommodations

Our family of four will stay in a single room at a Value resort. More expensive resorts offer greater accommodations and services, but the Value hotels are nothing to sneeze at.

> **Bottom Line:** $607.00

> **Hidden Costs:** Off-property hotels offer larger rooms with more amenities for the same or lower charges.

> **Hidden Savings:** You are on property, so buses are free, and you're closer to the parks and get all the benefits of staying here, including extra park hours that are exclusively for resort guests as well as the Disney Magical Express.

Tickets

Walt Disney World tickets are not a simple one-ticket, one-day purchase situation. You have worlds of options, all covered in Chapter 4. For now, assume that our family of four will just get basic Magic Your Way tickets for six days, assuming that they cannot use park access on their arrival day.

> **Bottom Line:** $1,076.00

> **Hidden Costs:** Park hopping or water park features add to the price of the tickets, and hotel surcharges increase the cost.

> **Hidden Savings:** For our family of four, it is likely they would not have the time to visit a park on their departure date either, reducing the tickets to five days, and lowering costs further.

Dining

In Chapter 12, you can learn more about the Disney Dining Plan. This can save many different vacation groups a good amount of money.

So how do we come up with a budget for food? Well, for our example family, the Disney Dining Plan is definitely the way to go, with a vacation-long cost of $899.76. But let's assume another $30 per day in family spending here, to cover the second meal not included in the standard dining plan, and the occasional soda and snack.

As for your own budget, the math is actually easy. Look at all the restaurant reviews in Chapters 13 to 15 for those where you plan on dining. Calculate your expenses there and then add any other expected dining.

There is one faster alternative: Assume $75 per adult per day and $50 per child per day. However, here we will assume the dining plan cost plus the $30 for the family per day.

> **Bottom Line:** $1,008.72
>
> **Hidden Costs:** Snacks and drinks sneak up on you at every corner.
>
> **Hidden Savings:** Taking some drinks and snacks with you into the park can save as much as $40 or $50.

Incidentals

Did you really think you would get by without buying some Mickey-imprinted goodies? No, you will need some general spending money to buy toys, trinkets, clothing, and the occasional poncho if you are caught in a downpour. It's best to assume the worst and plan for $10 per person per day.

Also keep in mind for your own budgeting, stroller rental costs around $20 a day, although, again, there are deals to be had. Usually when you rent one in a park, you get a receipt to get a free rental at any other park on the same day.

Other incidentals include locker rental (usually $7 per day, with a $2 refund with key return), gift purchases, and all the other things that Disney throws your way to try to get you to buy. Believe me, it's like trying to get a kid past the candy at the grocery store check-out!

Bottom Line: $280

Hidden Costs: Stands are selling things at every corner, making it hard to say no every moment of your vacation.

Hidden Savings: Give kids a one toy–one shirt budget for the whole trip. Let them make the final selection. They get the fun; you save some money.

Total Bottom Line

Add them all up and you get a figure just over $3,700. Yes, $3,700 seems a bit large for a family of four, but this is, as I mentioned earlier, a starting point, with high estimates. There are *many* ways to reduce this total, and for you it may already be lower, especially if you are not flying here. But the number is a good one to help you gauge your estimated costs.

Cost-Saving Strategies

So how do you get this number down? Really, it's fairly easy. First, keep an eye on the Sunday newspaper and the Disney website. Regular offers will bring significant savings, if you can be patient. In the last several years there have been offers that range from small savings to even a "buy four days, get three free" for a savings of well over $400. There are often packages that include the Disney Dining Plan for free, saving well over $500. Also, check your traditional vacation discount sources, such as AAA, AARP, and any offers available from your employer's HR department. Keep your eyes peeled.

Another strategy is to stay off property. If savings are the focus, many hotels cost far less than the Disney resorts. You lose some benefits, but they may be ones that you can live without. Check out the local prices and try the national travel websites like Expedia.

Summary

Hopefully by now you have your budget set. Look for new ways to lower your costs, but be realistic in your planning. Disney is not a cheap vacation, so don't assume you will be able to lower your costs unreasonably. With your budget in hand, you can now assess how good the deals out there really are.

Sample Budget Worksheet

Item	Model Family of 4	Your Estimated Cost
Transportation		
Airfare	$810.00	_____
Rental Car and Taxis		_____
Transportation Subtotal	**$810.00**	_____
Accommodations		
Hotel or Related Charge	$607.00	_____
Room Incidentals		_____
Accommodations Subtotal	**$607.00**	_____
Tickets		
Magic Your Way Tickets	$1,076.00	_____
Other Tickets		_____
Tickets Subtotal	**$1,076.00**	_____
Dining		
Disney Dining Plan	$798.72	_____
Groceries		_____
Meals		_____
Snacks/Incidentals	$210.00	_____
Dining Subtotal	**$1,008.72**	_____
Incidentals		
Stroller Rentals		_____
Souvenirs/Gifts	$280.00	_____
Locker Rentals		_____
Film		_____
Incidentals Subtotal	**$280.00**	_____
The Big Total!	**$3,781.72**	_____

Getting There

In This Chapter

- Decide how to get to Walt Disney World
- Master how to easily navigate the buses, boats, and monorails of Walt Disney World
- Learn how to lower your transportation budget

You can get to Walt Disney World and the Orlando area in so many ways. You probably already have an idea of what transportation mode you'll use. Many drive, if they live close by. Yet with airline prices traditionally lower to Orlando than to most U.S. cities, flying is typically within budget for those who don't live nearby.

This chapter looks at important transportation needs. I discuss how to get to Orlando, around Orlando, and around Walt Disney World.

Getting to Orlando

How you are getting to Orlando is probably something you have already decided. Whether driving or flying, know that Orlando is growing at a rapid pace, putting a strain on the highways, airport, and other transportation services. So plan accordingly, and make sure you give yourself plenty of time to move around.

Driving to Orlando

Regardless of where you're driving from, as you near Walt Disney World, the signage is clear and you should have no problem finding your resort. Just remember what area your resort is located in. For example, "Epcot Resorts Area" and "Downtown Disney Resorts

Area" are the first signs you see as you come from the north, indicating how to get to those areas. As you get closer, the signs become more hotel-specific. Here are the main exits off U.S. 4 that you want to keep an eye out for:

> **Exit 64 and Exit 65:**
>
> If you're coming from Tampa (exit 64) or Orlando (exit 65), use these exits to get to the Magic Kingdom–area resorts, the Animal Kingdom–area resorts, and the Wide World of Sports–area resorts.
>
> **Exit 67:**
>
> Take this for the Downtown Disney–area resorts and the Epcot-area resorts.
>
> **Exit 68:**
>
> Take this for hotels found on Hotel Plaza Boulevard or if you want to hit the Gooding's grocery store at the Crossroads Plaza shopping center.

Flying to Orlando

Playing host to almost 35 million passengers annually, the Orlando International Airport, known as MCO, is one of the busier airports in North America. The good news is that you have a lot of airlines and flights to choose from, and the prices are usually more competitive and lower than many other cities. The bad news is that the airport is usually crowded and the security lines are immense. If you're flying, ensure you give yourself plenty of time when heading home to get through security.

In addition to a number of international carriers, some of the domestic airlines that fly here include AirTran, Alaska, American, Delta, Frontier, JetBlue, Southwest, United, and US Airways.

Getting From the Airport to Walt Disney World

It's not too surprising that, with all the visitors to Walt Disney World, many businesses have popped up to help you with transportation from the airport to your hotel. The following are some of the ways to consider making the move to your resort.

Disney Magical Express

Disney Magical Express service is a resort perk started in 2005. If you stay at a Disney resort, you get a round-trip to and from the airport at no additional charge. (Note, the Swan and the Dolphin do *not* enjoy this service.)

How does it work? When you book your package, they send you an informational mailing that includes special luggage stickers. Attach them to your bags and check in at your home airport as usual. When you arrive, don't go to your baggage claim area, but instead make your way to Level 1 on the B side. When you get there, you will be directed to one of a dozen different lines to get onto your bus to Walt Disney World. The bus will then take you to your resort. There are usually a few resorts on each route, but the estimated 30–45 minute ride has never seemed to be too long.

It's important at this point to let you know that your bags are not making this bus ride with you. Bags are picked up by Disney staff, sorted based on the luggage stickers you put on them back home, and then brought to your resort separately. The bags can arrive as much as three hours later, so plan accordingly. Don't worry about having to wait around for your bags; they'll get to your room while you're out enjoying Walt Disney World. Do ensure you carry any essential medications with you in your carry-on. Also, pack your carry-on with whatever you'll need for that first afternoon (swim trunks for some pool time, children's nap or diaper needs, etc.).

HIDDEN MAGIC!

If you're a resort guest, you can actually check in for your return flight as early as 12 hours in advance and get your boarding passes at your resort. This free service works on the following airlines:

- AirTran
- Alaska
- American
- Delta
- JetBlue
- Southwest
- United
- US Air

When it's time to head back to the airport for your return flight, just check in at your resort desk and leave your bags. That's the last time you'll see them, so don't expect to be able to get to them. Do whatever you want that day, until you board a scheduled Disney Magical Express bus that takes you back to the airport around three hours before your flight.

Pros: Free service, no handling your bags.

Cons: Can't stop at the grocery store, and you won't get access to your luggage for up to three hours.

Bottom line: The service is free and relatively convenient. If you get it as part of your vacation package, you definitely should use it.

Taxis

Cabs run you at least $50 to $60, before tip, from the airport to the Disney area, but you can fit in as many people as the cab will hold.

Pros: Straight to your resort; bags are with you.

Cons: A lot more expensive than the free Magical Express.

Bottom line: Probably not your best choice, but ideal if you are working on a company expense account. Still, probably better than a shuttle.

Shuttle Services

A shuttle runs around $30 per person for a round-trip. The downside to the shuttle is that you can't guarantee that you won't have tons of stops before arriving at your resort.

Pros: Low cost.

Cons: If your stop is the last on the run, it could take an extra hour or more to get to your resort.

Bottom line: Not the best choice, but cheaper, as long as the Magical Express is not an option.

Limo and Town Car Services

Limousine services could be your great secret. For about $120 round-trip, before tips, you can fit a family of four into a nice town car and get direct service to your resort in style.

Some of the better limousine services, like Quicksilver Tours (www. quicksilver-tours.com; 1-888-GO-TO-WDW or 1-888-468-6939), will make a free 30-minute stop at an area grocery store for you to stock up on supplies. If you have a room with a fridge—or, better yet, a kitchenette—this can save you the cost of the ride in reduced food costs. Quicksilver, in particular, offers not only a luxurious ride, but they even have booster seats and child safety seats if needed (just let them know in advance). I use them every time I bring my family to town.

Pros: Nicer vehicles, personalized service, and that convenient grocery stop.

Cons: Not many cons here, unless you could travel for free on the Disney Magical Express.

Bottom line: By far the best non-free choice out there.

Rental Cars

Lots of options exist, so pricing them is up to you. However, you may find that you don't need a car. If you're staying at a Disney resort, you have a free ride to and from the airport, as well as free transportation around Walt Disney World. And if you're staying at a hotel elsewhere, you'll probably find that they have shuttles to the parks, thus reducing your need for a car. Be absolutely sure that you need one before making the reservation.

DID YOU KNOW?

Rental cars are available at the Orlando International Airport (MCO) from Alamo, Avis, Budget, Dollar, Enterprise, Hertz, L & M, National, Payless, and Thrifty, but you can get some on property as well. You can pick up rental cars at the following easily accessible Walt Disney World locations, although you can have one delivered to any Disney-owned hotel as well:

- Alamo National at Shades of Green Resort, Dolphin Resort, Car Care Center, and the Buena Vista Palace Hotel
- Avis at the Hilton on Hotel Plaza Boulevard
- Budget at the Doubletree Hotel on Hotel Plaza Boulevard
- Dollar at the Holiday Inn on Hotel Plaza Boulevard
- Enterprise at the Royal Plaza Hotel

Getting Around Walt Disney World

So you've now gotten to Walt Disney World, but how do you get around? Disney has an elaborate web of transportation services that are free to use and will get you where you need to go. First, let's look at the different transportation types.

Monorail

A Disney icon, the monorail is still as cool as it was in the 1970s. There are two basic loops for the monorail:

Monorail Route 1:

Circles around the lagoon in front of the Magic Kingdom with stops at the Transportation and Ticket Center, the Polynesian Resort, the Grand Floridian Resort, the Magic Kingdom, and the Contemporary Resort. There are express trains that stop only at the Magic Kingdom and the Transportation and Ticket Center, and a resort line that hits all the stops, including the resorts.

Monorail Route 2:

Takes guests between the Transportation and Ticket Center and Epcot.

Note that on the first loop, there are both express trains to the Magic Kingdom as well as ones that stop at the resorts.

Bus

The fleet of buses, or "motor coaches" in Disney-speak, is the main mode of transportation throughout Walt Disney World. For the most part, they run you between a resort and the attractions, water parks, and nightlife areas. They are usually on a 20-minute interval, so you shouldn't have to wait too long between buses. There's a key hub for buses at Downtown Disney where you can make a transfer. If there are no direct buses to your destination (such as when going from one resort hotel to another), just grab a bus to this hub and switch over to a bus headed to your destination.

DID YOU KNOW?

Cabs can be called to all Disney resorts. A short 10-minute cab ride from an Epcot-area resort to the Animal Kingdom Lodge costs $15, so know that the cost is significant, and the availability can be somewhat spotty.

Buses are usually the least desirable of the three transportation vehicles, just because they're usually more crowded and are not as fast or scenic. But they're well run and pretty darn reliable. And if they break down (as one I was riding on did on a recent trip), they get replacements out quickly.

Boat

Boats connect several different resorts and attractions. These can be a relaxing and scenic way to get from place to place, and I highly recommend that you take them if they're convenient. These are the major ones to remember, though others exist in the Magic Kingdom area:

Boat Zone 1:

Hollywood Studios to Swan and Dolphin hotels, Swan and Dolphin hotels to BoardWalk, BoardWalk to Yacht and Beach Club hotels, Yacht and Beach Club hotels to Epcot, and then it goes in reverse order.

Boat Zone 2:

Boats launch between the Magic Kingdom and the Grand Floridian, Polynesian, Wilderness Lodge, Contemporary, and Fort Wilderness resort marinas. Routes change regularly to meet demand.

There are also boats between the resorts in this zone.

Boat Zone 3:

Downtown Disney to Saratoga Springs, Old Key West, and Port Orleans resorts.

Boat Route 4:

Transportation and Ticket Center to Magic Kingdom.

Getting from Place to Place

The following chart shows how you will get from one place to another. This is a reference, but always ask a cast member if you're not sure.

Your Resort	Magic Kingdom	Epcot	Hollywood Studios	Animal Kingdom	Downtown Disney	Typhoon Lagoon	Blizzard Beach	To Another Resort
Animal Kingdom Lodge	Bus	Bus	Bus	Bus	Bus	Bus	Bus	Bus to Animal Kingdom (day) or Downtown Disney (night), transfer to bus to resort.
Beach & Yacht Club Resorts	Bus	Boat/Walk	Boat	Bus	Bus	Bus	Bus	Walk or boat to BoardWalk Inn, Swan, and Dolphin. For others, bus to Downtown Disney, transfer to bus to resort.
BoardWalk Inn & Villas	Bus	Boat/Walk	Boat	Bus	Bus	Bus	Bus	Bus to Downtown Disney, transfer to bus to resort.
Contemporary Resort	Monorail	Monorail (transfer at TTC)	Bus	Bus	Bus	Bus	Bus	Monorail to Grand Floridian or Polynesian. For others, monorail to Magic Kingdom, transfer to bus to resort.
Grand Floridian Resort	Monorail	Monorail (transfer at TTC)	Bus	Bus	Bus	Bus	Bus	Monorail to Contemporary or Polynesian. For others, monorail to Magic Kingdom, transfer to bus to resort.
Polynesian Resort	Monorail	Monorail (transfer at TTC)	Bus	Bus	Bus	Bus	Bus	Monorail to Grand Floridian or Contemporary. For others, monorail to Magic Kingdom, transfer to bus to resort.
Wilderness Lodge	Boat	Bus	Bus	Bus	Bus	Bus	Bus	Boat to Fort Wilderness. Boat to Magic Kingdom and transfer to monorail to Contemporary, Polynesian, and Grand Floridian. For others, bus to Downtown Disney, transfer to bus to resort.
WDW Dolphin & Swan	Bus	Boat	Boat	Bus	Bus	Bus	Bus	Walk/Boat to BoardWalk Inn and Yacht & Beach Clubs. For others, bus to Downtown Disney, transfer to bus to resort.
Caribbean Beach Resort	Bus	Bus	Bus	Bus	Bus	Bus	Bus	Bus to Downtown Disney, transfer to bus to resort.
Coronado Springs Resort	Bus	Bus	Bus	Bus	Bus	Bus	Bus	Bus to Animal Kingdom (day) or Downtown Disney (night), transfer to bus to resort.
Port Orleans Resort	Bus	Bus	Bus	Bus	Boat	Bus	Bus	Bus or boat to Downtown Disney, transfer to bus to resort.
Pop Century Resort	Bus	Bus	Bus	Bus	Bus	Bus	Bus	Bus to Downtown Disney, transfer to bus to resort.
All-Star Resorts	Bus	Bus	Bus	Bus	Bus	Bus	Bus	Bus to Animal Kingdom (day) or Downtown Disney (night), transfer to bus to resort.
Fort Wilderness	Boat	Bus	Bus	Bus	Bus	Bus	Bus	Boat to Wilderness Lodge. Boat to Magic Kingdom and transfer to monorail to Contemporary, Polynesian, and Grand Floridian. For others, bus to Downtown Disney, transfer to bus to resort.
Saratoga Springs Resort	Bus	Bus	Bus	Bus	Boat	Bus	Bus	Bus or boat to Downtown Disney, transfer to bus to resort.
Old Key West Resort	Bus	Bus	Bus	Bus	Boat	Bus	Bus	Bus or boat to Downtown Disney, transfer to bus to resort.
Shades of Green	Bus	Bus	Bus	Bus	Bus	Bus	Bus	Bus to Downtown Disney, transfer to but to resort.

Transportation chart.

Summary

That's the transportation world in a nutshell. By now, you should have an idea of how you'll get to Orlando, how you'll get to Walt Disney World, and how you'll get around once you're here.

Buying Tickets

In This Chapter

- Learn how the Walt Disney ticket system works
- Discover different ticket options
- Decide what your best ticket choice is and where to buy them

Disney tickets seem like a complex structure of different ticket types, archaic options, suspect discounts, and other confusions leading to a tangled web of prices. Yes, when you start bundling tickets with vacation packages and receiving discount ticket offers, it seems to get even more confusing, but it's really a fairly simple part of the overall plan.

First, you need to figure out what tickets and ticket options you need. I help you do that in this chapter. I also help you determine which ones are not ideal for you so you can avoid them. Finally, I help you understand where the best places are to buy tickets, and how you should compare buying tickets by themselves versus as a part of an overall vacation package.

Okay, ready to go?

Magic Your Way Tickets

Let's start with the basics. To get into any of the big four parks of Disney World, you need to begin with a *Magic Your Way* ticket, which gives you basic access to a single park for each day of your ticket's duration. Pick anywhere from 1 day to 10 days, based on how long you will be staying. This is what I refer to as the base ticket. It is nontransferable, and you have to use all the days on the tickets within 14 days after your first use.

> **MICKEY-SPEAK**
>
> **Magic Your Way** is the name of Disney's base park ticket. This base ticket isn't anything different than what you or anyone else would buy at the gate upon arriving at the park.

This base ticket gives you access to one park per day. As an example, if you use your ticket to go into the Magic Kingdom, that's the *only* park where it will work for that whole day. Of course, the next day you can use your ticket at another park, or you can use it to go back to the Magic Kingdom, if you want. However, no matter what, you are getting into just *one park per day*. What if you want to visit more than one park in a day? We'll get to that.

So what do I mean by "nontransferable"? Well, whenever you enter a park with your ticket, you put your finger on a scanner. It verifies that only you can use that ticket. You cannot pass it off to your brother, cousin, neighbor, and so on. Here are a few other interesting things to remember about your ticket:

- If you stay at a Disney resort, the ticket is actually pro-grammed on your room key.

- Everyone in your Disney resort room must purchase the same ticket type, including the same options.

- Your resort key/Magic Your Way ticket is also your pass into the parks for the *Extra Magic Hours.*

- You'll need your Magic Your Way ticket to get *FASTPASS* vouchers in the parks, so you'll have to keep the ticket within easy reach. Everyone with a ticket can use FASTPASS; there is no option that you need to buy to get to use this service.

- The more ticket days you purchase, the lower the per-day cost will be.

One other important consideration is your arrival and departure days. Consider whether you have the time on either day to adequately visit a park. If not, you can reduce your overall cost without limiting your vacation fun by buying fewer overall ticket days. You can do plenty of other things on these partial days at Walt Disney World (which we review in Chapter 5), and this can save you hundreds of dollars.

MICKEY-SPEAK

Extra Magic Hours are explained in greater detail later in the book, but they are basically a perk for resort guests, who get exclusive access to the parks before or after standard operating hours, making for a less crowded environment.

The **FASTPASS** ticket system also is explained later in the book in greater detail. Basically, it's a ticket perk that lets you avoid long lines for some of the more popular rides by getting a ticket for an expedited line at a prescheduled time later in the day.

So that's the basic ticket you'll need. Now you need to figure out how many days you'll need to complete step one in choosing tickets.

Magic Your Way Optional Add-Ons

You have your base ticket for the number of days you plan on visiting the parks. Now comes the interesting part. You can add any of three different ticket options to your Magic Your Way base ticket. As you add them, you add to the cost of your ticket, so ensure you're definitely going to need them.

Option 1: Park Hopper

The Park Hopper lets you go to multiple theme parks (but not water parks) in a single day for every day on your ticket. So you could go to the Magic Kingdom in the morning, Animal Kingdom in the afternoon, and Epcot in the evening, if you were so inclined. The cost of adding this feature is $35 for a 1-day ticket, and $55 for anywhere from a 2- to 10-day ticket, regardless of duration (for any guest, either adult or child), so the more days you'll be in Walt Disney World, the better an idea it is to add this to your ticket options.

Who should use it?

- Adult-only groups

- Families with teens

- Groups who want to visit one park during the day and dine at a restaurant at another park in the evening

Who should avoid it?

- Families with smaller children who probably won't make it to more than one park per day anyway

Option 2: Water Park Fun and More Option

The Water Park Fun and More option gives you access to many of Walt Disney World's other attractions. With this option you get admission to:

- Blizzard Beach Water Park

- Typhoon Lagoon Water Park

- DisneyQuest Indoor Interactive Theme Park

- ESPN Wide World of Sports Complex

- Disney's Oak Trail Golf Course (9-hole walking course)

So how many visits do you get to these added attractions? It is a simple rule to follow:

- 1-day Magic Your Way Ticket = 2 Water Park Fun and More admissions

- 2- to 10-days Magic Your Way Ticket = Same number of Water Park Fun and More admissions

So if you have a 6-day ticket, you get 6 Water Park Fun and More admissions.

You don't get the Park Hopper option with this option, but you can visit any of these attractions with your option admissions.

Regardless of the length of your stay, the cost of adding this feature is $55 (for each guest, both adult and child), so the longer your stay, the better an idea it is to add this to your ticket options.

A great way to determine whether this will be a good option is to compare the $55 cost to the number of times you think you will visit the water parks or other features. Basically, if you know you will visit the water parks at least twice, it is worth it—otherwise, it's probably not.

Who should use it?

- Adult-only groups planning on several water park visits
- Families with younger teens who plan on visiting the water parks

Who should avoid it?

- Families with smaller children
- Groups not planning on visiting the water parks

Option 3: No Expiration Date

This option makes your tickets valid indefinitely, letting you bring back the ticket and use the leftover days whenever you want. The cost increase can vary, but unlike the other options, the cost gets higher the more days you have on your base ticket.

Who should use it?

- Anyone from central Florida
- Someone who frequently travels to the area
- Those with a Disney vacation planned in the next few years

Who should avoid it?

- Anyone who is remotely uncertain of when they might return and those who know they won't be back anytime soon

DISNEY DON'T

Don't think that you can save your unused ticket days on a standard pass for a future vacation. Regardless of how many days you choose for your ticket, you have only the 14 days from the first day you use your ticket to use all the days on your ticket. The only exception is if you purchase the No Expiration option.

What Options Should I Buy?

Well, it's really up to you what options you choose. Of course, we show suggestions with each option, but it's important to consider your particular group needs. Here are some general things to keep in mind.

- *Families with small children* find that they rarely are able to hit more than one park in a day. They also find that they need to use part of their days to go back to their hotels for either naps or pool time. The chance to use the Park Hopper or the water park option is pretty infrequent, so why pay for them?

  - Recommendations: Park Hopper: No
  - Water Park Fun and More: No

- *Families with teens* often find the Park Hopper to be of some value, especially if the teens are very active. But the water park option is even more valuable, if they like water sports and will go regularly to the water parks.

  - Recommendations: Park Hopper: Yes
  - Water Park Fun and More: Yes

- *Adult-only groups* find the Park Hopper invaluable, as they often need to change parks on any given day for a change of scenery or for dining plans, especially at Epcot. The water park option can be valuable if they plan to go to the water parks repeatedly, but that's not a sure thing.

  - Recommendations: Park Hopper: Yes
  - Water Park Fun and More: Maybe

- I think the No Expiration option has little to do with your group type and more to do with geography. If you know you'll be back within two years, do it. If not, you might be wasting your money. I usually find that the option is one that's just not worth the extra cost, especially because there will be new deals for that next vacation. If you take the new deals, you still won't use the extra days on the second go-around.

Other Attraction Tickets

What if you want to just buy a water park ticket for a day? You can do that; here's the cost.

Use these prices to determine whether the Water Park Fun and More option is one worth adding.

Attraction	Child's Ticket (3–9)	Adult's Ticket (10+)
Typhoon Lagoon	$44	$52
Blizzard Beach	$44	$52
DisneyQuest	$38	$44

The Bottom-Line Cost of Your Ticket

The following shows the ticket pricing as purchased online from Disney for 2012. Prices will surely change sometime in the future, but this chart should give you a solid figure for budgeting purposes.

To get to your price, simply select the number of days you will visit, and find the correct column. If you are going to add options, you will see them in the same column, in the second set of rows. For each person in your party, add the base cost with all options that you desire. Do this for each person, and then add up all your prices for your final total.

	1 Day	2 Day	3 Day	4 Day	5 Day	6 Day	7 Day	8 Day	9 Day	10 Day
Magic Your Way Base Ticket										
Children (ages 3-9) Total Cost										
	$83.00	$164.00	$226.00	$239.00	$250.00	$260.00	$270.00	$280.00	$290.00	$300.00
Per Day Average										
	$83.00	$82.00	$75.33	$59.57	$50.00	$43.33	$38.57	$35.00	$32.22	$30.00
Adult (10+) Total Cost										
	$89.00	$176.00	$242.00	$256.00	$268.00	$278.00	$288.00	$298.00	$308.00	$318.00
Per Day Average										
	$89.00	$88.00	$80.67	$64.00	$53.60	$46.33	$41.14	$37.25	$34.22	$31.80

Park Hopper Option: Add $57 per person to your total cost ($35 if you are only getting a 1-day ticket).

Water Park Fun and More Option: Add $57 per person to your total cost.

No Expiration Option: Added cost varies.

2013 online ticket prices (does not reflect 6.5% sales tax).

Special Ticket Packages

Where *can* you get special ticket packages? As mentioned in earlier chapters, packages that include hotel rooms, meal plans, and other elements will usually lower your overall trip cost. But it's not always clear whether that cost reduction is from the tickets, from the dining plan, or from the hotel. In reality, it really doesn't matter.

The important thing is that you determine in this chapter how much your tickets will cost if you purchase them individually. Then you will have a figure to use when comparing different vacation packages to see just how good a deal they really are.

If you decide to buy the tickets separately, where's the best place to buy them? Here are some pointers:

- **Online ticket vendors:** A lot of people are selling Disney tickets online, and they all claim to have the best deal. For most of them, I say buyer beware. Many advertise their prices as being lower than the gate prices at the parks, and they are. But they are rarely, if ever, lower than the price of buying them directly from www.disneyworld.com.

Example: In a recent review of a popular ticket seller's prices, all those ticket prices were higher than that of the Disney park website.

DID YOU KNOW?

Annual theme park passes are available as well. Standard ones that give you access to the four theme parks go for $574 per child or adult. Premium ones that also give you access to the water parks and DisneyQuest cost $699 per child or adult.

- **Human resources programs:** Some companies offer employee benefits programs that can save you on tickets. Make sure you check with your HR department for any such deals.

  Example: A recent site visit to one such company saved around $20 to $25 on each adult ticket for a 6-day stay.

- **Travel services companies:** Everyone asks about AARP, AAA, and other similar organizations. Sometimes you can save at these organizations, so make sure you check them. Sometimes, however, you don't. Be sure you're also looking at the direct purchase prices, too. Of all of them, AAA seems to have the most regular discounts.

  Example: A recent visit to one of these organizations found prices that were exactly the same as at www.disneyworld.com.

So what do you do? Go to the source! I get the price at www.disneyworld.com, and then I look at the vacation packages from a few different sites and organizations. I don't look at more than three because the savings rarely gets to be more than about $100 per trip, and my time is worth more than that. Yours probably is, too. The key here is to get that ticket cost so that you can compare the value of different packages; don't get too consumed in chasing the deals at this point.

Summary

So that's the ticket situation in a few easy steps. Pick the number of days you want to visit the parks. Decide whether you need to visit more than one park a day. Consider whether you need to visit the water parks. Plan far ahead, and perhaps save some of your days for a return visit. Finally, make sure you have a solid idea of what tickets will cost you so you can weigh the value of different vacation packages. I'll bet you thought that was going to be *much* more painful, didn't you?

Vacation Strategies

In This Chapter

- Learn about special kid-friendly ideas to make the trip even better
- Discover great ways to make the trip fun for adults
- Save time and money with simple ideas

As you've seen, a vacation to Walt Disney World has a lot of options, as well as places to spend money. But you probably don't have an unlimited budget, and you're there for only a limited amount of time. So how do you make the most of both? I walk you through some of the best ideas I know of to save one or the other (or both!). I also let you know about some of the general services available that might be of interest to you.

General Trip-Planning Strategies

Let's start with strategies that work for any kind of traveling party, whether or not kids are involved. Make sure you have your Weekly Schedule Card from the Appendix section handy so that you can make any necessary changes. So what are some general trip-planning strategies that can help you in your overall planning? Let's look at a few key ones.

Important Strategy #1: Plan Your First Day's Activity

Odds are, the day you arrive in the Orlando area, you will not be getting there first thing in the morning, rested and ready for a day at a theme park. For most, it's an afternoon arrival via plane, with some time needed to settle in to the hotel. Remember, of course, that if you hit a park, you will "spend" one day of your tickets, so it may be better to save that for another day when you can go for the whole day.

Plan something different that will start the vacation off with a bang! Some ideas include:

- Hit your hotel pool for a relaxing dip.
- Try kick-starting your Disney experience with a character meal or dinner show.
- Take your first monorail ride!
- Visit Downtown Disney or the BoardWalk for some nightlife.

DID YOU KNOW?

Looking for some specific recommendations, or have a question not answered in any of the guidebooks? Then ask a mom (or dad)! Disney started the Disney World Moms Panel to help. Go to www. disneyworldmoms.com and you can ask specific questions to the panel of moms and dads from around the world. They bring a range of different experiences, and the mom or dad who is an "expert" on your question will try to get you a reply. I was on the panel in 2009, 2010, and 2012. I recommend it highly!

Important Strategy #2: Plan Your Parks and Meals

Flexibility and spontaneity can make the vacation fun, but you should still work a little advance planning into your days at Disney. Plan what parks you intend to visit on each day of your trip, as well as at least some of your meals.

My recommendations for how to pick what park to go to on what day are the following:

- **Busy season:** If you are visiting during a busy time of the year (when schools are NOT in session or during the holidays), then I would avoid whatever parks have the morning and evening Extra Magic Hours on that day.

- **Moderate season:** If you are visiting during a moderate time of year, then avoid the morning Extra Magic Hours, but consider the evening ones if your party is old enough to stay up and enjoy them.

- **Light season:** If you are visiting during the lighter crowd times of the year (while schools are in session), then go on days where parks have morning or evening Extra Magic Hours to enjoy this extra time.

- **Non-Disney resorts:** If you are staying at a non-Disney resort where you don't get the opportunity to take advantage of Extra Magic Hours, then always avoid the parks that have them on that particular day to avoid the largest crowds.

- **Park order:** It doesn't matter what order you visit the parks, but I recommend that first-time visitors start and finish their trip at the Magic Kingdom.

- **How many days per park:** I recommend 2 days at the Magic Kingdom and 1 day each at the other three parks. If you don't have 5 days, I would visit the Magic Kingdom twice, and then pick other parks to visit.

- **Animal Kingdom evening:** There is less to do in this park at night, as the animals head to bed. An Animal Kingdom park day is a great one to pair with an evening visit to Downtown Disney, the BoardWalk, or a resort for a special dinner.

DISNEY DON'T

Rumor has it that Heelys are banned at all Florida theme parks. These tennis shoes with retractable mini-rollerskate wheels in the heels are very popular, but apparently present a risk to other guests. Make sure you pack other shoes for the kids on this trip.

Once you have the general agenda of what park you will visit on which days, you should plan some of your meals. You should get your character meals, dinner shows, and romantic soirées planned and reserved ahead of time.

DISNEY DON'T

Don't forget to pack all the essentials! Shorts, swimsuits, sunglasses, and sandals—that's all you need, right? Wrong! Make sure you take into account the low evening temperatures for the time of year you're visiting: a pair of slacks and maybe a sweater could transform an uncomfortably cold night into a perfect evening out. Other things you should consider packing:

- A handy list of mail and email addresses—some attractions have kiosks where you can send themed email postcards free of charge.
- Comfortable walking shoes for everyone!
- Sunscreen, lip balm, hats, sunglasses, and ponchos.
- One autograph book per child, as well as a big pen (so that characters can grip them).
- Pool shoes for the water parks.
- Earplugs for kids who are scared by loud noises.
- Backpack or fanny pack for carrying necessities into the parks.

Other General Strategies

There are a great many strategies that help any kind of group, regardless of age, group size, or budget. Here are a few.

- Consider using an Orlando-area grocery delivery service, like GardenGrocer.com, that can deliver groceries to your room, helping you save on your food budget!

- If you can stop at a grocery store, do so. Stock up on drinks, snacks, and breakfast foods to have back in the room. Doing so can save you a ton of money in the long run.

HIDDEN MAGIC!

Refillable resort mugs can be a great deal. These mugs allow you to get free soda refills in your resort as often as you wish. At around $15 each, these smaller mugs do require a lot of refilling to pay for them, but it can pay off if you plan a lot of resort pool time. They are a great souvenir, too.

- Can't stop at a grocery store? Mail a box of supplies ahead to your room. You may not be able to ship bottles of soda, but a box of cereal, some dry packaged snacks, and other items will save you food budget dollars and lighten your bags.

- If you have to take a backpack into the park anyway, pack snacks and beverages. Packing a lunch is not out of the question, either. You can always stow it away in a locker or your stroller once you get to the park. Again, the cost savings can be significant.

- Best Friends Pet Care, an extensive kennel facility at Walt Disney World, has air-conditioned kennels for a variety of animal types. You can get more information at www.wdw. bestfriendspetcare.com or at 1-877-4-WDW-PETS. This is not your neighborhood kennel, offering an amazing array of facilities and packages. Reservations are required.

DID YOU KNOW?

In many theater seating attractions, people elbow others out of the way to get to the front of the crowd, waiting by the doors that lead to the theater. Let them go! In most cases, being in the middle of the crowd means you will sit in the middle of the theater, where 3-D effects are best and the view of all characters is guaranteed. Let the piggies sit on the sides, where they deserve to be!

Strategies for Families

If you're bringing kids to Walt Disney World, you're in the majority. That does not mean, however, that you always have to be in the longest lines and at the busiest restaurants. The following sections describe some strategies that can help you avoid crowds and maximize the fun.

Before You Leave

I've had friends surprise their kids by not telling them they were headed to Walt Disney World until they literally were there, and it was great. But you can have fun at the other extreme by following these strategies:

- Let your kids help with the planning. Allow them to select the hotel from a few that you have picked within your price range. Let them choose a few of the restaurants, and have them help in filling out the Trip Cards, selecting what attractions to hit and which to miss.

- Print out a sheet of ID labels with your name, home address, cell phone number, etc. After you label any of your items you are taking with you, keep a few extra so that toys and other items that you buy while you are there can be marked as yours as well.

DID YOU KNOW?

If you want some keepsake photos from your trip but don't want to carry around a camera, Disney's PhotoPass service can help. Disney photographers around the parks will take your picture and then give you a card. From then on, whenever one of them takes your picture, you give them your card to swipe. When the trip is over, you just visit the website to view your pictures (www.disneyphotopass.com) for 30 days, and you can let friends view them as well. The site lets you crop, resize, and add borders and captions. You can even create holiday cards, mouse pads, mugs, and shirts.

Items can be pricy, but if you had a lot of pictures taken, it can be a better deal to have them send you all the unedited pictures on a CD for between $100 and $200.

A new option, PhotoPass Plus, allows you to have any pictures taken at character meals and attractions that take ride photos added to your account. Visit a PhotoPass Plus booth while at Walt Disney World to find out more.

- Try some craft projects. Have your kids make "lost child" name tags or lanyards that they can wear in the parks. This is functional and fun.

- Prepare your kids for all the walking that they will do in the parks by starting a family walk every evening for the two or three months leading up to your trip. You can build their endurance, ensuring that they enjoy more of the trip!

- If you're going to surprise your kids, have some planning materials ready for when you break the good news. Let them do some of the planning by selecting rides in some parks, choose some of the no-reservation-required meal destinations, and list what characters they want to meet.

- Let your kids plan a day at the parks. A neat new feature from Disney's website lets you create a customized theme park map. You can print them out at home as well as have them printed for you. The maps take a few weeks to arrive, but they can be a perfect excitement builder.

- Buy an autograph book and a fat pen if you have kids who will want to meet their favorite stars. You can probably get a cheaper book at home; just be sure it's big enough and opens easily. Characters with large padded gloves and children with little hands will appreciate the book and pen being large and easy to work with.

- Know your child's height before you go and determine what rides you can't let them experience, avoiding some disappointment ahead of time.

Once You're There

When you get to Walt Disney World, use these strategies to make the trip more enjoyable for you and your children:

- When you arrive, make sure you get your resort's recreational activities calendar. This will tell you what is going on at your resort while you are there, and can alert you to free movie nights, ceremonial activities, and other entertainment that you might have otherwise overlooked!

- Make sure that most days include a pool visit or nap in the afternoon. Despite their apparently endless supply of energy, younger kids will tire out, and if you don't plan for that, you will have some very unpleasant moments.

- Each theme park has a complimentary Baby Care Center where you can retreat to an air-conditioned calm zone. There are TVs running Disney movies, toys, baby-changing areas, and other conveniences that can allow you to calm an upset child or rest a tired one. Use them to refresh younger children.

- Use the Rider Switch feature at any height-restricted attraction. In this, you get a pass from the attraction attendant by the standby entrance. The first parent goes on the ride, via the standard line. When they are done, the second parent uses the Rider Switch pass, getting in the FASTPASS line, regardless of time of day. Whatever parent is not riding can take the kids to do something else. This way both adults get a chance to try some of the thrill rides and roller coasters.

- Identify an easy-to-find landmark. This can be a place where you can meet if separated, or to rejoin the group at a predetermined time.

DID YOU KNOW?

Need a doctor while at Walt Disney World? While Disney resorts can help you out, there is also a physician's group that makes house calls to the resorts. Call 407-399-3627.

There is also an urgent care hospital that provides complimentary transportation. Centra Care (407-938-0650) has multiple locations.

What about filling that empty prescription? Turner Drugs delivers; just call 407-828-8125.

- Plan a character meal. This is a must-do for almost every child.

- Consider the children's activity centers or baby-sitting services as a way to get some away-from-the-kids time, without ruining the fun for them. A sane mommy and daddy equals a happier vacation for all!

HIDDEN MAGIC!

Many of the Deluxe resort hotels at Disney have children's activity centers for kids age 4 to 12. These provide an ideal way for you to keep the kids entertained while you get an adult's night out. They get dinner, movies, activities, and fun. Make reservations by calling 407-WDW-DINE (407-939-3463). No, you do not have to be a guest of the actual hotel for your kid to enroll, but you do have to be a Disney resort guest. Usually you have to pay about $12 per hour per child, and reservations are necessary.

- In-room baby-sitting is available, known as Kid's Night Out. Call 407-828-0920 for reservations. Guess what? They don't just baby-sit! They can actually take the kids out to attractions, if you want them to. Typically, rates run around $14 per hour for one child, and additional kids are just a couple dollars more per hour. This is not a Disney-run program, but a local Orlando service that is very popular with regular guests.

After You Get Home

Capture that magic! Have kids make albums of their trip, complete with photographs, tickets, menus, hotel and park maps, and anything else you can think of. If you need some extra scrapbooking materials, visit Disney's Wonderful World of Memories store at Downtown Disney.

Vacation Strategies for Adults

Disney World is not just for kids; in fact, it is now considered the number one honeymoon destination in the United States. There's plenty of fun to be had for adult groups, as well as romance for couples who are so inclined. There are also some strategies that will help you shorten line-waiting time, see more of the park, and enjoy the trip as a full vacation. The following are some pointers to remember when preparing for your visit.

- Some rides have single rider/standby lines that are much shorter than the regular ones. Sure, you're not sitting next to your friend on the ride, but that's for only a few minutes, and you can shave hours off your total line-waiting time.

- Close down the park! Stay late and enjoy smaller crowds, shorter lines, and fewer kids.

- Eat at non-standard meal times (lunch at 2, dinner after 8) to get quieter meal settings and easier-to-get reservations.

- Try the Richard Petty Driving Experience, a spa treatment, or a round of golf for a mostly child-free time.

Nightlife

There's a great deal more nightlife than you might expect in the Walt Disney World area. Knowing a few places to spend a night out can help bring adults a little sanity.

- **Hotel lounges**—Not all hotels have a lounge, and those that do are usually smaller and quieter, making them an ideal place for a romantic cocktail or for a small gathering.

- **Theme parks**—The four theme parks are not exactly nightclubs, but they can be a nice place to lounge around and enjoy the Florida nights. The best of these is Epcot's World Showcase, and only the Magic Kingdom is alcohol-free.

- **Downtown Disney**—The nightlife here has taken a hit since the closing of the nightclubs of Pleasure Island. But dancing, music, and drinks can still be had at places like Raglan Road, Bongos, and House of Blues. Find out more in the Downtown Disney chapter.

- **BoardWalk**—Not quite the wild party that you might be wanting, the BoardWalk still has a few adult-only retreats that are fun, as well as family-friendly entertainment on the walk itself. Learn more in the BoardWalk chapter.

HIDDEN MAGIC!

Where are some of the best clubs? Here are my picks, though there are certainly more:

- Pub crawl: Trying the beers of the World at Epcot World Showcase
- Live music: House of Blues at Downtown Disney
- Rowdy singing: Jellyrolls at the BoardWalk
- Sports bar: ESPN Zone at the BoardWalk
- Live entertainment: Yehaa Bob at the River Roost Lounge in Port Orleans Riverside Resort

Romance

Romantic dining spots and private getaways in Walt Disney World are surprisingly numerous. Fireworks give you a great backdrop for an evening stroll. Other activities and events help set the mood, including private boating excursions, spa services, and opulent suites. Here are just some of the romantic options available at Walt Disney World:

- Dinner at Victoria & Albert's at the Grand Floridian Resort (formal), California Grill at the Contemporary Resort (casually elegant), or Le Cellier in Epcot (cozy)

- Cocktails at Todd English's bluezoo (contemporary elegance)

- Private boating
- A nighttime walk along the BoardWalk

DID YOU KNOW?

Disney World florists can deliver flowers or snack baskets to a room, but they can do a great deal more as well! In 2009, they added room decoration packages that can be themed to a specific event (first visit, engagement, wedding, etc.), and can include anything ranging from a 3-foot-tall Mickey to cookie bouquets, Hidden Mickey books, and all sorts of other great surprises. Visit www.disneyflorist.com.

Summary

There are a lot of time- and money-saving strategies out there, and these are just a few. As long as you plan ahead and are ready for a few surprises, you'll have a great time.

Choose Your Castle: Picking Your Resort Hotel

Walt Disney World has dozens of resort hotels on its property, and the Orlando area sports hundreds more accommodation selections. Should you stay at a Disney resort or stay elsewhere? If you are staying "on property," what kind of resort should you select? With so many choices at your fingertips, I help you quickly sort through the options and pick the place for you. Welcome to your castle!

Walt Disney World Resorts

In This Chapter

- Learn about the different hotel options at Walt Disney World
- Discover the benefits of staying on property
- Learn about the Disney resort seasons and how the charges change

A large part of the expense and the experience of a vacation to Walt Disney World is where you lay your head at night. I know what you're thinking: what does it matter where we stay when we'll spend so little time there? That's what I explain in this chapter, providing you with my suggestions and some options to match the varying needs of your particular travel party.

As you read this and the other chapters in this part of the book, you'll see that I am partial to staying at the Disney-owned resorts. But that's not to say this is the right solution for all visitors. Of course, there are literally thousands of accommodation options in the greater Orlando area, so covering them all here is out of the question. Instead, you find an overview of several of the best options for someone visiting Walt Disney World. So I do offer some non-Disney recommendations, pointing out the benefits and costs of staying at these alternatives.

Introduction to Disney Hotels

Let's start by considering the hotels on Disney property. These resorts provide certain benefits available only to guests staying *on property*, and they are all found in the immediate vicinity of the attractions.

> **MICKEY-SPEAK**
>
> Staying **on property** means staying at one of the resorts located on Disney property. These resorts, and their guests, enjoy some special treatment at the Disney parks, so the status can matter a great deal. Most are owned and operated by Disney, but a few are not; the benefits vary based on these distinctions, so be aware of what kind of on-property resort you are considering.

Disney classifies its resorts into the following categories:

- Deluxe Villa
- Deluxe
- Moderate
- Value
- Campgrounds
- Other select deluxe hotels

There are also a few other special resorts on Disney property: the Hotel Plaza Boulevard near Downtown Disney, the Shades of Green hotel for U.S. military personnel, and a new high-end Waldorf Astoria/Hilton complex at Bonnet Creek. These are covered in greater detail in Chapters 10 and 11.

What do the different categories really mean? The following sections provide a synopsis, including information on the other types of resorts on Disney property. Also take a look at Appendix C of this book. It has pictures of resort rooms from several of these different categories.

Deluxe Villa Resorts

Largely driven by the growth of the Disney Vacation Club, the Disney time-share program, this category of resort is growing more rapidly than any other. These resorts offer a greater array of room types, designed to support larger groups, cater to longer stays, and provide for those special needs that a standard room cannot address. Disney owns all of these resorts, so they get you all the benefits of staying at a Disney resort, as listed later in this chapter. Learn more about these resorts in Chapter 10.

Deluxe Resorts

Deluxe resorts are the high end of the Disney lodging experience. These resorts offer a greater range of amenities and services. The rooms are larger, and the overall experience is certainly more upscale than other types of lodging. These resorts enjoy better locations on the property, with quicker access to certain parks or entertainment areas. As an example, all but one of them enjoys transportation to a theme park via a short walk, a monorail trip, or a boat ride, all of which are preferable to a bus trip. You'll get all the benefits of staying at a Disney-owned resort, as listed later in this chapter. You can find out more about what perks they do and don't offer when you read their reviews in Chapter 7.

> **HIDDEN MAGIC!**
>
> If you are staying at a Disney resort, be sure to ask for the resort's recreational activity flyer when you check in. Many of the Disney resorts have fun, family-friendly activities going on all the time that you may not have heard about. Mostly found at the Deluxe and Moderate resorts, but also at Fort Wilderness and occasionally at the Value resorts, activities include treasure hunts, poolside entertainment, and free outdoor movie screenings complete with bonfires and other surprises.

Moderate Resorts

These resorts offer nearly comparable-sized rooms to the Deluxe resorts at a greatly reduced rate, but they usually have fewer amenities available. The greatest drop-off is in dining options and transportation, where most rely exclusively on bus service to get to the parks and other locales. Within this group, the level of services varies, with each having something special to attract you. Recently added to this category were the Cabins at Fort Wilderness, which offers a family a unique accommodation option that is largely overlooked by most visitors. You'll get all the benefits of staying at a Disney-owned resort, as listed later in this chapter. Learn more about these resorts in Chapter 8.

Value Resorts

These resorts are one of the great options, bringing on-property accommodations down to the price range that most of us can afford. Amenities drop off greatly, but the Disney machine makes sure to deliver top quality even if the price tag is a bit lower. Bus service is the standard transportation and there are no table-service restaurants at these resorts, but they do have many of the necessities—and they deliver them with flair. Disney owns all of these resorts, so they get you all the usual benefits, as listed later in this chapter. Learn more about these resorts in Chapter 9.

> **DID YOU KNOW?**
>
> Starting in 2009, guests have been able to go through the check-in process for their Walt Disney World resort from the comfort of their own home! Starting up to 10 days before they arrive, they can check in, make special requests, and get all that process out of the way. When you arrive, you pick up your packet and get right to the fun. They will even text you when your room is ready!

Campgrounds

Disney Campsites at Fort Wilderness have long been the RV enthusiast's dream, offering ideal sites, affordable rates, and great amenities. The sense of community here also adds to the experience. Read more about these in Chapter 10.

Other Select Deluxe Hotels

The Swan and Dolphin hotels, located behind the BoardWalk, are on Disney property but are not run by Disney. These two massive teal-and-orange Starwood resorts are run by Westin (Swan) and Sheraton (Dolphin) and are hard to miss. They are often home to conventions, and while there are some perks for those on Disney property that you do not get here, there are other side benefits that you can read about in Chapter 11.

Shades of Green

This resort is in a class by itself, as it serves U.S. military personnel and retirees exclusively. Learn more about this resort in Chapter 11.

Hotel Plaza Boulevard

This area adjacent to Downtown Disney is home to seven hotels with names that you may recognize, such as Hilton, Best Western, and Courtyard. These hotels are on Disney property, but each enjoys different benefits and perks than the standard Disney-owned resort. We cover the benefits in more detail when we review them in Chapter 11.

Benefits of Staying on Property

So why should you stay at a Disney property? Well, Disney is interested in getting as many of your vacation dollars as possible while you're here, and they'll give you perks to convince you that your accommodations budget should go to them as well. Some of these perks are great ones; others are not so important to most guests. You need to weigh which ones offer some value to you and which do not. The following sections outline the major ones.

Disney Magical Express

When you arrive at the Orlando International Airport (MCO), you never have to touch your bags—you just jump on a bus that takes you to your resort. Here is how it works.

> Disney mails luggage stickers to you before you leave on vacation. Place them on your luggage when checking in at your home airport. When you arrive at the Orlando airport, simply go to the Magical Express reception area and you are guided to your Magical Express bus. The bus whisks you to your resort. All the while, Disney grabs your bags at the airport, transports them to your resort, and drops them off in your room.

That is right, they gather your bags for you, and you never even have to pick them up! Bags typically arrive in your room within three hours. The return trip to the airport at vacation's end includes baggage handling again, along with advance airline ticketing for select airlines. It's a great savings, in both dollars and headaches.

> **Good for:** Anyone, because taxi service can run $30 to $60 per person.

> **Avoided by:** If you are part of a large group and want to make a stop by a grocery store to stock your kitchenette, you're better off taking a limo that allows for such stops than taking a cab later.

> **Value:** If you're flying to Disney, assume that you'll save a minimum of $30 for the round-trip per-person charge. If you're driving, you obviously do not need this perk.

Extended Theme Park Hours

Extra Magic Hours allow guests to enter select parks on certain days an hour ahead of all other guests, and to stay at other parks after standard closing hours. These Extra Magic Hours mean you're in the park with a slightly smaller crowd to contend with, and you get more time to enjoy all those rides and shows.

> **Good for:** Again, just about anyone can take advantage of the hours. Even if you're not an early riser, the evening hours are a nice way to enjoy smaller crowds, lower temperatures, and less pressure to get it all done in the standard hours.
>
> **Avoided by:** Almost nobody!
>
> **Value:** It's hard to put a dollar amount on it, but if you can take advantage of three Extra Magic Hours sessions in a week's visit, I would estimate the value at approximately half a day's worth of whatever you're spending on tickets.

Disney Resort Transportation

You can enjoy free usage of the buses, boats, and monorails that interconnect the Walt Disney World parks, resorts, and other facilities.

Come on, who are we kidding here? In reality, the transportation is open to everyone. You do, however, need to consider that staying on property means you're not driving to the parks and incurring a daily parking charge of $14.

> **Good for:** Everyone.
>
> **Avoided by:** Nobody.
>
> **Value:** $14 per day.

Charging Privileges

Basically, wherever you are, you can charge merchandise, food, drinks, and other purchases to your room.

> **Good for:** Most people enjoy this perk, especially those who don't like carrying lots of cash or their credit cards. It's also preferred by international guests, many of whom like to have all bills kept together.

Avoided by: This isn't hurting anyone, though you will definitely want to monitor usage.

Value: I wouldn't apply a dollar value to the perk, but it's a nice convenient feature.

Package Shipping

No, they're not shipping items home for you, but they're helping you get through your day in the park. This perk helps you when you buy something at a Walt Disney World–area store. Instead of having to carry purchases around all day long, they will ship them back to your resort room. It takes over a day, so you can't do it on your last few days of your vacation, but it's a great help if you find a gift early in the morning and don't particularly want to carry it around on roller coasters the rest of the day, or rent a locker to stow it in.

Good for: Guests who plan on buying lots of items, especially in the parks.

Avoided by: Visitors staying three days or less.

Value: Renting a locker is a minimum of $5, so that's what you save per day when you buy something to be shipped to your room.

Disney Dining Plan

The Disney Dining Plan is another way for Disney to get more of your money. (There are several actual plans in the program.) They again do it in a way that probably makes good sense for you, so don't look at it with a jaded eye. This program is an optional extra charge, but it's not necessarily a bad thing, as most find this to be a great money saver in the long run. As you will find out in Chapter 12, the dining plans allow you to prepurchase meals at a good rate, and if the costs work out, it's a great convenience and money saver.

Good for: Guests who plan to have a lot of table-service or counter-service meals and whose daily per-person food budget is more than $40.

Avoided by: Guests who keep their food budget under $30 a day or who plan on having a lot of meals away from Walt Disney World.

Value: The examples in Chapter 12 have a sample family of four saving over $20 per day in food costs on the basic plan.

The Bottom Line for On-Property Perks

What's the bottom line? Well, as explained here, it all depends on your particular needs. You will likely find that a combination of these perks offers a savings or benefit worth a certain amount. A number of intangibles should be considered as well. Your morning trips to the parks will be shorter, you won't have to worry about your car, you won't have to pay for parking, etc. With smaller children you can get back to your resort for naps and pool time more quickly. I also feel that the Disney resorts really get you in the Disney mood with their decor, service, and general ambiance. You are immersed in the Disney experience your whole trip, instead of just for the eight or so hours a day that you visited the park from a non-Disney hotel. These intangibles always bring me back to the Disney resort experience, even when it may cost me a few extra bucks per day.

As you consider your accommodation selection, you can revisit your budget planning, outlined in Chapter 2, and adjust the value of different packages based on what these perks will do for you.

Understanding Disney Resorts

Disney runs its resorts its own special way, with unique customs and practices that may seem odd to the active traveler. Understanding them can help you get through the cloud of confusion they can create.

Disney Rate Seasons

Disney charges different nightly rates depending on the anticipated demand for rooms. They used to have four basic rate seasons, but that has been replaced by as many as 20. Yep, 20. But don't let that sound confusing to you. The basic rules still apply. Weekends are more expensive than weekdays. Holidays and summer break are more expensive than when kids are in school.

Here is how the seasons seem to hit, throughout the year:

- January through mid-February: Value
- Mid-February through end of February: Peak

- March through mid-March: Regular

- Mid-March through April: Peak

- May through mid-July: Regular

- Mid-July through September: Value

- October: Regular

- November through December: Fall

Note that the following holidays throughout the year raise prices: Disney Marathon (January), Martin Luther King Day, President's Day, Easter, Independence Day, Columbus Day, Thanksgiving, Christmas, and New Year's.

The following is the order, from most to least expensive, of the rate seasons from Disney:

- Holiday (Christmas through New Year's Day)

- Easter

- President's Weekend

- Peak Season

- Thanksgiving

- Independence Day

- Columbus Day

- Regular Season

- Martin Luther King Day

- Disney Marathon

- Fall Season

- Value Season

As a frame of reference, the lowest cost room rate was anywhere from 63 percent to 50 percent of the highest. In the Grand Floridian resort in 2012 that meant that going on a Value Season weekday ($460/day) as opposed to a Holiday Season day ($730/day) would save you $270 per day. As another example, a Value hotel room can range from as low as $84 a night to as high as $169 a night. That means the price can be literally double its lowest rate when you travel during certain holidays.

To be sure of what season your travel dates are in, simply visit the resort's webpage at **www.waltdisneyworld.com,** then select **Room Types & Pricing.** From there you can see when the different season rates apply for that particular resort.

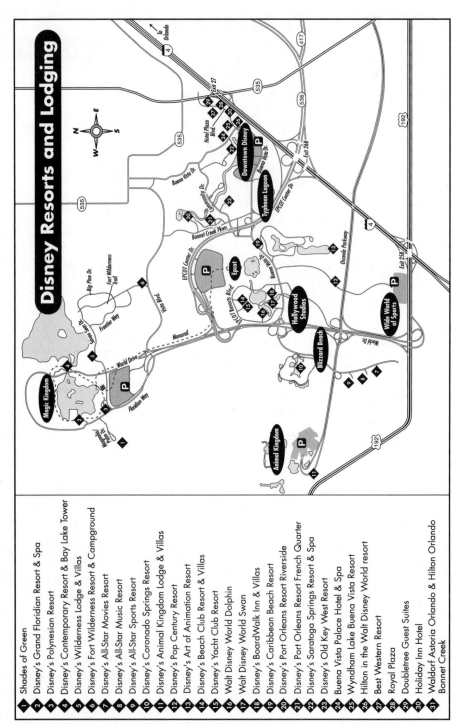

Disney Resorts and Lodging

1. Shades of Green
2. Disney's Grand Floridian Resort & Spa
3. Disney's Polynesian Resort
4. Disney's Contemporary Resort & Bay Lake Tower
5. Disney's Wilderness Lodge & Villas
6. Disney's Fort Wilderness Resort & Campground
7. Disney's All-Star Movies Resort
8. Disney's All-Star Music Resort
9. Disney's All-Star Sports Resort
10. Disney's Coronado Springs Resort
11. Disney's Animal Kingdom Lodge & Villas
12. Disney's Pop Century Resort
13. Disney's Art of Animation Resort
14. Disney's Beach Club Resort & Villas
15. Disney's Yacht Club Resort
16. Walt Disney World Dolphin
17. Walt Disney World Swan
18. Disney's BoardWalk Inn & Villas
19. Disney's Caribbean Beach Resort
20. Disney's Port Orleans Resort Riverside
21. Disney's Port Orleans Resort French Quarter
22. Disney's Saratoga Springs Resort & Spa
23. Disney's Old Key West Resort
24. Buena Vista Palace Hotel & Spa
25. Wyndham Lake Buena Vista Resort
26. Hilton in the Walt Disney World resort
27. Best Western Resort
28. Royal Plaza
29. Doubletree Guest Suites
30. Holiday Inn Hotel
31. Waldorf Astoria Orlando & Hilton Orlando Bonnet Creek

Walt Disney World hotel locations.

Hotel Locations

Most Disney resorts are labeled by the area of Walt Disney World where they are located. Areas include the Magic Kingdom, Epcot, Animal Kingdom, Downtown Disney, and Wide World of Sports areas.

These labels help you identify what attractions you will be closer to, but do not impact what kind of amenities are available to you. What does this matter to you? Probably not a lot, but if you know that you will spend a great deal of time in one area recreationally, getting a resort in that area would be a good idea.

Hotel Comparison

What are the differences among the Disney properties? Following is a brief chart of some of the key differences for the Disney properties, not including those on Hotel Plaza Boulevard.

Disney Rooms

The rooms at Walt Disney World have a variety of amenities and comforts that are pretty standard in hotels around the world. But certain practices are only catching up to the Kingdom. You should be prepared for your stay here so that you appreciate what you're paying for.

Just because you may be paying top dollar for a room at Walt Disney World, don't expect excessive luxury. Two identical rooms in New York City and Des Moines, for example, would charge different rates because of their locations. Similarly, your room at the resort may be like a standard hotel room in your hometown, but remember that the extra charge here is based on getting other kinds of benefits for your money. First, you are at the premier vacation spot in the world. Second, you are closer to the parks than the less expensive off-property resorts.

Hotel	Rating	Standard Room Rates	Villa Room Rates	Dining Table Service	Counter Service
Deluxe Resorts (Chapter 7)					
Animal Kingdom Lodge	4	$265-$620		X	X
Beach Club Resort	5	$335-$925		X	X
BoardWalk Inn	4	$345-$910		X	X
Contemporary Resort	4	$315-$910		X	X
Grand Floridian Resort & Spa	4.5	$460-$1160		X	X
Polynesian Resort	4.5	$405-$1045		X	X
Wilderness Lodge	4	$265-$650		X	X
Yacht Club Resort	5	$335-$1015		X	X
Moderate Resorts (Chapter 8)					
Caribbean Beach Resort	3	$159-$314		X	X
Coronado Springs Resort	3	$164-$289		X	X
Port Orleans Resort French Quarter	3.5	$159-$279		X	X
Port Orleans Resort Riverside	3.5	$159-$319			X
Cabins at Fort Wilderness Resort	3	$285-$455		X	
Value Resorts (Chapter 9)					
Pop Century Resort	3	$89-$189			X
All-Star Movies Resort	2.5	$84-$184			X
All-Star Music Resort	3	$84-$184	$198-$375		X
All-Star Sports Resort	2.5	$84-$184			X
Art of Animation Resort	TBD	TBD-$179	$249-$425		X
Deluxe Villas & Campgrounds (Chapter 10)					
Bay Lake Tower (Contemporary)	4	$415-$710	$515-$2605	X	X
Animal Kingdom Villas	4	$300-$810	$435-$2345	X	X
Beach Club Villas	5	$345-$580	$500-$1265	X	X
BoardWalk Villas	4	$345-$580	$500-$2345	X	X
Old Key West Resort	3	$315-$465	$435-$1795	X	X
Saratoga Springs Resort & Spa	3.5	$315-$465	$435-$1795	X	X
Treehouse Villas (Saratoga Springs)	3.5		$595-$980	X	X
Villas at Wilderness Lodge	4	$355-$535	$485-$1260	X	X
Fort Wilderness Resort & Campground	2.5	$46-$125*		X	
*These reflect campsite rental rates, not rooms					

Room Service	Resort Amenities						Transportation		
	Beach	Marina	Spa	Fitness Centers	Playgrounds	Child Activity Centers	Monorail	Boat	Bus
X			L	X	X	X			X
X	X	X	L	X		X		X	X
X			L	X	X			X	X
X	X	X	L	X	X		X	X	X
X	X	X	X	X		X	X	X	X
X	X	X		X	X	X	X	X	X
X	X	X	L	X	X	X		X	X
X	X	X	L	X		X		X	X
L	X	X			X				X
L	X	X	L	X	X				X
L		X			X			X	X
L		X			X			X	X
	X	X			X			X	X
P					X				X
P					X				X
P					X				X
P					X				X
P									X
X	X	X	L	X	X		X	X	X
X			L	X	X	X			X
X	X	X	L	X		X		X	X
X			L	X	X			X	X
X		X		X	X			X	X
X			X	X	X			X	X
X					X			X	X
X	X	X	L	X	X	X		X	X
	X	X			X			X	X

Resort Amenities   Transportation

Disney hotel comparison chart.

Other Accommodation Options in Orlando

If you're looking for some non-Disney properties, where should you look? Well, with more than 350 hotels in the area, not to mention townhomes for lease, timeshares, and more, there are too many choices to consider them all. In Chapter 11, I show you three nearby areas to consider and list a few of my favorite hotels.

The Disney Vacation Club

Disney has been promoting its time-share program for some time now, and its growth is hard to miss, especially when you visit Walt Disney World. The resort growth here has been largely tied to the program, and it also offers some non–Orlando-based options. Resorts in the Disney Vacation Club are listed in Chapter 10.

In addition to several locations throughout Walt Disney World, Disney also has locations in Florida, Hilton Head, Hawaii, and the Disneyland resort in California. For more information about this program, visit www.disneyvacationclub.com.

Summary

Admittedly, we covered a lot of different topics in very short order here. The topics that matter, however—namely, the specifics about all the on-property and select off-property hotels—are covered adequately in the other chapters in this part of the book, so for now you have a good understanding of the advantages of staying on property, what the Disney Vacation Club is, and what different options are available to you.

Deluxe Resorts

In This Chapter

- Learn about Disney's Deluxe resorts
- Select the theme and location that are right for you
- Find out what room and resort amenities are available

When you start to take a closer look at the resort options at Walt Disney World, it's always smart to start at the top and work your way down. Starting at the top means beginning by looking at the Deluxe-class resorts. These are the cream of the crop, and if they are within your budget, they can really make your already great vacation even better. They are well-themed complexes that transport you to a different place or time, including the national parks of the American West, a coastal Florida resort from the 1800s, a great safari lodge on the African plain, an Atlantic seaside resort, a futuristic high-rise, and more. They are definitely the first-class section of the Disney hotel world.

These top Disney resorts offer you the best-in-class rooms, amenities, locations, and decor for your accommodation choice. Within the class, there are also some distinct differences, so you can pick the one that is most suited to your specific needs. Some offer expansive pools, others are just a walk away from nightlife venues, and still others are prized for being just a quick monorail ride from the Magic Kingdom.

Now of course, the cost is there, too. These resorts can get pretty pricey. But if they're within your budget, the advantages to staying at one of these resorts will become evident.

What Is a Deluxe Resort?

Deluxe resorts offer the best of everything—and charge for it as well. The advantages largely fall into four groups: room size and features, resort features, hotel location, and dining options. Let's take a look at just what these benefits are and what they might mean to you.

Room Size and Features

Deluxe resort rooms are larger than the rooms at the Moderate and Value resorts. How much larger, and who cares? Well, a good deal larger, and, believe me, you will.

First, room size. The rooms offer a larger overall space, which is great if you have four or more people to a room. This gives you more space for your luggage, clothes, and purchases.

HIDDEN MAGIC!

Want to add that special touch to your stay? Contact the Disney World Florist and have a bouquet of flowers or candy waiting, or, better yet, have them decorate the room! Visit www.disneyflorist.com to see what they have to offer.

Second, room features. The bathrooms are nicer, featuring, in most cases, multiple sinks. The entryways have larger closets with closing doors, as opposed to an exposed rod. The TVs are larger, with most of the recent room renovations placing flatscreens in the rooms. Refrigerators are standard in the room, and a Pack 'N Play crib can be put in your room at no charge just by asking in advance. You often get a veranda or patio, offering you somewhere to relax when the kids are asleep. It sure beats sitting on your own bed in the dark.

Resort Features

These resorts have more to offer when you leave the room as well. It starts from the moment you check in, where grand lobbies make you feel immediately welcome. Some of the resorts offer more shopping than just the standard souvenir shop found in most hotels. There are also concierge desks and concierge floors for that extra support that can make all the difference.

Recreation is next. Sure, all the resorts have pools, but the Deluxe pools are larger and carry the theme of their host resort, complete with volcanoes, sandy horizon pool entrances, lazy rivers, water slides, and poolside bars. Some resorts have beach areas and marinas; others have tennis courts, spas, volleyball courts, and health clubs. All of them have something extra.

> **HIDDEN MAGIC!**
>
> So what are my favorite Deluxe resorts? Well, they're all pretty good, but here's a breakdown of some different reasons why one might be your best choice.
>
> - **Best resort for little kids:** Disney's Polynesian Resort
>   Being on the monorail gets you to the Magic Kingdom quickly, which is where you likely will spend the majority of your days. The atmosphere is fun for boys and girls.
>
> - **Best resort for tweens:** Disney's Wilderness Lodge
>   While it's nice to be at one of the monorail resorts, the Lodge is a lot of fun and is still just a quick boat ride from the Magic Kingdom and the outdoor fun of Fort Wilderness.
>
> - **Best resort for teens:** Disney's Beach Club Resort
>   Access to the best Deluxe resort pool, as well as a quick walk to Epcot and the BoardWalk make this Deluxe resort great fun. And the atmosphere is more relaxed and low-key than its sister Yacht Club.
>
> - **Best resort for just adults:** Disney's Yacht Club Resort
>   Nightlife is just a short walk away, and the proximity of the Epcot World Showcase and its restaurants makes it ideal. A more upscale, sedate setting gets you away from kids more than at other locales.
>
> - **Best value:** Disney's Wilderness Lodge
>
> - **Most exotic:** Animal Kingdom Lodge
>
> - **Most luxurious:** Disney's Grand Floridian Resort & Spa

Hotel Location

At Walt Disney World, location is king. It starts with being able to get to a theme park by boat, foot, or monorail. These are all far preferable to buses because they can get you there in a faster, less crowded, and more scenic fashion. One of the resorts (Animal Kingdom Lodge) does not enjoy this benefit, but it has many other unique features.

Another advantage to location is the view. Looking out your resort room to see Cinderella Castle is not just a nicety; it can heighten the excitement for kids of all ages. Looking out onto one of the area lakes, catching a nearby park's fireworks from your room balcony or a hotel public space, and just being in the middle of it all adds immeasurable value to your overall experience.

Dining Options

The increased dining options that you will find in a Deluxe resort are another underestimated value. You're going to be tired after a day at the parks. Being able to dine at your own resort instead of having to go elsewhere to forage is amazingly important. These resorts have more table-service restaurant options, ranging from fine dining to more casual offerings. They have counter-service food courts as well, and also feature lounges, character meals, and a more complete room service menu.

Bottom line: The features go on, but these few give you an idea of how you can improve your stay with a Deluxe hotel reservation. These resorts will cost you more, but they make for an entertaining stay that complements any Disney vacation.

Deluxe Resort Pros

- Significantly wider menu of amenities, both in room and resortwide
- Better locations that shorten your travel to the theme parks
- Larger rooms

Deluxe Resort Cons

- Extremely expensive rooms
- Less luxurious rooms than in similarly priced national chains

The Walt Disney World Deluxe Resorts

Let's look at the Deluxe resorts. Review the themes, features, and benefits of each of these unique resorts. Don't underestimate how much the theme of your resort can make your stay even more special.

Disney's Animal Kingdom Lodge

Overall Rating: ★ ★ ★ ★ ☆
Location: Animal Kingdom area
Price Range: $265–$620 for a standard room

Transportation: Buses to all theme parks, water parks, and Downtown Disney.

Special Features: The savannah animal-viewing areas, warm and inviting public spaces intended to get guests to socialize.

Room Types: Large rooms sleep 4 to 5, with two queen-sized beds and a day bed or one king-sized bed and a day bed, or a queen-sized bed with bunk beds. Suites for up to 8 guests also are available.

Best Room Locations: Stay as close to the main lobby as you can. The further you get out on the wings of this hotel, the more walking you have to do. The rooms that overlook the savannah animal-viewing areas cost extra but are popular. Realize that the resort can't guarantee that you will see animals at any given time; they kind of work on their own schedule. But it can be a unique experience when you're enjoying a room service breakfast and a zebra trots by. My personal opinion is that you can see them down the hall in the public viewing areas as easily as you can from your own veranda, so save the extra dough. Just make sure you're not in a room overlooking the Uzima pool if you can help it, as the added noise can be a distraction.

Dining: The lodge has three restaurants and a great lounge. The high-end Jiko—The Cooking Place is one of the best fine restaurants in all of Orlando, providing African-inspired cuisine and a range of South African wines. Boma—Flavors of Africa is a wildly popular and better-than-average buffet that has both kids' standards and some African-flavored choices making it a great deal of fun. The Mara has food-court dining and is located adjacent to the pool. The Victoria Falls lounge just off the lobby is a nice place to grab a cocktail after a long day at the parks, with several fruity drink specials and cushy seats that you can sink into and relax.

Atmosphere: The Animal Kingdom Lodge is like staying in an extremely large African safari outpost. The entry hall is a massive, multistory space decorated with colorful tribal masks, native art, and safari artifacts. The hall opens upward for several stories, and one entire side is made of windows looking out onto an African plain.

This savannah area really makes this a unique resort. A variety of animals roam free just feet from guest rooms and a public viewing area. Animal guides are regularly around to talk to guests about the care of the different animals, as well as provide interesting facts about their species.

Animals roaming the Animal Kingdom Lodge savannah.
Photo © Disney.

The theme is carried throughout the rest of the resort, with occasional animal-viewing verandas, fireplace-gathering areas, and a pool that is reminiscent of an African watering hole. As ambiance goes, it's one of the warmer, better-themed resorts in all of Walt Disney World, and it has won numerous awards. It doubles both as an ideal place to stay with kids and as a high-quality resort for adults. The theme and special features make it fun and exciting, keeping kids in a Disney mood. For adults, it has a kind of "rough" elegance that can't be denied and is certain to be appreciated.

Despite winning numerous awards as a top resort destination, the Animal Kingdom Lodge only scores a 4 out of 5 rating largely due to it only having bus service within the Disney transportation system. That, and the resort's remote location, make it a sometimes less than ideal choice for first-time visitors to Walt Disney World. It is, however, still one of my favorite resorts, due to the great atmosphere, superb dining, and unique animal vistas.

Special Activities: The Animal Kingdom Lodge has a lot of great added features. The Arusha Rock Savanna Outlook provides great views into the animal habitat and is often manned by staff who can answer questions, and sometimes even have night vision goggles that you can borrow to get a better view of the animals. The Simba Clubhouse child activity center is a great place to entertain your 4- to 12-year-old for a few hours at night. For only $12 an hour they get supervised care and activities, as well as dinner, while you take a well-deserved adult night out. Finally, guests of the lodge can go on special dawn or dusk safaris to get some great animal-viewing experiences.

Disney's Beach Club Resort and Yacht Club Resort

Overall Rating: ★ ★ ★ ★ ★
Location: Epcot area
Price Range: $335–$1,015 for a standard room

Transportation: Walk to Epcot and the BoardWalk; boat to Hollywood Studios; buses to all other theme parks, water parks, and Downtown Disney.

Special Features: These two intertwined resort hotels are in walking distance to Epcot and the BoardWalk, and are just a boat ride away from Hollywood Studios. This alone is of great appeal to any guest. The real highlight here, however, is the pool. Shared by the two resorts, it's the best one in all of Walt Disney World. It's like a wandering river, meandering around to create numerous private areas where you don't have to have other guests constantly walking through your lounging area. There's also a section of the pool with a sandy-beach entry for a near-oceanlike experience. A nearby ship-wreck serves as the scenic start to a great water slide, too.

Room Types: Large rooms sleep 4 to 5, with two queen-sized beds or two double beds or a king-sized bed. Other rooms have the same configurations with a day bed as well. Suites for up to 8 guests also are available.

Best Room Locations: Rooms to the Epcot side (east) of the Beach Club Resort are quieter and allow you to avoid public spaces when leaving for the BoardWalk or Epcot. For the Yacht Club Resort, you are best served getting rooms to the far west side to avoid public space noise.

Dining: These two hotels are lucky, in that they have not only a good complement of their own restaurants, but also the restaurants of the BoardWalk, the Swan and Dolphin hotels, and the pavilions of the Epcot World Showcase all within a short walk. It's an embarrassment of riches. But let's focus on the restaurants in these two resorts. The most popular is the Cape May Café, which starts the day with a character breakfast buffet and then serves a seafood buffet at night. The Yachtsman Steakhouse serves a decent steak, and the Beaches & Cream Soda Shop makes for a more casual food stop. The Captain's Grille (formerly the Yacht Club Galley) also offers nice standard American fare. The food court experience that you get at most other Disney resorts is not as fully featured here, but still good for some grab-and-go dining.

Atmosphere: These two resorts are reviewed together because they are essentially the same resort, sharing many of their facilities and amenities. But once you're inside, certain decor and atmosphere nuances create slightly different moods for your stay.

The Beach Club provides a great middle ground between formal and fun as the decor provides an understated elegance to your stay. The muted colors help set the tone in one of the best stays in all of Walt Disney World. The cozy registration hall leads to quiet halls and well-appointed rooms.

Where the Beach Club decor is a bit more muted and relaxed, the Yacht Club has a very upper-crusty New England look that is very appealing. Elegant hues of blue and gold accent the bead board trim, while ship models and nautical items decorate the public spaces.

The bottom line is that the conveniently quick transportation to two theme parks and the BoardWalk means that I can avoid lots of the transportation headaches, and the decor in the Yacht Club makes me feel like I'm staying at an elegant resort commensurate with how much I'm spending on the room. Oddly enough, however, the Beach Club is very popular, and the Yacht Club is the least popular of all Deluxe resorts. Go figure.

Special Activities: The Sandcastle Club child-care center is great for any 4- to 12-year-olds whose parents need a few hours of peace and quiet at night. Per-child charge is $12 an hour and includes a buffet dinner. The Albatross Pirate Cruise for 4- to 10-year-olds is another daytime excursion that can be an unexpected and thrilling surprise for any budding pirate.

Disney's BoardWalk Inn

Overall Rating: ★ ★ ★ ★ ☆
Location: Epcot area
Price Range: $345–$920 for a standard room

Transportation: Walk to Epcot and the BoardWalk; boat to Hollywood Studios; buses to all theme parks, water parks, and Downtown Disney.

Special Features: The resort's location is just about perfect. You can walk or take a boat to both Epcot and Hollywood Studios. You also have the BoardWalk and all of its perks right outside your door. There's a public hall for games, separate from the standard hotel arcade.

Room Types: Large rooms sleep 4 to 5, with two queen-sized beds or a king-sized bed. Other rooms have the same configurations with a junior-sized day bed as well. Suites for up to 8 guests also are available.

Best Room Locations: Garden-view rooms offer the best blend, giving you peace and quiet in your room, and the fun of the BoardWalk just a few paces away. If you have teens, they may get a treat from a view of the BoardWalk, but it might not be worth the trade-off for the evening noise level.

Dining: All the dining is on the BoardWalk, with a good array of choices. At the high end is the Flying Fish Café, offering the best seafood at Walt Disney World. Kouzzina (formerly Spoodles) takes care of more of the daily needs of a family, with newly updated cuisine inspired by the cultures of the Mediterranean, particularly Greece. There are also other choices, like the pub environments of the Big River Grille & Brewing Works and the ESPN Club, as well as counter foods at the BoardWalk Bakery and in stands along the walk itself.

A special benefit here are the bar choices, starting with a nice, small lounge inside the resort that is a perfect and quiet escape from a long day. You also have the nearby bars of the BoardWalk, like Jellyrolls and the Atlantic Dance Hall. This is a far better selection than at any other resort hotel.

Atmosphere: The BoardWalk Inn harkens to a quieter day, transporting you to the Atlantic seaboard resort towns like Coney Island. This truly unique resort sits astride the actual BoardWalk that serves as a relaxed nighttime diversion in the Walt Disney World landscape. The promenade of bars and restaurants gives you a nice retreat from your room, especially if you're traveling with just adults. But families will also find this to be an ideal spot, with the G-rated entertainment and great dessert offerings.

Inside, the decor carries the theme further, with a whitewashed elegance that doesn't get too frilly. The registration hall is smaller than found in most Deluxe resorts, making it a cozier gathering place, with interesting curios like a miniature carousel. The pool is also very fun, decorated in bright reds and whites, with a circus theme that makes it better than most.

Special Activities: The BoardWalk Inn special activities are largely based on the location, with all the action going on at the BoardWalk. But also remember that many of the activities at the nearby Yacht and Beach Club (like the Albatross Cruise) are ones that guests of the BoardWalk can enjoy as well.

Disney's Contemporary Resort

Overall Rating: ★ ★ ★ ★ ☆
Location: Magic Kingdom area
Price Range: $315–$910 for a standard room

Transportation: Monorail to the Magic Kingdom and Epcot; buses to all other theme parks, water parks, and Downtown Disney.

Special Features: Are you kidding me? A hotel with a monorail running through it—how cool is that? Being located just minutes away from the Magic Kingdom is a huge perk. You can walk or take a monorail there. You can even monorail to Epcot, making it one of the more park-accessible resorts. The resort also has a marina, complete with a lot of water sports.

Room Types: Large rooms sleep 4 to 5, with two queen-sized beds and a day bed or one king-sized bed and a day bed. Suites for up to 8 guests also are available.

Best Room Locations: I prefer the view to the west toward Seven Seas Lagoon and the Magic Kingdom. But views to the east and Bay Lake are very serene and beautiful, too, so it's hard to go wrong. Either way you want to be in the main tower, as opposed to the less expensive but less fun Garden Wing rooms. If you are going to spend the money to stay here, you want to spend a bit more and be in the atmosphere of the tower.

Dining: Two of the best restaurants of their respective types are found here. California Grill, perched atop the hotel, is a fantastic high-end restaurant with excellent food and views to match. Chef Mickey's is a character meal spot with a top-notch buffet that has better food than most buffets. There's a food court as well, for that quick bite or to grab some snacks. The Wave restaurant adds another table-service dining choice that is inconsistent in its experience, but has a larger, easier-to-access bar setting.

Atmosphere: I don't care how old you are; it's pretty hard not to be impressed when you see the monorail running through the middle of the hotel. That really sets the mood for the modern ambiance that the hotel conveys. The recent extensive lobby and public area refurbishment has not warmed up the somewhat cold ambiance, but the stores are better and more fun to browse. The halls are sparsely decorated, but the view down into the main area is better than some cheap abstract art on a wall. The rooms, once decorated like they were out of a bad 1970 sci-fi movie, have now been completely renovated, with a classic new look that is more, well, contemporary. The completely revamped rooms have flatscreen TVs, dark-wood furniture, and more comfortable beds of the kind that most major upscale chains are rolling out. The rooms seem more like what you should be getting for the price paid. Bottom line is that this legendary hotel is one that will amaze kids with its public spaces, despite the cold ambiance, and comfort you with its rooms.

Special Activities: There are not a lot of special resort-specific events here, but the views, marina-based boat rentals, and the location really makes up for that.

Disney's Grand Floridian Resort & Spa

Overall Rating: ★ ★ ★ ★ ☆
Location: Magic Kingdom area
Price Range: $460–$1,160 for a standard room

Transportation: Monorail to the Magic Kingdom and Epcot; buses to all other theme parks, water parks, and Downtown Disney.

Special Features: Marina, full spa, monorail, specialty meals, and more high-end dining options. Considered the luxury resort of all Deluxe hotels, it has the top shops, rooms, suites, and everything else of any resort here.

Room Types: Large rooms sleep 4 to 5, with two queen-sized beds or one king-sized bed. Most rooms also include a day bed. Suites for up to 8 guests also are available.

Best Room Locations: Any room with a view of Cinderella Castle is nice but comes at a premium, as there are not very many. If you can choose a building, choose the lake views from Conch Key or Sago Cay, and then Boca Chica.

Dining: Why are there so many restaurants here? Because you're paying for them, so you deserve them! Victoria & Albert's is the most elegant of all restaurants at Walt Disney World, with personalized menus and cuisine that is beyond compare. Citricos (Mediterranean) and Narcoossee's (seafood) prove that the premier resort has more than one quality restaurant for your enjoyment. 1900 Park Fare brings a series of unique character experiences at breakfast, dinner, and even high tea. The tea is extremely special for your little princess—and expensive, at more than $200 for one adult and one child. The Garden View Lounge proves that the resort really thinks that everyone should enjoy high tea. For more casual dining, there is the Grand Floridian Café. Then there's the standard counter-service site (Gasparilla Grill & Games) that all Disney resorts have. There are even a few small lounges for evening drinks with great views of the lake. Your restaurant selections are numerous, the quality is mostly excellent, and if you pay to stay here, you earned it.

Atmosphere: This is the flagship resort at Walt Disney World. The expansive resort is a pristine sight to see, with its contrasting white walls and windows set under the vivid red rooftops. The Victorian structure is decorated inside with muted light hues and a frilly elegance that makes it a perfect stay for families with a budding princess. It can seem a bit antiseptic to me, but the decor is undeniably elegant and well executed.

Taking its inspiration from the Atlantic seaside resorts that popped up along the Florida coastline during the 1800s, the amenities and particularly the shopping certainly honor that spirit of a high-end resort destination. Every detail is done to perfection.

Special Activities: The Mouseketeer Club child-care center is great for any 4- to 12-year-olds to visit for supervised activities and dinner while their parents enjoy the Disney nightlife. Per-child charge is $12 an hour and includes a buffet dinner. The daytime activities for 4- to 12-year-olds include the Grand Adventures in Cooking program, the Wonderland Tea Party, and Disney's Pirate Adventure.

Disney's Polynesian Resort

Overall Rating: ★ ★ ★ ★ ☆
Location: Magic Kingdom area
Price Range: $405–$1,045 for a standard room

Transportation: Monorail to the Magic Kingdom and Epcot; buses to all other theme parks, water parks, and Downtown Disney.

Special Features: The Polynesian has a great array of dining options, with several entertaining choices that are ideal for families. The monorail access to the Magic Kingdom and Epcot, as well as the recently renovated rooms, takes this resort from being one that I used to steer people away from back to being a great choice. The Hawaiian theme is just so much fun for kids, and romantic for adults.

Room Types: Large rooms sleep 4 to 5, with two queen-sized beds and a daybed. Suites for up to 8 guests also are available.

Best Room Locations: The Tuvalu, Fiji, Tokelau, Hawaii, Tahiti, and Samoa buildings all offer great rooms that are not a long walk from the Great House. Choose any of these if you can get a lake view. Just make sure if you have kids who need afternoon naps that you are not facing south toward the parking lot in the Rarotonga, Aotearoa, Tonga, or Rapa Nui buildings; the noise level from the nearby Richard Petty Driving Experience can make napping nearly impossible, possibly creating a major issue for the duration of your vacation!

Dining: 'Ohana has been a great addition to this resort, with a perfectly themed character breakfast (Lilo and Stitch, as well as Mickey and friends) and an entertaining dinner experience complete with a ukulele player who guides children through dances and limbo competitions like the Pied Piper. There's a bit more toned-down table-service dining at the underrated Kona Café, the counter-service convenience of a newly renovated Captain Cook's Snack Company, and the *Spirit of Aloha* show's luau atmosphere to bring you a very wide spectrum of dining options. The lounge, located just off the lobby by the entrance to 'Ohana, may be small, but they create some fruity drinks that have become a mainstay of long-time visitors.

Atmosphere: One of the original resort hotels at Walt Disney World, this Polynesian-themed set of hotel buildings had become so dated that many visitors chose other resorts. A comprehensive room makeover in 2006 has made staying here a good choice again. Flatscreen TVs, comfier beds, and better furnishings have made all the difference. The public spaces in the Great Ceremonial House have also been redone, and the improvements there make this resort almost as appealing as the newer ones, like the Animal Kingdom Lodge. Although the lobby, complete with waterfall and tropical flowers, is a cozy and exotic treat during quieter times, its smaller size (compared to that of newer Deluxe resorts) makes it a bit manic when busy. Still, the hotel is a very appealing option because of the monorail access, the proximity to the Magic Kingdom, the romantic grounds, and the fun, sometimes campy Polynesian decor. If they could only get a Trader Vic's restaurant in here, the Hawaiian homage would be complete!

Special Activities: The Neverland Club child-care center at the Polynesian consistently rates as the best resort child-care activity center at Walt Disney World. Fun for 4- to 12-year-olds includes lots of supervised activities and dinner in the spacious facility. Per-child charge is $12 an hour and includes a buffet dinner.

Looking for a nice setting for watching the fireworks from nearby Magic Kingdom? Head down to the resort's beach for a relaxed setting, where music is piped in from the park.

Disney's Wilderness Lodge

Overall Rating: ★ ★ ★ ★ ☆
Location: Magic Kingdom area
Price Range: $265–$650

Transportation: Boat to the Magic Kingdom; buses to all other theme parks, water parks, and Downtown Disney.

Special Features: The decor and great restaurants are both worthy features, as is the pool, with its nearby geysers and the rocky stream feeding it. The lodge also enjoys some of the least expensive Deluxe-class rooms available. But being only a boat ride away from the Magic Kingdom is by far the best feature to this resort.

Room Types: Large rooms sleep 4 with two queen-sized beds or one queen-sized bed and bunk beds. Suites for up to 8 guests also are available. Rooms with one king-sized bed instead of the two queen beds also are available.

Best Room Locations: Be certain that you do *not* have a room that looks out onto the main lobby. The high noise level generated by the Whispering Canyon Café in the evenings makes it hard to get young children to sleep early. If you can, get to the left side of either wing; as it projects out to the lake, your views will improve.

Dining: The lodge enjoys one of the best fine restaurants (Artist Point) and perhaps the best non–character restaurant experience for kids (Whispering Canyon Café), where the food is good and the fun is better. There's also a counter-service restaurant (Roaring Forks Snacks) for quick bites or breakfast before a day at the parks.

Atmosphere: Designed in the spirit of the large national park lodges of the western United States, the Wilderness Lodge greets you with a cavernous lobby that is alive with log-cabin warmth. The stories-high lobby has exposed wood beams and stained-wood decor accented with totem poles and an enormous stone fireplace that set the scene. An indoor creek that eventually runs outdoors to the pool (or at least appears to) adds a nice accent to this warm and inviting open space. After the lobby takes your breath away, the man-made geysers, the rocky stream leading to the pool, and the other well-executed small touches will help convince you that you have arrived out West at the likes of Yellowstone or Yosemite.

Special Activities: The Chip 'n Dale's Campfire Sing-A-Long at the nearby Fort Wilderness is a popular evening event for families as you gather round the fire and enjoy a Disney movie in the great outdoors.

> **DID YOU KNOW?**
>
> During the holidays, each resort has a special decor that will knock you over. Huge Christmas trees are set in the lobbies of most resorts, a gigantic African-themed holiday display is a delight in the lobby of the Animal Kingdom Lodge, and many others have creative creations dreamed up by their kitchen staff. Perhaps the most fun, though, is the giant gingerbread house built as a store in the lobby of the Grand Floridian. You can actually buy a smaller gingerbread house from this store. The store made out of gingerbread might actually be larger than my first apartment in college.

Summary

Those are the Deluxe resorts. There's no doubt that they're expensive. But if you can afford them, they add an element of luxury, convenience, and comfort that will undoubtedly improve your overall vacation experience. Within the group are distinct differences, providing different benefits for different travel groups, so let the resort you select be a major attraction in your overall stay.

Moderate Resorts

In This Chapter

- Learn about Disney's Moderate resorts
- Select the theme and location that are right for you
- Find out what room and resort amenities are available

So the Deluxe resorts seem a little too pricey, but you still want more than some cheapo room at the end of your theme park day? Moderate resorts at Disney are a truly great compromise for most guests, offering most of the amenities that they require, but keeping the costs a bit more reasonable along the way.

What Is a Moderate Resort?

Moderate resorts are wonderfully themed, well-appointed hotels that provide more than bare-bones accommodations but don't make you feel like you need to take out a second mortgage. And you might find that many of the amenities "lost" are ones that you would never have had time to take advantage of on this trip anyway, so why pay for them?

The rooms are a bit smaller than those in the Deluxe resorts, but only by a bit. They still offer larger spaces and the in-room amenities that you might want. Some of these resorts now offer hyper-themed resort rooms, transformed into Pirate or Princess themes that are heavily detailed and are typically worth the premium pricing. Most now have mini-refrigerators as standard. The resort amenities, however, do drop off a bit. There are no character meals here, but you can go to other resorts and parks for that. The real drop-off in benefits may be in the transportation, where you have to use bus routes to all parks. The buses aren't horrible; they just aren't monorails. For most, it's an easy concession to save over $100 a night on the room.

Bottom line: The Moderate resorts may not be the least expensive rooms in all of Walt Disney World, but for many (if not most) guests, they're the perfect deal. Sure, they're not as inexpensive as the Value resorts. And sure, they're not as featured as the Deluxe resorts. But the middle ground that they provide is perfect for most guests to the Magic Kingdom.

Moderate Resort Pros

- Large pools and some restaurant selection
- Larger rooms
- $100 less per night than a Deluxe resort

Moderate Resort Cons

- Bus transportation to all parks
- Limited in-room and resort amenities
- No on-site character meals

The Walt Disney World Moderate Resorts

Time to learn about the Moderate resorts. The differences between each are more than in just the decor, so look for what is right for your group.

Disney's Caribbean Beach Resort

Overall Rating: ★ ★ ★ ☆ ☆
Location: Epcot area
Price Range: $159–$314 for a standard room

Transportation: Buses to all theme parks, water parks, and Downtown Disney.

Special Features: The Caribbean Beach Resort is the most centrally located of the Moderate resorts, translating to shorter bus trip times, on average. You also will enjoy the largest rooms in the Moderate resort class. Finally, a main pool refurbishment makes for a more themed and enjoyable stay.

Room Types: Large rooms sleep 4 with two double beds. New to the resort are a limited number of Pirate-themed decorated rooms. The beds are carved to look like pirate ships. The furniture looks like treasure chests and other bounty. The drape separating the bathroom looks like a pirate ship sail. At an upcharge of around $25, these rooms are ideal if you have a young buccaneer in your family.

There are king-sized beds available, with one king replacing two doubles.

Best Room Locations: Anything with a view of the lakes that run through the center of the resort is preferable, especially the Aruba or the Old Port Royale Centertown areas. The latter is best if you are planning on dining in the resort, as that is where the restaurants are found.

Dining: Shutters at Old Port Royale and the Old Port Royale Food Court offer the sole dining options here. The indoor food court is fun because the decor is intended to make you feel like you're at a Caribbean outdoor market, but with the benefits of being in a clean, air-conditioned space.

Atmosphere: The atmosphere here is intended to transport you to the Caribbean, and with the hot Florida sun playing its part, it seems to do a fair job. The brightly colored structures seem like some of the nicer white-washed buildings of the tropical isles. The sun-drenched ambiance tells you to take it easy.

This well-spread-out resort surrounds a lake, providing some quieter settings, with the buildings gathered in several small groupings. This resort has smaller pools, but more of them than at most other resorts. The Custom House serves as the check-in hall, but the real resort amenities are found by the Old Port Royale area on the other side of the lake, so the closer you are to that area, the better off you'll be.

Disney's Coronado Springs Resort

Overall Rating: ★ ★ ★ ☆ ☆
Location: Animal Kingdom area
Price Range: $164–$289 for a standard room

Transportation: Buses to all theme parks, water parks, and Downtown Disney.

Special Features: The Coronado Springs Resort is home to a rather significant convention space. This can play out in your favor: a morning bus ride may be lighter, with most of the resort guests heading to conference rooms instead of theme parks. The resort also has a beauty salon and health club, and can provide spa treatments, something no other Moderate resort provides.

Room Types: Large rooms sleep 4 with two queen-sized beds. Suites also are available that can room up to 6, and king-sized beds are available with one king replacing the two queen beds.

Coronado Springs Resort.
Photos © Disney.

Best Room Locations: The Ranchos are best if you're looking for a lot of pool time, while the Casitas give you quicker lobby and restaurant access. My favorite location, however, is the Cabanas, where I'm close to both, but in a quieter setting by not being too close to either.

Dining: Maya Grill has an improving menu, with more and more truly Mexican-inspired cuisine. This table-service offering and the counter-service dining at the Pepper Market are well-themed, fun places to eat and should take care of all your faster dining needs. A wealth of nightclubs makes this a great location for adult-only groups as well, with Rix as the lead locale for fun.

Atmosphere: The Mexican-themed decor is expertly executed in a fashion that really provides a relaxing and historical view of our neighbor to the south. The public spaces, particularly the check-in area, are warm and classic in their appeal, becoming fun and festive when you move to the food courts. The large pool even sits in the shadow of a large Mayan pyramid. The quietly warm atmosphere, paired with the spa services, make this a great place for romantic couples to get away.

As Moderate resorts go, this is a great option, although the convention crowds can be a bit of a negative. But higher ratings at other Moderate resorts come from the value of certain amenities, not from shortcomings here. This is an excellent selection.

Disney's Port Orleans Resort French Quarter

Overall Rating: ★ ★ ★ ✬ ☆
Location: Downtown Disney area
Price Range: $159–$279 for a standard room

Transportation: Boat to Downtown Disney, buses to all theme parks and water parks.

Special Features: The resort has boat access to Downtown Disney, which can truly be a great connection to the rest of the Walt Disney World properties because it serves as the bus-transfer location. The Scat Cat's Lounge also provides a nice addition to the site, as not all resorts have a lounge, which can be a nice retreat for adults.

> **DID YOU KNOW?**
>
> A big plus to the Port Orleans resorts is the boat access to Downtown Disney. This is especially nice if you have a group that plans on enjoying some of the nightlife and shopping and the thought of a long bus ride back to your resort sounds painful.

Room Types: Large rooms sleep 4 with two double beds. Some rooms have a trundle bed as well, sleeping 5 guests. Some king-sized beds are available as well.

Best Room Locations: Rooms facing the waterway from buildings 2, 5, and 6 provide for nice views and fast access to bus and boat transportation.

Dining: The Sassagoula Floatworks and Food Factory Food Court is a fun counter-service destination decorated with float art and giant masks. The Scat Cat's Lounge also adds a nice adult-relaxation location that you won't get at a Value resort.

Atmosphere: Drop yourself into the world of Mardi Gras festivities as you are immersed in a perfect New Orleans atmosphere. Think of it as Bourbon Street without so many drunks. It comes complete with a lounge, verandas for many rooms, and a relaxed open space that will help you wind down at the day's end. The boat access to Downtown Disney and its nightspots seem to speak to the entire Bourbon Street way of life.

Of all the Moderate resorts, this is the one I recommend most to adult-only parties. It has all the benefits of the other part of Port Orleans, but is smaller and less busy than that part of the resort. All I can say is *laissez les bon temps rouler* (let the good times roll)!

Disney's Port Orleans Resort Riverside

Overall Rating: ★ ★ ★ ✬ ☆
Location: Downtown Disney area
Price Range: $159–$319 for a standard room

Transportation: Boat to Downtown Disney, buses to all theme parks and water parks.

Special Features: The resort has boat access to Downtown Disney, which can truly be a great connection to the rest of the Walt Disney World properties because it serves as the bus-transfer location. Additionally the inviting open spaces are popular with families for general exploration and quiet walks at day's end.

Room Types: Large rooms sleep 4 to 5, with two queen-sized beds and an optional Pack 'N Play crib. Some king-sized beds are available as well.

Best Room Locations: The Magnolia Terrace building provides for quick access to the pool, as well as bus and boat transportation.

Atmosphere: The decor is intended to be more like rural Louisiana, with two sections, Alligator Bayou and Magnolia Bend. The former has smaller units that make you feel like you are near the swamplands, while the latter speaks to manors of the Old South. Although the New Orleans part of Port Orleans may seem to offer more touristy ambiance, this land is better for offering more vistas and public spaces worth exploring. You still get the same boat access to Downtown Disney, a lounge, as well as a table-service restaurant, giving you a bit better of an amenities menu than in the French Quarter part of the resort. Of all the Moderate resorts, this is the one I recommend most to families traveling with children.

Special Activities: The seasonally available Campfire on the Bayou is a fun and free night out for families, complete with sing-a-longs, stories, and even s'mores (for a small charge). You can also go fishing, rent a surrey bike, or go on a horse-drawn carriage ride (all at a charge).

HIDDEN MAGIC!

So what is my favorite Moderate resort? Each has something just a bit unique to offer, so these might be some reasons to choose one over the others.

- **Best resort for little kids:** Caribbean Beach
- **Best resort for tweens and teens:** Port Orleans Riverside
- **Best resort for adults:** Port Orleans Resort French Quarter
- **Best value:** The Cabins at Fort Wilderness
- **Most exotic:** Coronado Springs

The Cabins at Disney's Fort Wilderness Resort

Overall Rating: ★ ★ ★ ☆ ☆
Location: Magic Kingdom area
Price Range: $285–$455 for a standard cabin

Transportation: Boat to Magic Kingdom; buses to all other theme parks, water parks, and Downtown Disney. Note that you will need to take an initial internal shuttle ride to get from your cabin to either the boat dock or the bus station.

Special Features: The Cabins provide a unique set of accommodations previously overlooked by a majority of Walt Disney World guests. These cabins sleep up to 6, have a full kitchen and maid service, furnish a grill and deck, and bring you far closer to nature than any other Moderate resort. At the same time, they have all the items you would expect in a hotel, such as cable TV, daily housekeeping, phone, a full bathroom, and air-conditioning. The resort amenities are similar in that they have the standards such as pools and restaurants, but also a marina, horse-riding stables, and outdoor entertainment venues for campfires, twilight movies, and nature walks.

Room Types: Wilderness Cabins come with a full kitchen and sleep 6 guests, with a double bed and two bunk beds in the main bedroom, and a pull-down double Murphy bed in the living room.

Best Room Locations: The Cabins are all at the south end of the Fort Wilderness property, which makes them far from all the resort-area amenities and the water transportation to the Magic Kingdom. Still, there is a pool in this area, and cabins in the 2500 or 2600 loops place you near that pool as well as near one of the internal bus transportation stops.

Atmosphere: The cabin mood is set up well, with exposed wood walls and handmade wood furniture that is upholstered with warm, western Native American prints. The rustic feel is an ideal frame for windows that look out on forested areas in one of the rare secluded resort spots in all of Walt Disney World. The public building takes you further from the modern cabin feeling into a more historical look at old forts from the Western expansion—or at least what the expansion of the Old West looked like on Davy Crockett shows of the '50s.

Summary

Disney can bring some sanity to your accommodation budget. You may have slightly longer transportation times on the way to the parks in the morning, but the impact is minimal and the savings are significant.

Value Resorts

In This Chapter

- Learn about Disney's Value resorts
- Select the theme and location that is right for you
- Discover the pitfalls of different room locations, and learn how to avoid them
- Find out what room and resort amenities are available

The honest truth is that, no matter what travel discounts you land, a Walt Disney World vacation is unlikely to be cheap. Thank goodness Disney realized that we were not all born of robber barons and endowed with trust funds when they created the Value resorts! These lower-cost options may not have all the amenities of a Deluxe resort, but they make up for it with explosively fun decor and a vibrant atmosphere that is always buzzing with families. They also offer significant advantages over their similarly priced non–Disney property competitors that make them appealing options.

What Is a Value Resort?

Walt Disney World has five Value resorts located in two areas. All feature a central building for registration, shopping, dining, and transportation. The cozy guest rooms are located in three-story buildings covered with massively oversized decorations themed to the different resorts. There are two types of rooms. The standard rooms are designed to hold four, and offer the very basic hotel amenities you might expect. Two double beds (with a few single king rooms available), a pair of chairs with a small table, and a TV on a small chest of drawers pretty much round out the furnishings. The bathroom holds a bath/shower and a toilet, with the sink separately located out by the closet. It may seem sparse, but do you need more?

Another room type is now widely available at these resorts. Based on the Family Suites rooms that were tested (and are still available) at the All-Star Music Resort, the Art of Animation Resort will be 75 percent Family Suites. These suites offer a separate master bedroom with a queen-sized bed, a living room, a dining area, two separate bathrooms, and a kitchenette area, all providing accommodations for up to 6 guests. They do this with a double-sized sleeper sofa and a double-sized Murphy bed in addition to the master bedroom. The kitchenette has a mini fridge, microwave, sink area, and coffeemaker. Now mini-refrigerators are being added to all Value resort rooms during their renovation. You can also request cribs, bed rails, or hair dryers. Laundry facilities are located in separate buildings on the grounds and next to the pools. The resorts also have a gift shop, food-court dining, arcades, in-room pizza delivery (no other room service available), playgrounds, pools, and bus service to all the parks and Downtown Disney.

Over the top decor at the Value Resorts.
Photos © Disney.

Bottom line: These resort options are ideal for families on a budget. They all get a thumbs-up for being good at what they are: affordable and adequate accommodations that immerse you in the Disney experience.

Value Resort Pros

- Affordable cost
- Vibrant decor, an attraction in itself for families with children
- Food court and pizza service, offering more affordable food options

Value Resort Cons

- Smallest rooms in all of Walt Disney World
- Bus-only transportation
- Noisy public areas

The Walt Disney World Value Resorts

Let's look at each Value resort. Keep an eye on the decor of each resort, as that can be the biggest differentiator, and can make your choice easy based on what your kids like best.

Disney's Pop Century Resort

Overall Rating: ★ ★ ★ ☆ ☆
Location: Epcot area
Price Range: $89–$189 for a standard room

Transportation: Buses to all theme parks, water parks, and Downtown Disney.

Special Features: Visually extravagant decor, lakeside ambiance for select rooms.

Room Types: Small rooms for 4 include two double beds. Some single king rooms also are available.

Best Room Locations: The '60s B Hall, overlooking the lake. A room overlooking the large lake is the ideal choice for its view as well as the quieter setting, if you can get it. Rooms by a pool or playground are noisy, and a room far from the main building can add a fairly long walk to get to the bus transportation that takes you to the parks.

Dining: Food court, in-room pizza delivery. No room service.

Atmosphere: Everywhere you look, you are surrounded by oversized icons of the past century, with buildings dedicated to decades from the 1950s to the 1990s. Vivid story-high letters on each building shout out the lingo of the era, paired with relevant giant objects like a life-size foosball set, giant Mr. and Mrs. Potato Heads, and an immense Big Wheel.

Disney's All-Star Movies Resort

Overall Rating: ★ ★ ✭ ☆ ☆
Location: Animal Kingdom area
Price Range: $84–$184 for a standard room

Transportation: Buses to all theme parks, water parks, and Downtown Disney.

Special Features: Visually extravagant decor.

Room Types: Small rooms for 4 include two double beds. Some single king rooms also are available.

Best Room Locations: Toy Story hall #10. A room overlooking a pool or playground can add significant unwanted noise. The wrong room also can add a fairly long walk to get to the bus transportation that takes you to the parks.

Dining: Food court, in-room pizza delivery. No room service.

Atmosphere: Dive into the silver screen as you swim in a pool themed on *The Mighty Ducks*, complete with an immense duck goalie mask and giant hockey sticks. Elsewhere are giant reminders of many of your children's favorite movies, including a three-story-tall Woody (from *Toy Story*) who even has Andy scrawled on the bottom of his boot. The decor here might well be the most appealing to small children of all the Value resorts, and that means more than you might imagine when it comes to getting them into the Walt Disney World mood. Other buildings are themed to *101 Dalmatians*, *Fantasia*, and *Herbie the Love Bug*.

This resort could be the best Value resort for families with younger children, particularly those who are heavily into Disney movies.

Disney's All-Star Music Resort

Overall Rating: ★ ★ ★ ☆ ☆
Location: Animal Kingdom area
Price Range: $84–$184 for a standard room, $198–$375 for Family Suites

Transportation: Buses to all theme parks, water parks, TTC, and Downtown Disney.

Special Features: Visually extravagant decor and Family Suite rooms.

> **DID YOU KNOW?**
>
> Washers and dryers each cost $2 per load, with detergent available for $1 out of the vending machine. The view is ideal: you can do laundry and watch kids in a pool at the same time.

Room Types: Small rooms for 4 include two double beds. Some single king rooms also are available. Family Suites for 6 plus a crib include a queen-sized bed, two chairs that fold out to single beds, and one couch that folds out to a double bed.

Best Room Locations: The Calypso halls #1 and #10. As with all the All-Star Resorts, pools and playgrounds can add a lot of noise to your life. Other rooms can add a fairly long walk to get to the bus transportation that takes you to the parks.

Dining: Food court, in-room pizza delivery. No room service.

Atmosphere: Only giants could wield these monstrous musical instruments. Buildings are themed to Calypso, Jazz, Rock, Country, and Broadway, complete with instruments, giant cowboy boots, and other decorations. Although this resort's decor has the least "pop" of all of the resorts, it might be preferable for a group with teens or no kids, as it might seem a bit less childish in its environment.

The unique feature of the Family Suites will certainly increase interest in this resort. If you're traveling in a group of five, six, or seven, this might be the best choice because of the suites.

Disney's All-Star Sports Resort

Overall Rating: ★ ★ ★ ★ ☆
Location: Animal Kingdom area
Price Range: $84–$184 for a standard room

Transportation: Buses to all theme parks, water parks, TTC, and Downtown Disney.

Special Features: Visually extravagant decor.

Room Types: Small rooms for 4 include two double beds. Some single king rooms also are available.

Best Room Locations: Go for rooms in the Surfing hall #6, facing away from the pool. As with all the All-Star Resorts, pools and playgrounds can add a lot of noise to your life. Other rooms can add a fairly long walk to get to the bus transportation that takes you to the parks.

Dining: Food court, in-room pizza delivery. No room service.

Atmosphere: Surfing, basketball, tennis, football, and baseball are the themes here. The decor is pretty worn. The tennis halls are particularly beaten up. But the sports can still be fun, and seeing kids walking up to three-story-high football helmets and 30-foot-high basketball hoops can provide some humorous reactions.

> **HIDDEN MAGIC!**
>
> The decor here can be an attraction unto itself. Send older kids out on sightseeing walks while younger siblings nap. Give them a camera to capture some of the sights that they think are the most outrageous.

The resort benefits from being the first bus stop of the All-Star Resorts. This means your kids might stand a chance of getting a seat on otherwise-packed buses.

Disney's Art of Animation Resort

Overall Rating: Not rated yet
Location: Epcot area
Estimated Price Range: $TBD–$179 for a standard room,
$249–$425 for Family Suites

Transportation: Buses to all theme parks, water parks, TTC, and Downtown Disney.

Special Features: New Family Suites allow for more flexible accommodations for larger families on a budget. Rooms take specific movie theming to a wonderful extreme.

Room Types: Small rooms for 4 include two double beds. Some single king rooms also are available. Family Suites for 6 plus a crib include a queen-sized bed, two chairs that fold out to single beds, and one couch that folds out to a double bed.

Best Room Locations: Family Suites will be in buildings themed to *Lion King, Cars,* and *Finding Nemo.* The fourth set of buildings, themed to *The Little Mermaid,* will be standard rooms. The best rooms will enjoy the common lake that is shared with the Pop Century Resort.

Dining: Food court, in-room pizza delivery. No room service.

Atmosphere: While the other Value resorts took theming to a new level, this resort takes it to another universe. You will never feel like you are in a "value" resort when you are here. The public spaces are as well executed as with other Values, but with even a greater adherence to a single story. You are *in* Radiator Springs (*Cars*) or under the sea (*Finding Nemo*).

HIDDEN MAGIC!

So what is my favorite Value resort? The truth is, they are mostly similar, but if given a choice, there are some differences.

- **Best resort with kids:** Art of Animation Resort
- **Best resort for adults:** Art of Animation, for the food court

Summary

Value resorts are great at what they do, and they don't pretend to be more than what they are. They provide affordable on-property accommodations with a fun flair and the basic amenities that most guests need, as well as valuable Disney Resort guest benefits. What a smart way to spend your money!

Deluxe Villa Resorts and the Disney Vacation Club

In This Chapter

- Find out what extras you get in a Deluxe Villa resort
- Discover the world of Disney's Disney Vacation Club (DVC) time-share program
- Review the camping alternatives of Fort Wilderness

So you say you have a big group? Okay, let's move on from traditional hotel rooms to something a bit more industrial strength! Accommodations in the Deluxe Villas category offer you larger spaces for larger groups. Studios as well as one-, two-, and three-bedroom villas are available, and the choices go on from there. Many of these are also Disney Vacation Club resort properties, a time-share program that offers resort hotels throughout Walt Disney World and also at other locations throughout the United States. Perhaps the most important benefit for the majority of the accommodations offered here are the in-room kitchenettes. Not only is it convenient to have some of the features available in your room, but if you can genuinely expect to eat a few meals there, you'll dramatically reduce your vacation cost. Some of these choices are connected to resorts we have already reviewed in previous chapters, so you should already have an idea of what the atmosphere and location are like. If you need a bit more than the average hotel room can offer, these could be the right solution for you.

What Is a Deluxe Villa Resort?

These resorts are designed with the knowledge that many parties visiting Walt Disney World can be larger than the fictional family of four that we used as our model in the budgeting chapter. When you have as many as 12 in your group, you have an alternative accommodation solution that keeps you all together. So what are the differences from standard rooms? A greater variety of accommodation types including multiple bedroom suites, a variety of kitchen types, and time-share programs are just a few.

Remember, too, that while these are typically part of the Disney Vacation Club time-share program, you can book them like any other Disney resort at Walt Disney World without being a participant in the program.

The Fort Wilderness campsites are listed in this chapter as well. They are not, however, in the Deluxe Villa category, and they are not affiliated with the Disney Vacation Club. However, they offer accommodations that are different from a simple hotel room, so this is as good a place to discuss them.

Deluxe Villa Resort Pros

- Rooms with kitchens available
- Multiple-bedroom suites to keep your family together
- Time-share investment opportunities available

Deluxe Villa Resort Cons

- Limited locations
- Time-share investment opportunities available

What Is the Disney Vacation Club?

The Deluxe Villa group of resorts at Walt Disney World is very much intertwined with the Disney Vacation Club. However, Disney's answer to time-shares takes its leave from the standard business with a sales pitch that is less high pressure and a product that is well known. If time-shares are of interest to you, you should know that their properties are not just at Walt Disney World; they also have beachfront resort properties in Vero Beach, Florida; Hilton Head, South Carolina; and Oahu, Hawaii.

Looking to buy in on the Disney Vacation Club? First off, you'll want to visit its website, at www.disneyvacationclub.com. You can also check out some of the time-share reseller sites to see if you can buy from someone else. One that focuses on Disney time-shares is www.dvcbyresale.com.

HIDDEN MAGiC!

Which of these should you choose? Make sure you review the sister resorts, if they apply, to get an idea of whether the resort area is right for your party. But what if I had to choose?

- **Best resort for kids:** The Villas at Disney's Wilderness Lodge
  You have to love the closeness to the Magic Kingdom and Fort Wilderness Lodge, as well as the great pool!

- **Best resort for just adults:** Saratoga Springs Resort & Spa
  A quick boat ride gets you to all the Downtown Disney restaurants and nightlife.

Deluxe Villa Resorts

The Deluxe Villa resorts are a great alternative to the standard hotel room. For those villas tied to a Deluxe resort, follow the ratings for those rates in Chapter 7. Let's dig into the different offerings here to see what is right for you!

Bay Lake Tower at Disney's Contemporary Resort

Location: Magic Kingdom area
Price Range: Studios: $415–$710; Villas: $515–$2,605

Room Types: Studios sleep 4 with a queen bed and double sleeper. One-bedroom villas sleep 5 with a king-sized bed, a queen sleeper, and a single sleeper. Two bedroom villas sleep 9 with a king-sized bed, two queen-sized beds, a queen sleeper, and a single sleeper. Three-bedroom Grand Villas sleep 12 with a king-sized bed in the master room, two queen-sized beds in the second room, two queen-sized beds in the third room, and a queen sleeper and a double sleeper in the living room.

Best Room Locations: Views of the Magic Kingdom are undoubtedly the prime spots, but the Bay Lake views on the other side are scenic as well, if not a venue for watching the fireworks.

Special Features: DVC members staying here can access the Top of the World Lounge, which offers tremendous views of the Magic Kingdom fireworks.

For information on the transportation, atmosphere, special features, and dining at this resort, see the review of Disney's Contemporary Resort in Chapter 7.

Disney's Animal Kingdom Villas

Location: Animal Kingdom area
Price Range: Studios: $300–$810; Villas: $435–$2,345

Room Types: Studios and one-, two-, and three-bedroom villas provide accommodations for up to 12.

In the Jambo House, studios sleep 4 with a queen-sized bed and double sleeper. One-bedroom villas sleep 4 to 5 with a king-sized bed, queen sleeper, and single sleeper. Some one-bedroom value villas have a king-sized bed and queen sleeper only. Two-bedroom villas sleep 8 to 9 with a king-sized bed, two queen-sized beds, a queen sleeper, and single sleeper. Some two-bedroom value villas are a combination of a studio and one-bedroom value villa and sleep only 8. Three-bedroom villas sleep 12 with a king-sized bed in the first bedroom, two queen-sized beds in the second bedroom, two queen beds in the third bedroom, and a queen sleeper in the living room.

In the Kidani Village, studios sleep 4 with a queen-sized bed and double sleeper. One-bedroom villas sleep 5 with a king-sized bed, a queen sleeper, and single sleeper. Two-bedroom villas sleep 9 with a king-sized bed, a queen-sized bed, double sleeper, a queen sleeper, and double sleeper. Three-bedroom villas sleep 12 with a king-sized bed in the first bedroom, two queen-sized beds in the second bedroom, two queen beds in the third bedroom, and a queen sleeper in the living room.

Best Room Locations: Jambo House and Kidani Village are the two phases of the Animal Kingdom Villas. The first phase, Jambo House, involved converting some of the existing Animal Kingdom

Lodge floors on one wing into Disney Vacation Club rooms. One concern here is transportation time from your room to either the lobby of the Animal Kingdom Lodge or other transportation hubs. Your best bet is to either ask for a room as close as possible to that original lobby, or get a room in the new Kidani Village area near the lobby of that expansion. Otherwise, the obvious consideration is whether or not you have a view of the savannah that has been built around this resort. As with the original resort, the animal-viewing areas are popular and provide unique experiences that are the single largest draw for this resort.

For information on the transportation, atmosphere, special features, and dining at this resort, see the review of Disney's Animal Kingdom Lodge in Chapter 7.

Disney's Beach Club Villas

Location: Epcot area
Price Range: Studios: $345–$580; Villas: $500–$1,265

Room Types: Studios sleep 4 and come with a queen-sized bed and double sleeper. One-bedroom villas sleep 4 and come with a king-sized bed and a queen sleeper. Two-bedroom villas sleep 8 and come with a king-sized bed in the first room, a queen-sized bed and a double sleeper or two queens in the second room, and a queen sleeper or double sleeper in the living room.

Best Room Locations: Rooms as close to the rest of the Beach Club are best, shortening your walk time to the parks, pool, and boats.

For information on the transportation, atmosphere, special features, and dining at this resort, see the review of Disney's Beach Club Resort in Chapter 7.

Disney's BoardWalk Villas

Location: Epcot area
Price Range: Studios: $345–$580; Villas: $500–$2,345

Room Types: Studios sleep 4 and come with a queen-sized bed and double sleeper. One-bedroom villas sleep 4 and come with a king-sized bed and queen sleeper. Two-bedroom villas sleep 8 and come with a king-sized bed, a queen-sized bed and double sleeper, and a queen sleeper. Three-bedroom villas come with a king-sized bed in the first bedroom, two queen-sized beds each in the second and third bedrooms, and a queen sleeper in the living room.

Best Room Locations: Garden-view rooms offer the best blend, giving you peace and quiet in your room and the fun of the BoardWalk just a few paces away. If you have teens, they may get a treat from a view of the BoardWalk, but it might not be worth the trade-off of the evening noise level.

For information on the transportation, atmosphere, special features, and dining at this resort, see the review of Disney's BoardWalk Inn in Chapter 7.

Disney's Old Key West Resort

Overall Rating: ★ ★ ★ ☆ ☆
Location: Downtown Disney area
Price Range: Studios: $315–$465; Villas: $435–$1,795

Room Types: Studios sleep 4 and come with two queen-sized beds. One-bedroom villas sleep 4 and come with a king-sized bed and a queen sleeper. Two-bedroom villas sleep 8 and come with a king-sized bed, a queen-sized bed, and double sleeper or two queen beds, and a queen- or full-sized sleeper. Three-bedroom villas come with a king-sized bed in the first bedroom, two queen-sized beds in the second bedroom, two full-sized beds in the third bedroom, and a queen sleeper in the living room.

Best Room Locations: Most rooms overlook the golf course, and the view is far more preferable to a pool view, which is usually noisier. The closer you are to the Hospitality House, the closer you are to the boat service to Downtown Disney.

Transportation: Boat to Downtown Disney, buses to all theme parks and water parks.

Special Features: Boat access to Downtown Disney is a nice feature for shopping enthusiasts and those seeking some nightlife.

Dining: Olivia's Café provides adequate table service, and Good's Food to Go has the resort counter service you will like, but with Downtown Disney so nearby, you'll want to go there as often as possible.

Atmosphere: The island feel of the resort is relaxing, and the studios and villas offer pretty much the same thing as most of the other resorts in this class. This is yet another good location for adult groups, due to the proximity to Downtown Disney.

Disney's Saratoga Springs Resort & Spa

Overall Rating: ★ ★ ★ ☆ ☆
Location: Downtown Disney area
Price Range: Studios: $315–$465; Villas: $435–$1,795; Treehouse Villas: $595–$980

Room Types: Studios sleep 4 and come with one queen-sized bed and a double sleeper. One-bedroom villas sleep 4 and come with a king-sized bed and a queen sleeper. Two-bedroom villas sleep 8 and come with a king-sized bed, two queen-sized beds, a queen sleeper, and a single sleeper. Treehouse villas sleep 9 and come with a queen-sized bed in the first bedroom, a queen bed in the second bedroom, one set of bunk beds in the third bedroom, and a queen sleeper and single sleeper in the living room. Three-bedroom villas come with a king-sized bed in the first bedroom, two queen-sized beds in the second bedroom, two queen beds in the third bedroom, and a queen sleeper in the living room.

Best Room Locations: The best choices are rooms in The Springs area, adjacent to the Carriage House, which houses the restaurants, spa, and other central amenities. These rooms are also a quick walk to the boat launch to Downtown Disney. A secondary choice is Congress Park rooms, only if they have a water view of Downtown Disney.

Transportation: Boat to Downtown Disney, buses to all theme parks and water parks.

Special Features: This resort has a great location across the lake from Downtown Disney. Part of the resort is the new Treehouse Villas. These are all new, but are inspired by similar accommodations that used to exist here many years ago. The great central clubhouse really exudes a clubby and fun ambiance.

Dining: The Artist's Palette is a good general-purpose dining option, but the real treat here is the nice mix of offerings at the Turf Club. Better still is getting you over to Downtown Disney for all the dining options found there.

Atmosphere: Saratoga Springs transports you to the refined world of upstate New York horse racing. The atmosphere here is more subdued and quieter than at other resorts, although it's not unfriendly to families. The wooded Treehouse Villa locales offer a more secluded, serene stay as well. It is almost like two resorts in one.

The Villas at Disney's Wilderness Lodge

Location: Magic Kingdom area
Price Range: Studios: $355–$535; Villas: $485–$1,260

Room Types: Studios sleep 4 and come with one queen-sized bed and a double sleeper. One-bedroom villas sleep 4 and come with a king-sized bed in the bedroom and a queen sleeper in the living room. Two-bedroom villas sleep 8 and come with a king-sized bed in the first bedroom, two queen-sized beds in the second bedroom, and a queen sleeper in the living room.

Best Room Locations: The closer the villa is to the rest of the Wilderness Lodge, the shorter the walks to the bus and to the boats. Ask to be as close as possible.

For information on the transportation, atmosphere, special features, and dining at this resort, see the review of Disney's Wilderness Lodge Resort in Chapter 7.

DISNEY DON'T

It sure is great that you're getting a kitchenette in your room, but ensure you don't plan on buying all your food at a Disney store. Plan on a grocery store stop on the way to the resort. If you're coming from the airport, consider one of the limo services that throw in a free 30-minute grocery store stop with their fee.

Disney's Fort Wilderness Resort & Campground

Overall Rating: ★ ★ ☆ ☆ ☆
Location: Magic Kingdom area
Price Range: Campsites: $48–$126

Room Types: Some campsites accommodate up to 10 with tents or pop-up campers, and include electricity, water, cable, and internet (for a fee) connections. Full campsites accommodate up to 10 with tents and RVs, and include electricity, water, cable, sewer, and internet (for a fee) connections.

Best Room Locations: All locations are very scenic, so try to get as close to the water as possible. The lower the campsite number (100s being the lowest, 2800s being the highest), the better.

Transportation: Boat to the Magic Kingdom, buses to all other theme parks, water parks, and Downtown Disney.

Special Features: The campsites let you bring your RV home along with you. The resort features include horseback riding, an animal petting area, and a marina.

Dining: Fort Wilderness is home to two popular dinner shows, *Hoop Dee Doo Musical Review* and the seasonal *Mickey's Backyard BBQ*, both of which you should try to include in your visit. But for those more regular meals, you can visit Crockett's Tavern and Trail's End Restaurant, both of which offer some good and comparably reasonably priced casual dining.

Atmosphere: While the campsites do set the mood for a more rustic setting, Disney has done an admirable job to make it comfortable. They don't allow the low-frills environment to be an excuse for lower-quality, lesser-upkeep efforts or poorer amenities. This area is fun, active, and a great option for someone wanting an alternative to a hotel.

Special Activities: A great variety of outdoor activities abound, including horseback riding, archery lessons, campfires, outdoor movies, seasonal hayrides, and sleigh rides. You can also rent a golf cart here that can make getting around to all the activity areas much easier.

Summary

If you need something more than two beds, a television, and a bathroom, here you go. If you have an RV, it can now have a Disney address! These great choices open up a variety of accommodation options, and do so in great style, or with access to the great outdoors.

Hotel Plaza Boulevard and Orlando Resorts

In This Chapter

- Learn about the Hotel Plaza Boulevard choices
- Get inspired by the Swan and Dolphin
- Read up on the hotel reserved for members of the U.S. military
- Find out what other Orlando-area resorts are good choices, as well as bad

Sometimes the Disney-owned resorts are just not the right thing for you. That doesn't mean you're relegated to staying in some fleabag motel an hour away. There are literally thousands of choices in the Orlando area, and in this chapter I walk you through some of the best of them.

Hotel Plaza Boulevard

Hotel Plaza Boulevard has been a fixture on the Walt Disney World map since the earliest days of the Magic Kingdom. When there were simply not enough rooms in the area, Disney invited select companies to build hotels on their property, and thus sprung up the Hotel Plaza Boulevard.

Located next to Downtown Disney on the southeast corner of the Walt Disney World property, this outcropping of hotels brings an excellent alternative to the Disney resorts. Typified by better rates but less Disney-themed decor, these hotels include national chains and smaller operations.

An important distinction to consider with these hotels is that, although they are on property, they don't share all the same perks as a Disney resort. While none enjoys the Disney Magical Express, some of them do enjoy other special privileges, so look into what each one offers you. Some important things to remember:

- Sometimes the deals here are really great.

- The rooms are usually comparable in size and quality to the Deluxe resort rooms found at Disney resorts.

- You can earn and use existing points from hotel reward programs at Hilton, Marriott, and Best Western to book rooms.

HIDDEN MAGIC!

So what is the best option on Hotel Plaza Boulevard?

- **Traveling with kids:** The Regal Sun Resort
- **Adult party:** Buena Vista Palace Hotel & Spa
- **Best overall:** Buena Vista Palace Hotel & Spa

Let's look at these choices. I list them from west to east, with the first ones located most closely to the Downtown Disney area.

Buena Vista Palace Hotel & Spa

Website: www.buenavistapalace.com
Address: 1900 Buena Vista Drive, Lake Buena Vista, FL 32830
Phone: 1-866-397-6516

Special Features: Formerly a Wyndham resort, this Luxury Resorts Hotel (LXR) is one of the nicer Hotel Plaza choices, complete with a full spa, contemporary rooms, Sunday breakfast character meals, and a very posh ambiance. It also offers complimentary transportation to all the theme parks. Along with the Hilton, it ranks as one of the higher-end choices on Hotel Plaza Boulevard.

Hilton in the Walt Disney World Resort

Website: www.hilton.com
Address: 1751 Hotel Plaza Boulevard, Lake Buena Vista, FL 32830
Phone: 407-827-4000

Special Features: The Hilton offers free shuttles to all theme and water parks, and a Disney character breakfast. The hotel is one of the nicer properties, and guests can also enjoy the privilege of Extra Magic Hours, a rare and big plus. It's the closest hotel to Downtown Disney, which is just a short walk away. This resort is not to be confused with the new Hilton that is paired with the Waldorf Astoria at nearby Bonnet Creek.

Wyndham Lake Buena Vista Resort

Website: www.wyndhamlakebuenavista.com
Address: 1850 Hotel Plaza Boulevard, Lake Buena Vista, FL 32830
Phone: 1-800-624-4109

Special Features: Formerly known as the Grosvenor, then the Regal Sun Resort, the Wyndham Lake Buena Vista Resort is one of the original hotels in this area. It hosts Disney character breakfasts, has a better-than-average kid-friendly pool complex, and offers complimentary shuttles to all four theme parks.

Holiday Inn Hotel

Website: www.holidayinn.com
Address: 1805 Hotel Plaza Boulevard, Lake Buena Vista, FL 32830
Phone: 407-828-8888

Special Features: Typical standard two-bed rooms, but recently was redone from top to bottom. I have not stayed here yet, but it looks to be a good lower-cost choice.

Royal Plaza in the Walt Disney World Resort

Website: www.royalplaza.com
Address: 1905 Hotel Plaza Boulevard, Lake Buena Vista, FL 32830
Phone: 407-828-2828

Special Features: The hotel has a much improved decor, but it still lags behind the Palace and the Hilton for luxury. Features include free breakfast for kids 10 and under, as well as free transportation to the Disney parks.

Best Western Lake Buena Vista Resort Hotel

Website: www.bestwestern.com
Address: 2000 Hotel Plaza Boulevard, Lake Buena Vista, FL 32830
Phone: 407-828-2424

Special Features: This is a pretty standard hotel, but it offers complimentary theme park shuttles.

Doubletree Guest Suites in the WDW Resort

Website: www.hilton.com
Address: 2305 Hotel Plaza Boulevard, Lake Buena Vista, FL 32830
Phone: 407-934-1000

Special Features: This is a Hilton hotel chain, so if you have a frequent guest program there, you might be able to use points to stay or earn points while there. Complimentary transportation is provided to all parks and Downtown Disney, and the rooms are all suites.

Other Resorts on and near Walt Disney World Property

There are a few other resorts located on Walt Disney World property or immediately adjacent. Some offer the very highest of luxury, others bring unparalleled locations, and there is even one that honors the service of the American military.

Walt Disney World Dolphin

Website: www.waltdisneyworld.com or www.swandolphin.com
Address: 1500 Epcot Resorts Boulevard, Lake Buena Vista, FL 32830
Phone: 407-934-4000

Location: Epcot-resort area, just a quick walk from the BoardWalk.

Transportation: Boat to Epcot, Hollywood Studios, and the BoardWalk; buses to all other theme parks, water parks, and Downtown Disney.

Special Features: You get to enjoy Extra Magic Hours, which is a big perk. You can earn Starwood hotel loyalty reward points when you stay here, something you can't do at a Disney resort. Being walking distance away from the BoardWalk and a boat ride from Epcot and Hollywood is also a big perk. Note that this is a fairly large convention hotel, so you might find yourself in the midst of that kind of crowd.

Room Types: Large rooms sleep 5 with two double beds.

Best Room Locations: Rooms facing the Swan hotel can give you nighttime views of fireworks from Epcot or Hollywood Studios. Note, the higher the floor, the better.

Dining: The Dolphin has a better high-end restaurant selection than the Swan, with Shula's Steak House and the über-trendy night-club/restaurant, Todd English's bluezoo.

Atmosphere: Both the Dolphin and the Swan were designed by Michael Graves, but they're distinct from each other in their moods, if not their color palettes.

Inside, the circus-tent interior decor of the lobby sets the mood for the more child-friendly and fun atmosphere. Beach decor accents throughout the halls and even rooms keep the mood light.

> **DISNEY DON'T**
>
> The Dolphin and the Swan are operated by the Starwood group—namely, by Sheraton and Westin. Because of that, some of the perks to staying on property are not available to guests here. These change frequently, but for the time being the benefits that you do **not** get here now include the following:
>
> * Disney Magical Express
> * Charge-to-your-room privileges

Walt Disney World Swan

Website: www.waltdisneyworld.com or www.swandolphin.com
Address: 1200 Epcot Resorts Boulevard, Lake Buena Vista, FL 32830
Phone: 407-934-4000

Location: Epcot-resort area, just a quick walk from the BoardWalk.

Transportation: Boat to Epcot, Hollywood Studios, and the BoardWalk. Buses to all other theme parks, water parks, and Downtown Disney.

Special Features: You get to enjoy Extra Magic Hours, which is a big perk. The Westin Heavenly Beds are just that: a piece of heaven. You can also earn Starwood hotel loyalty reward points when you stay here, something you can't do at a Disney resort. Being walking distance away from the BoardWalk and a boat ride from Epcot and Hollywood is also a big perk.

Room Types: Large rooms sleep 5 with two queen-sized beds.

Best Room Locations: Rooms facing the Dolphin benefit from a more serene view, but the ones facing the other direction often can get a nice nighttime view of the fireworks from one of the parks.

Dining: The dining here is not as diverse as at the Dolphin, but it doesn't have to be with so many choices nearby.

Atmosphere: Where the Dolphin provides upscale kid-friendliness, the Swan is decidedly more adult-friendly.

If forced to pick between the two resorts, I would say that the edge goes to the Swan for the *amazingly* comfy beds, the fact they have queen beds and not doubles and the more serene ambiance. The Dolphin wins out on dining options and kid-friendly atmosphere. Let this be your guide when selecting between the two.

Waldorf Astoria Orlando

Website: www.waldorfastoriaorlando.com
Address: 14200 Bonnet Creek Resort Lane, Orlando, FL 32821
Phone: 407-597-5500

Location: Bonnet Creek, on the southern edge of Walt Disney World.

Transportation: Bus shuttles to all theme parks, water parks, and Downtown Disney.

Special Features: This is unquestionably the height of luxury in the Walt Disney World area. The only other Waldorf Astoria outside of the famed one in New York City, it brings a contemporary flair to the fine surroundings. If money is no object, this is where you will want to stay. The resort also has a spa and Rees Jones–designed golf course. This resort is linked to the Hilton Orlando Bonnet Creek resort, and they share a great deal, including a moderately sized convention facility between them.

Room Types: Large rooms sleep 4 with two queen-sized beds.

Best Room Locations: Select rooms in higher floors can provide views of literally all of Walt Disney World, including fireworks at night. Simply breathtaking.

Dining: The famed Bull & Bear is a high-end steakhouse with more variety than you might anticipate. Oscar's takes care of your other breakfast and lunch needs in a brighter setting. Lounges and pool-side bar/grills offer more options throughout the day.

Atmosphere: While the famed Waldorf Astoria name may invoke a metropolitan and possibly stuffy image of what passes for luxury, banish that thought from your mind. The resort blends elegance with a relaxed, sun-tinged comfort that does not betray the NYC original.

Hilton Orlando Bonnet Creek

Website: www.hiltonbonnetcreek.com
Address: 14100 Bonnet Creek Resort Lane, Orlando, FL 32821
Phone: 407-597-3600

Location: Bonnet Creek, on the southern edge of Walt Disney World.

Transportation: Bus shuttles to all theme parks, water parks, and Downtown Disney.

Special Features: Not to be confused with the Hilton on Hotel Plaza Boulevard, this resort shares property and many amenities with the luxurious Waldorf Astoria Orlando. This may be the single best-kept secret in the Walt Disney World area. It blends the obvious luxury of its sister resort with a warmer, more family-friendly ambiance. It shares the convention facility, golf course, restaurants, and spa. But it has a much better pool complex, and more restaurant selections. I am not shy in saying that this is my favorite hotel in the Walt Disney World area.

Room Types: Large rooms sleep 4 with two queen-sized beds.

Best Room Locations: Facing west is best, with the view of some parks in the distance, and the golf and pool complexes.

Dining: While you can wander over to the Waldorf Astoria for steak at the Bull & Bear, your selections here with poolside, counter service, and other dining are more convenient. Two highlights are La Luce and Harvest Bistro, which are both simply fabulous.

Atmosphere: This resort oozes contemporary luxury that would make a family with small children, a business meeting, and a couple on a romantic getaway all feel perfectly at home at the same time.

Shades of Green

Are you in the Army, Navy, Air Force, or Marines? Well, Disney has a hotel just for you! Shades of Green is an AFRC hotel exclusively reserved for military personnel and their families. Make sure you consider this option if you're coming to Walt Disney World. Shades of Green is available to eligible members of the U.S. Armed Forces community, Department of Defense civilians, and their families. Managed by Disney, it offers all the same benefits as a traditional Disney resort. Room rates are dependent upon military grade and type of room but traditionally range from $76 to $116. The rooms are comparable to those at a Disney Moderate resort. Check out their website for more information, or call their reservation desk from Monday through Friday from 0830 to 1700 hours (see, I know a little military-speak!), at 1-888-593-2242.

Location: Magic Kingdom area
Website: www.shadesofgreen.org
Address: 1950 W. Magnolia Palm Drive, Lake Buena Vista, FL 32830
Phone: 1-888-593-2242

Special Features: AAFES General Store and great room rates.

Room Types: Large rooms have two queen-sized beds.

Orlando-Area Hotels

In a recent online search for rooms in the Orlando area, more than 350 hotels came up. Needless to say, I can't review them all, and probably shouldn't even try. A few things I share here can help you with planning if you're looking to stay off Disney property but still want to make sure you're getting the best deal possible. Let's look at some of the areas you might look in for accommodations.

Celebration/Kissimmee Area

This is the best location for getting to the parks as quickly as possible, especially Animal Kingdom and Magic Kingdom.

- Celebration Hotel (www.celebrationhotel.com; 407-566-1844)
- Gaylord Palms (www.gaylordhotels.com/gaylordpalms; 407-586-0000)

Lake Buena Vista Area

This area is great for getting to Downtown Disney. Please note that while I recommend these resorts, the Nickelodeon Suites has received many guest complaints that it is noisy and not particularly clean. But the appeal of the characters demands it be listed here.

- Nickelodeon Family Suites by Holiday Inn (www.nickhotel.com; 1-800-344-3959)
- Sheraton Vistana Resort (www.starwood.com; 407-239-3100)

 HIDDEN MAGIC!

So what are your best options off property?

- **Traveling with kids:** Hilton Orlando Bonnet Creek
- **Adult party:** Waldorf Astoria Orlando
- **Best overall:** Hilton Orlando Bonnet Creek

International Drive

Hotels in this area are ideal if you're attending a convention at the Orange County Convention Center or will visit Universal Studios and other theme parks. The traffic is very heavy and will cause longer commute times to Disney.

- The Peabody Orlando (www.peabodyorlando.com; 407-352-4000)
- Embassy Suites Hotel Orlando International Drive South (www.embassysuitesorlando.com; 407-352-1400)

Summary

With literally hundreds of hotels to choose from in the Orlando area, as well as all the other choices, no doubt this is just a drop in the proverbial bucket. But with choices that are good for kids and adults, as well as options in areas where you may have some other plans, you've got an idea of some good choices, as well as places to look for other options.

Feast Like Royalty: Dining at Walt Disney World

Dining at theme parks has moved beyond burgers and pizza, and you will definitely enjoy the changes. But with some prices that can shock even the wealthy, you need to plan ahead. In Part 3, I show you what culinary options have sprung up throughout Walt Disney World and how you can get the most from your dining dollar. You learn about the craze known as character meals, and you consider money-saving options, including dining plans and top-notch meals that come at bargain-basement prices. Bon appétit!

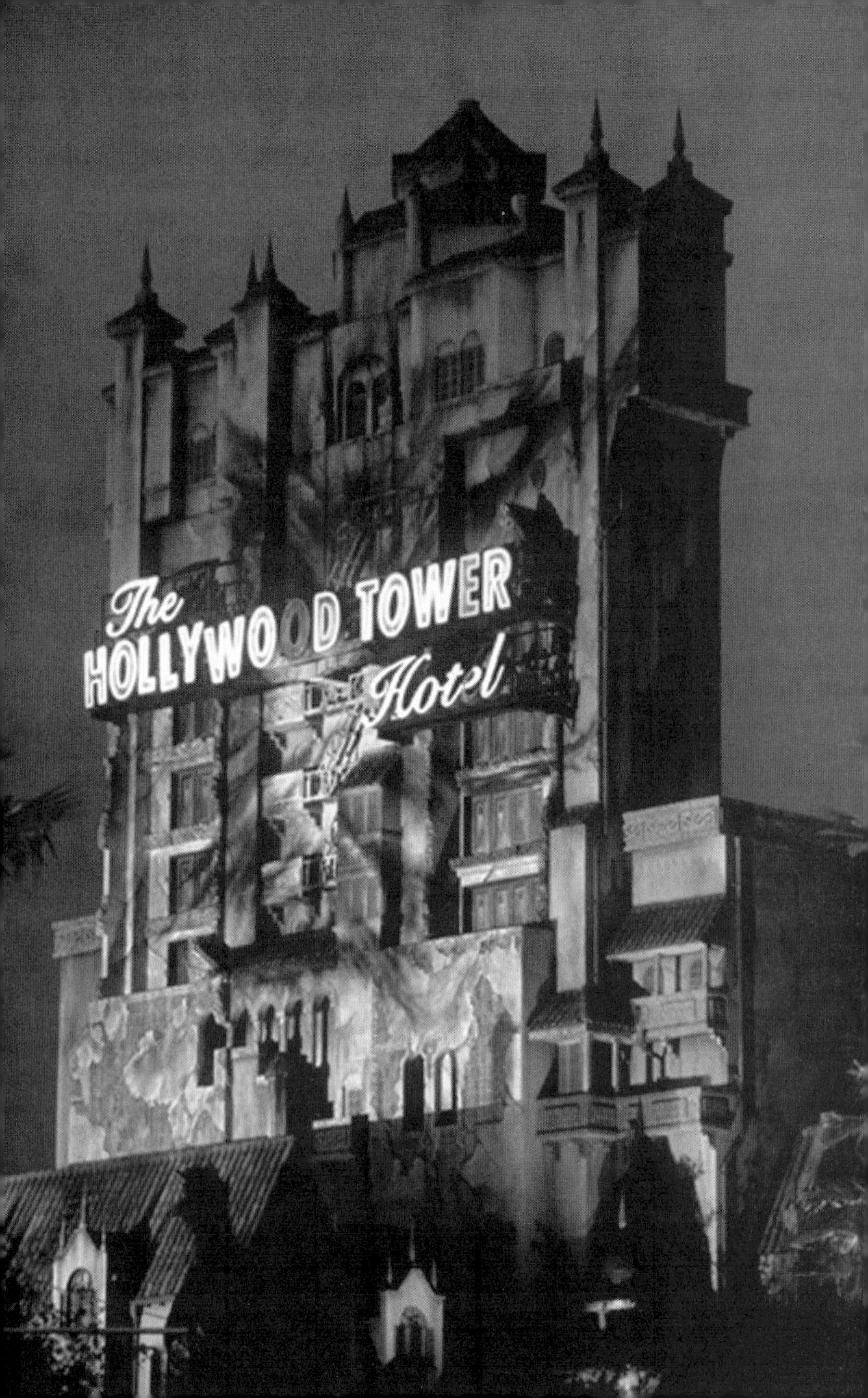
The
HOLLYWOOD TOWER
Hotel

Dining at Walt Disney World

In This Chapter

- Find out about restaurants all around the world (Disney World, that is!)
- Figure out what choices are best for your taste buds
- Learn about how to meet Disney characters at mealtime
- Understand what the Advance Dining Reservations and Disney Dining Plan programs are all about

If your idea of theme park food variety is having cheese added to your hamburger, you're in for a big surprise. Walt Disney World has grown over the years to include an amazing array of dining selections. There are counter-service fast-food joints, elegant fine-dining restaurants, and food stands with everything from soft drinks and ice cream to fresh fruit and roasted turkey legs. You can select cuisines from all around the world or some really great American classics. You may also be surprised by a growing effort to bring more healthful choices to the parks and to meet specialty diet requirements.

Making your dining arrangements ahead of time is important, and Disney restaurant reservations are not exactly like the ones you get back home. I show you how their system works so you know what you're getting and can plan accordingly. Another important factor is cost. While there are dining options to fit all cost ranges, it can be easy to overspend if you don't pay attention. Because the right meals can make a vacation, underestimating your true food costs could just as easily ruin it.

So why is planning important? Well, some restaurants are so popular that you have to make reservations months before you arrive if you want to get in. And managing your food budget is even more important so that you can enjoy as many of these special dining experiences without having to feel the pain on your credit card later. Let's get started!

Making Advance Reservations

Let's start by looking at the Advance Dining Reservations system at Walt Disney World.

Making a Reservation

Making reservations is easy. Almost all of the restaurants accept reservations via one central line. The system is easy. Simply call 407-WDW-DINE (407-939-3463). Tell them what restaurant you'd like to go to, the number of people in your party (even those under 3), the desired time, and so on. Ensure you write down your confirmation number. In the back of this book you'll find a card designed just for this purpose, so you can keep all your reservation confirmation numbers in one place for easy reference.

You can now also make dining reservations via the Walt Disney World website. Just find the restaurant of your choice and you will be able to request your day and time for a party of up to 10. It will even make recommendations of alternatives, if your restaurant is fully booked, though to date the suggestions, because they are computer generated, are not always very appropriate. They may not be of the same kind of dining experience or cost level.

Advance Reservations Defined

Now exactly what you get with an advance reservation is a bit more complex. Basically, your advance reservation schedule means that when you arrive and check in, you are placed ahead of anyone who is waiting for a table but doesn't have an advance reservation. Because they accept only a limited number of advance reservations per hour, it is in most respects exactly like a standard reservation. But don't think that an 8 P.M. advance reservation means that there's a gleaming table sitting there waiting for you; you may still have to wait a bit.

All of that being said, this system runs pretty much like a normal reservation. Rarely have I had to wait more than 10 to 15 minutes after my advance reservation time.

When to Make a Reservation

Nearly all of the restaurants, including character meals, accept reservations as far out as 180 days in advance. If you are staying at a Disney resort you can make your plans for up to 10 days of your stay in one call. So, in essence, if you are staying for 10 days, you can make some of your reservations for meals as far out as 190 days!

> **DISNEY DON'T**
>
> Don't get caught out in the cold. The following are some of the more popular meals reservations at Walt Disney World, so you'll need to make a little extra effort to secure them.
>
> - Dinner at Le Cellier
> - Breakfast at Cinderella's Royal Table
> - Lunch at the Crystal Palace
> - Dinner at 'Ohana
> - *Spirit of Aloha* show
> - *Hoop Dee Doo Musical Review*
> - California Grill
> - Restaurant Akershus (Princess meals)
> - Dinners on certain holidays (New Year's, Christmas, Thanksgiving)
> - Dinners at restaurants with a view of fireworks

Here are some simple rules:

- Plan on calling 180 days out from your arrival day to make your reservations.

- For select popular meals, make sure you call on the morning that is exactly 180 days out, at 7 A.M. Eastern Standard Time, exactly when the lines open.

- Don't be discouraged if you don't get every meal that you want. Call back in a week or two, as well as a few weeks before your trip. Cancellations happen all the time, so you might get lucky.

- Write down your confirmation numbers! Take them with you to each meal, as it helps speed up the check-in process.

What Else You Should Know

Here are a few other tips to keep in mind:

- When making a reservation, if you are staying at a Disney resort, have your resort reservation number handy.

- Arrive at the restaurant 10 to 15 minutes before your seating time. That way, they get you in the queue at the right time. Some dinner shows, like the *Hoop Dee Doo Musical Review*, require that you arrive as much as 40 minutes ahead of time. This is because they have to seat the entire restaurant all at once, and they need people there early so the show can get started on time.

- For many meals, you need a credit card to make the reservation.

- During the holidays some restaurants add a holiday surcharge, especially buffets, so ask how much it costs when making reservations.

- Some of the more popular restaurants require a credit card charge to secure a seat year-round. This is to discourage people from blocking off meals and then not showing up, depriving others of the chance to eat there.

Disney Dining Plan

This has quickly become one of my favorite features of a Disney resort vacation package. It's available only to Disney resort guests and is a great value, in most cases. You'll still want to consider your overall dining plans and budget to see if it's right for you, but in the right instances, it can provide significant savings and a great deal of convenience.

How the Plan Works

With the plan, you pay a flat amount per person in exchange for a specific number of meals at Disney restaurants. There are now three basic plans, where for every hotel night of your stay, you get the following:

Deluxe Dining Plan

- Three meals, either quick service or table service

- Quick-service meals including an entrée, a dessert, and one drink; or a combo meal with drink, if applicable. At breakfast it is just the entrée and the nonalcoholic beverage.

- Table-service meals including an appetizer, an entrée, a dessert, and one drink; or a full buffet, if applicable

- Two snacks (ice-cream bar, popcorn, milk, or bottle of soda or water, to name a few)

- Resort refillable mug (only refillable at your Disney resort)

Standard Dining Plan

- One quick-service meal including one entrée, one dessert, and one drink; or a combo meal with drink, if applicable. At breakfast it is just the entrée and the nonalcoholic beverage.

- One table-service meal including one entrée, one dessert, and one drink, plus an appetizer for kids 3–9; or a full buffet, if applicable

- One snack (ice-cream bar, popcorn, milk, or bottle of soda or water, to name a few)

- Resort refillable mug (only refillable at your Disney resort)

Quick Service Dining Plan

- Resort refillable mug (only refillable at your Disney resort)

- Two quick-service meals including one entrée, one dessert, and one drink; or a combo meal with drink, if applicable. At breakfast it is just the entrée and the nonalcoholic beverage.

- One snack (ice-cream bar, popcorn, milk, or bottle of soda or water, to name a few)

- Resort refillable mug (only refillable at your Disney resort)

Note that the drinks included must be nonalcoholic. You can still buy wine, beer, or cocktails—or additional food items, for that matter—but you have to pay for them. But don't think that this is a restrictive plan. The menu item selection is complete, not some prechosen item list at each restaurant. And with more than 100 Disney restaurants included in the main plan, you'll rarely encounter a problem. Plus you don't have to use your meals in any particular order or on specific days; use them when you want to.

Other Considerations

Well, a few meals at Walt Disney World are more extravagant in their food or entertainment. For these, you have to redeem two of your table-service meal credits for just one meal. Furthermore, the two-credit charge at dinner shows like *Spirit of Aloha* gets you into Category 2 (of 3) seating, not the premiere Category 1 that sits closest to the entertainment. These restaurants include the following:

- Jiko—The Cooking Place
- Flying Fish Café
- California Grill
- *Hoop Dee Doo Musical Review* (Category 2 seating)
- *Mickey's Backyard BBQ*
- Citricos
- Narcoossee's
- *Spirit of Aloha* show (Category 2 seating)
- Artist Point
- Yachtsman Steakhouse
- Cinderella's Royal Table
- The Hollywood Brown Derby
- Le Cellier (dinner only)

Other plan considerations include:

- **Room Service:** You can use the dining plan credits for room service, but not for mini-bar charges, souvenir or refillable drink mugs, or nonfood merchandise (such as photos at character meals).

- **Children's Plan:** Kids ages 3 to 9 have to pick their meals from the children's menu, if one is available.

- **Toddlers:** Children under 3 cannot order the plan. But they are allowed to eat from one of the parent's plates, saving you from having to buy them a meal at many dining locations, like a buffet.

- **Everyone Is on the Plan:** You can't have some of your party on the plan but others not. Everyone in a room has to be on the plan, so you can't go cheap and share meals.

Where the Plan Works

Few restaurants don't honor the plan. Victoria & Albert's in the Grand Floridian Resort is one. Most new restaurants don't get added to the plan right away, but usually end up there eventually. Otherwise, coverage is extremely broad. As you read the restaurant reviews in the next chapters, look for the **D** symbol.

You can print out brochures for these plans from the Disney World website. Just look for the page titled "Why Stay at a Disney Resort Hotel?" under the "Plan" section.

How to Use It

Your room key will keep track of your meal redemption. Whenever you're dining, let them know you're on the plan when you're being seated or approaching the counter. Then give them your room key when paying the bill. The receipt will show how many credits remain for that particular kind of meal, a nice feature for tracking your progress.

When it comes to snacks, all you need to do is look for the Disney Dining Plan logo on cart stands or counter-service menus. The distinctive block logo with the DDP letters and a soda cup in it are easy to find and are next to all applicable snack selections.

MICKEY-SPEAK

When you see the **D** logo next to a restaurant in the dining chapters of this book, it means the restaurant is part of the Disney Dining Plan program.

Disney Dining Plan Costs

So what is the cost? The plans can change at any time, but it's safe to assume that it will cost, per person, per day, the following amounts:

- Quick Service dining plan: Adults $34.99/Children 3–9 $11.99

- Standard dining plan: Adults $51.54/Children 3–9 $15.02

- Deluxe dining plan: Adults $85.52/Children 3–9 $23.79

In peak seasons, the daily prices of these plans can rise from $2 to $4 per adult, and $1 to $2 per child. How does that compare to buying on your own? Let's take a quick look at one day on the plan with our fictional family of four (two adults, and two children, ages 6 and 8). That equates to two adult dining plans and two child dining plans.

How much would each plan cost for one day? And how does that compare to what you would get?

- Quick Service Daily Plan Cost: $93.96

  Comparable costs off the plan for a Quick Service Lunch and Dinner, and a snack: $95.44

- Standard Plan Comparison: $133.12

  Comparable costs off the plan for a Quick Service Lunch, Table Service Dinner, and a snack: $171.84

- Deluxe Plan Comparison: $218.62

  Comparable costs off the plan for a Table Service Breakfast, Lunch, and Dinner, and two snacks: $304.42

In all three examples the math certainly indicates that you can save some money. As the plans get more expensive, the savings seem to rise as well. However, does it really work out that way? This math all looks fine and good. But don't just compare the price to the cost. Compare what you would have bought normally to the cost. That's the real measure of the deal.

One important note: remember when calculating your food budget that you will still have other possible food costs that you will need to add, whether you choose to do a dining plan or not:

- Extra meals. You have the same number of days of vouchers as nights in your resort hotel, but you're probably there for one more total day, so you'll be buying some meals on that extra day.

- Breakfast, or whatever third meal you did not use. Plan to use credits for this meal on the Standard or Quick Service plan.

- Alcoholic beverages at meals.

- Not all plans cover all meals you might eat. Consider ALL your dining needs, not just what is on the plan. For instance the Quick Service plan only covers two meals.

- More snacks in the parks.

- Waters and sodas that you will drink to keep hydrated in the Florida sun.

- Gratuities are *not* included in the dining plan (with a few exceptions), so budget for that as well.

Which Plan for Which Family?

So should you go with the Deluxe, the Standard, or the Quick Service plan? It all depends on your group. Here are some basic suggestions:

- *Families with smaller children* are usually best off with the Standard or Quick Service. Why not the Deluxe? To make it pay off, you pretty much have to go to table-service restaurants for every meal, and most small children won't sit for that or eat that much food.

- *Adult-only groups and foodies.* People who are here for culinary adventures should consider the Deluxe. It pays off as long as you are going to all table-service dining choices.

- *Families with teens* can consider the counter-service option, especially if they are going to let their kids go off on their own. Breakfasts or lunches on the go are probably the norm already, and they can just use their Magic Your Way card to pay for their meals, meaning you don't have to give them cash!

Bottom Line

While they all seem to measure out as good deals, I think that you have to consider each with a guarded eye. For most families the Deluxe plan is too costly and too much food. They simply won't get to it all, so they are overspending even before they get to Orlando. It can be a good deal. No criticism there. But few can really make it worth their while.

The Standard and Quick plans can be right, if that's how you dine. But be sure that you are planning your meals to ensure that you are maximizing the plan. Overall, the dining plans seem to give savings to many different kinds of guests.

Comparing Character Meals

You may have heard about the famed character meals at Walt Disney World. In a nutshell, your dinner (or lunch, or breakfast, or high tea) hosts are Disney characters. From Mickey and Minnie, to the bevy of movie Princesses, to Lilo and Stitch, you have a wide array of characters from which to choose. During your meal the characters move from table to table, greeting the kids, signing autograph books, posing for pictures, and creating special moments that your children will treasure forever.

These character encounters have become a staple of most family vacations to Walt Disney World. They are also the most sought-after advance reservations, with few exceptions. But with more than a dozen to choose from, as well as the dinner show options that we review later in this chapter, which one is right for you?

Later in the respective chapters, we review the restaurants for cuisine and overall entertainment value, but let's do a little side-by-side comparison to get you started. The chart starting on the next page reviews the different features of the character meals and dinner shows.

DID YOU KNOW?

Are you wondering why there's a range of prices for the *Spirit of Aloha* show? Disney is testing different price ranges for different seating options. They have already mapped out the seating at the *Hoop Dee Doo Musical Review* and the *Spirit of Aloha* dinner show into three tiers each, with higher prices for better views of the show. I think that the $10 added cost per person makes choosing the best seating section a good idea, but for larger groups, that can be expensive. In the *Spirit of Aloha* show, the second tier offers good views and a bit more of the warm ambiance of the restaurant, so it's a good selection. The second tier in the *Hoop Dee Doo Musical Review* is also a good choice if you want to keep the costs down a bit.

Kids and Healthful Dining

Long before the fury over trans-fat oils hit the national media, Disney had been beset by concerns over the foods that they were dishing out to kids. The counter-service meals were all falling to the usual suspects, like burgers with fries, chicken strips, and mac and cheese. Don't get me wrong—these are all personal favorites, but even I know I can't eat them all the time.

Disney knew they had to do better, so they've started to incorporate more healthful children's menu items around Walt Disney World. Chicken pita pizzas with apples and a side salad, vegetable plates with yogurt and chicken salad, and broiled chicken strips with vegetables and yogurt have all become the new lead kid's meals. You can still get your kids the bad stuff usually, but when they're putting more healthful selections forward as their primary selections, it's much easier to get your kids to eat well while on vacation.

Restaurant	Location	Character Meals	Hosts
Cinderella's Royal Table	Magic Kingdom	B, L, D	Cinderella, Ariel, Snow White, Belle, and Aurora
The Crystal Palace	Magic Kingdom	B, L, D	Winnie the Pooh, Tigger, Eeyore, and Piglet
Akershus Royal Banquet Hall	Epcot	B, L, D	Ariel, Belle, Jasmine, Snow White, Sleeping Beauty, and Cinderella
The Garden Grill	Epcot	D	Mickey Mouse, Pluto, and Chip and Dale
Hollywood & Vine	Hollywood Studios	B, L	Disney Junior Stars
Donald's Safari Breakfast/Lunch	Animal Kingdom	B, L	Donald Duck, Pluto, Mickey Mouse, Minnie Mouse, and Chip and Dale
Cape May Café	Beach Club Resort	B	Goofy, Minnie Mouse, and Donald Duck
Chef Mickey's	Contemporary Resort	B, D	Mickey and Minnie Mouse, Donald Duck, Goofy, Pluto, and Chip and Dale
1900 Park Fare	Grand Floridian Resort	B, D	B-Mary Poppins, Alice in Wonderland D-Cinderella, Wicked Step-Sisters
'Ohana	Polynesian Resort	B	Lilo and Stitch, Mickey Mouse, Pluto
Gulliver's Grill	Swan Resort	B	Goofy and Pluto
Mickey's Backyard BBQ	Fort Wilderness	D	Mickey and Minnie Mouse, Goofy, Pluto, Chip and Dale, and a Country Stage Performance
Spirit of Aloha Show	Polynesian Resort	D	Hawaiian Luau Stage Show
Hoop Dee Doo Musical Review	Fort Wilderness	D	Western Stage Performance

2 = You must use two table service credits for a meal at this restaurant. B = Breakfast, L = Lunch, D = Dinner,

Character meals and dinner shows at Walt Disney World.

Disney Dining Plan	Character Grade	Cuisine	Serving Style	Cost Rating
yes, 2	5	American	À la Carte	$$$
yes	4	American	Buffet	$$
yes	5	B-American L&D-Norwegian/American	B-Family Style L & D-Buffet/À la Carte	$$$
yes	3.5	American	Family Style	$$
yes	3	American	Buffet	$$
yes	4.5	American	Buffet	$$
yes	3.5	American	Buffet	$
yes	5	American	Buffet	$$
yes	5	American	B & D-Buffet	$$
yes	3.5	American	Family Style	$$
	2	American	Buffet	$
yes, 2	4.5	American	Buffet	$$$$
yes, 2	NA	Polynesian	Family Style	$$$$
yes, 2	NA	American	Family Style	$$$$

T = Teatime. Character Grade 1-5, where 1 = worst experience and 5 = best experience.

Comparing Dinner Meals

As you can see, I also review the dinner shows. There aren't a lot of them, but they are popular. The *Hoop Dee Doo Musical Review* and the *Spirit of Aloha* show have been here for quite some time, always packing them in.

Author's Favorites

Everyone has their own cuisine favorites, so my choices will not always be the best for everyone. That being said, as you go through the next few chapters, you'll see what I consider to be the best of each park, the resorts, and the rest of Walt Disney World. My tastes lean to trying lots of new cuisines, and I also don't mind spending a bit to try them. What do I think are the absolute best? Here are my choices.

Best of Walt Disney World Dining

These are my very favorite overall Walt Disney World dining choices.

Best Overall Fine Dining—California Grill (Contemporary Resort): Fine dining, exceptional views, relaxed but elegant ambiance. Perfection.

Best Overall Character Meal—Restaurant Akershus (Epcot): This restaurant has an embarrassment of riches in the Princess department. The food is also quite good, offering some new tastes but letting you rely on American standards if that's your royal wish.

Best Overall Counter-Service Meal—Flame Tree Barbeque (Animal Kingdom): Excellent barbecue combined with tropically lush and luxurious dining ambiance makes for an unparalleled and affordable experience.

Best Overall Snack—Dole Whip (Magic Kingdom): To each his own, but this classic never fails to satisfy.

Best Dinner Show—*Hoop Dee Doo Musical Review* (Fort Wilderness): This long-running show is still one of the hardest reservations to get, and it combines good food and fun, kitschy entertainment.

Disney Dining Honorary Mentions

Some of these are not awards you'll see in a *Michelin Guide*, but they're important for Walt Disney World.

Best Fireworks Show Restaurant—Rose & Crown (Epcot): An outdoor seat is hard to score, but the view of *IllumiNations* is beyond compare, especially with a nice pint of English beer.

Honorary Mention—California Grill (Magic Kingdom) for a view of the Magic Kingdom show: A better view than at Rose & Crown, but the Epcot show is the better of the two.

Best Pizza—Via Napoli (Epcot): Pizza has been notoriously mediocre at Walt Disney World until this new pizzeria breezed in with crisp, Neapolitan-style pies.

Best Counter-Service Breakfast—Tonga Toast (Polynesian Resort): Originally only available at the Kona Café, you can now get this banana-stuffed French toast at Captain Cook's counter service as well.

Best Romantic Restaurant—Victoria & Albert's (Grand Floridian Resort): If white table cloth, over-the-top elegance is your cup of tea, then V & A is exceptional. It's expensive, but is the most elegant experience in all of Walt Disney World.

Most Over-the-Top Cocktails—Tambu Lounge (Polynesian Resort): The glasses are tiki gods and the drinks are all strong, fruity, and tasty.

Most Fun Dining at a Resort—Whispering Canyon Café (Wilderness Lodge Resort): The staff makes dinner so fun for kids— and the adults, too—that nobody wants a room near the place!

Most Fun Dining at a Park—50's Prime Time Café (Hollywood Studios): Don't tell Mom that you don't like green beans. We clean our plates in this family, young man!

Best Steakhouse—Yachtsman Steakhouse (Beach Club): The nearby Shula's (Dolphin Resort) might have a higher-end, more traditional experience, but the expense for value there is so extreme that Yachtsman is a better bet.

Best Seafood—Flying Fish Café (BoardWalk): Good-quality and innovative preparations make this the choice for seafood fans.

Most Exotic Restaurant Setting—Restaurant Marrakesh (Epcot): Welcome to the Kingdom of Morocco, showcasing authentic cuisine and complemented by live music and dancing.

Best Trendy Dining—Jiko—The Cooking Place (Animal Kingdom Lodge): The flavors explode from the food, and all those awards wouldn't lie.

Best Buffet—Tusker House (Animal Kingdom Theme Park): The food includes both a well-executed array of traditional cuisine at each meal, but also some wonderfully exotic and still approachable Indian and African inspired selections as well.

Honorary Mention—Boma (Animal Kingdom Theme Park): Inspiration for Tusker House, Boma offers a different setting for its African-inspired items that are alongside American standards.

Best Wine List—Jiko (Animal Kingdom Lodge): Sporting the largest South African wine list outside of South Africa, it's filled with great choices that are new to most wine connoisseurs.

Summary

You're probably going to disagree with at least one of my awards. That's a good thing because that means you found a favorite of your own. Either way, let's dig in and see what these restaurants are all about, shall we?

Dining in the Resorts

In This Chapter

- Uncover the dining surprises that await you at your resort
- Learn about entertaining and delicious meals at other resorts
- Find that perfect meal for you and your party

The Disney resorts are designed to make your stay more comfortable, and we all know the way to most people's hearts is through their stomachs. The restaurants that you find in the resorts cover the spectrum from quick-service food courts to ultra-elegant, white-tablecloth gourmet experiences. And unlike the typical restaurant selection in Hometown, U.S.A., there are numerous dining destinations that feel that entertainment is a necessary side dish to your entrées. In this chapter, I walk you through the table-service restaurants at the Disney resorts, reviewing their food, their fun, and the finances you need to afford them.

Restaurants reviews are listed with others from the same resort so that you can see all your choices together.

Dining at Deluxe Resorts and Deluxe Villas Resorts

The Deluxe resorts have some of the most innovative and entertaining dining I have ever experienced. There are also some fine-dining choices that rank as some of the best in the Orlando area, and can make a great vacation experience even better. When you are planning your vacation, look to these restaurants for some of your special group experiences. Remember, all the Deluxe resorts have counter-service restaurants, providing both quick service and complete meals, as well as grab-and-go convenience groceries.

Disney's Animal Kingdom Lodge and Villas

Boma—Flavors of Africa

Cuisine Type: American/African
Serving Style: Buffet
Breakfast: $ $ *Prix fixe*
Lunch: Not open
Dinner: $ $ Prix fixe
D: Yes
Rating: ★ ★ ★ ☆

Located off the main lobby of the Animal Kingdom Lodge, this buffet restaurant is one of the reasons why the resort is so popular. The noisy setting is surrounded by richly colored woods that carry the hotel theme but make for a slightly more serene dinner experience. Open for both breakfast and dinner, the biggest problem with this restaurant is that it is so popular that there is always a crowd waiting for a table—be sure you make reservations.

MICKEY-SPEAK

With **prix fixe,** you pay a flat price per person for the meal, not including alcoholic beverages. Buffets usually charge a flat price (different for children and adults), regardless of what you eat or how often you go back.

Breakfast is largely made up of American breakfast standards, including an omelet bar. There are also a few African items, including the *bobotie*, a South African dish that includes minced meats (corned beef, in this case), eggs, and a baked topping. This is a nice way to try something new without having to venture too far out of your comfort zone.

The buffet is an ideal dinner place for families, offering a wide selection of American items as well as several African-influenced foods. The adventurous in your family can try African-inspired soups and meats, as well as a nice array of other touches here and there, like the couscous. But for those not ready for a walk on the wild side, there are several standards, like mac and cheese, spaghetti, and chicken nuggets.

As meals go, you won't necessarily want to make a trip here if you aren't already staying at the resort. But if you're going out for dinner already, this could be the perfect combination of a good buffet meal with a visit to the scenic hotel. Many find the animal-viewing areas on the adjacent savannah a great place to wait for your table to become available.

Jiko—The Cooking Place

Cuisine Type: African fusion
Serving Style: À la carte
Breakfast: Not open
Lunch: Not open
Dinner: $ $ $ $
D: Yes—2
Rating: ★ ★ ★ ★ ★

A personal favorite, this expensive dining option is worth the cost. The Cooking Place, a display kitchen for some appetizers and salads, is an ideal place to sit if you are traveling alone because you can get recommendations from the knowledgeable staff. The rest of the ambiance is a bit too cool for my taste, especially after moving from the warm colors of the lodge, but it is comfortable and adequately upscale.

The cuisine is more heavily inspired by African flavors than at Boma. The wide array of appetizers can serve as a tapas-style dinner selection, with favorites including the light but flavorful flatbreads, the lentil pastilla, and the maize-and-sweet potato tamales. There's also a Taste of Africa sampler that's great for sharing. Not as easy to share, but exceptional, are the roasted butternut squash soup; the tikka-marinated tuna; and the cucumber, tomato, and red onion salad.

The entrées continue to amaze, with rich, well-balanced flavors. A popular selection is the tamarind-braised beef short rib, but there are several good choices.

Wine lovers will be interested in knowing that one of, if not the largest selection of South African wines outside of that country can be found here, with most available by the glass!

Sanaa

Cuisine Type: Indian
Serving Style: À la carte
Breakfast: Not open
Lunch: À la carte
Dinner: À la carte
D: No
Rating: ★ ★ ★ ★ ☆

The newest dining option at the Animal Kingdom Lodge, it's actually located in the new Deluxe Villa Resort Kidani Village. The cuisine is inspired by the nations along the old spice route, reflecting mostly Indian cuisine, but also has some African, Chinese, and even European influences.

Disney's Yacht and Beach Club Resorts and Villas

Dining at the Yacht and Beach Clubs is not limited due to the nearby options at the BoardWalk and Epcot World Showcase. Instead, there are a great number of choices that should make your stay delicious.

Cape May Café

Cuisine Type: American (B), seafood (D)
Serving Style: Buffet
Breakfast: ♛ $
Lunch: Not open
Dinner: $ $
D: Yes
Rating: ★ ★ ★ ☆ ☆

The buffet breakfast is a character meal with Goofy, Minnie Mouse, and Chip and Dale. The standard American breakfast selections are well prepared, if uninspired. This can be a far more convenient option than Chef Mickey's in the Contemporary if you are staying in one of the Epcot-area resorts.

The dinner buffet is all about seafood, as befitting the restaurant's name. Clams are the most popular item, but the mussels are good as well, and the barbecue ribs are good for those meat eaters in the crowd. It may not be the best seafood you can get, but it is comparatively affordable and plentiful.

Yachtsman Steakhouse

Cuisine Type: Steakhouse
Serving Style: À la carte
Breakfast: Not open
Lunch: Not open
Dinner: $ $ $ $
D: Yes—2
Rating: ★ ★ ★ ☆ ☆

This high-end steakhouse is a great place to get a great cut of beef. The ambiance is a bit airier than the recent spate of dark mahogany-lined men's club decors that you find elsewhere.

Obviously, you'll want to stick to the steak selections here, and the appetizers are all the usual suspects that you can count on. It's really a good steakhouse; though the nearby Shula's (Dolphin) has more cachet and Le Cellier (Epcot—Canada Pavilion) has a larger following.

Beaches & Cream Soda Shop

Cuisine Type: American
Serving Style: À la carte, counter service
Breakfast: Not open
Lunch: $
Dinner: $
D: Yes
Rating: ★ ★ ★ ☆ ☆

This extremely relaxed table-service restaurant is a popular choice for resort guests. It serves basic burger and sandwich fare well and affordably. But it is really known more for its soda-shop atmosphere that makes it a popular dessert destination, as ice cream flows out of here like water from a tap. The Kitchen Sink as well as the No Way Jose are both popular favorites, with the first requiring a whole can of whipped cream to finish off its gluttonous decadence.

Beaches is bumped from a 3 to 3.5 rating largely due to being the best dessert venue in all of Walt Disney World.

Captain's Grille

Cuisine Type: American
Serving Style: À la carte
Breakfast: $
Lunch: $
Dinner: $ $
D: Yes
Rating: ★ ★ ⯨ ☆ ☆

Formerly known as the Yacht Club Galley, the Captain's Grille is a slightly less chaotic alternative to the Beaches & Cream Soda Shop. This casual table-service restaurant sticks to burgers and sandwiches, with a tilt toward seafood, as the resort's theme implies. It's nothing special, but is a convenient choice if you're staying here.

Disney's BoardWalk Inn Resort and Villas

The restaurants at the Disney BoardWalk are reviewed in Chapter 15.

Disney's Contemporary Resort

California Grill

Cuisine Type: American
Serving Style: À la carte
Breakfast: Not open
Lunch: Not open
Dinner: $ $ $ $
D: Yes—2
Rating: ★ ★ ★ ★ ★

Arguably the finest restaurant in all of Walt Disney World, it combines excellent cuisine, casually elegant decor, an exceptional wine list, an educated wait staff, and a scenic penthouse view of the surrounding area, including the Magic Kingdom.

The food is California inspired, bringing a great variety of fresh flavors to the table. The grilled pork tenderloin with polenta is a signature dish, but with constant changes and additions to the menu, you should just let your taste buds make the selection. Sushi here is an exceptional shared appetizer and the bisque is excellent.

The atmosphere adds a final touch of elegance. Watching the sun set and the Magic Kingdom come to life adds a great backdrop to your dinner. But the best part is when the fireworks at the park start. The lights in the restaurant are dimmed, the soundtrack from the park is piped in, and you get a free show without having to be in the often-crowded park. If you're done with dinner, just grab a cocktail and head out to the outdoor walkway to watch under the night sky.

Resort casual attire is required (collared shirts and slacks).

Chef Mickey's

Cuisine Type: American
Serving Style: Buffet
Breakfast: 👑 $ Prix fixe
Lunch: Not open
Dinner: 👑 $ $ Prix fixe
D: Yes
Rating: ★ ★ ★ ☆

This certainly appears to be just another buffet serving as a backdrop to a character experience. Wrong again. The food at Chef Mickey's, while wholly American, doesn't play second fiddle to Mickey and friends; it is fairly well executed, especially when considering the volume of diners served. Breakfast includes a variety of the classics, as well as some good regional American breakfast favorites.

Dinner has meat-carving stations, seafood and pasta selections, and numerous sides. Children's options are naturally offered and are of superior taste and quality.

The character experience is wonderful. Mickey and his core friends are regularly available but not too overbearing. Older kids who are beyond all that will still find it cool that a monorail regularly runs overhead. However, if you're not looking for characters, you might find this meal difficult to get through, so search out another locale.

The Wave

Cuisine Type: American
Serving Style: À la carte
Breakfast: $
Lunch: $ $
Dinner: $ $ $
D: Yes
Rating: ★ ★ ★ ⯪ ☆

This posh new restaurant scores high in the ambiance factor at first, but the barren dining space can make it seem as if you made a wrong turn. The wine list is fairly good, and the trendy dessert samplers, which offer trios of smaller bites together, is refreshing. Overall this restaurant is an underwhelming locale with decent food but little reason to visit.

DISNEY DON'T

Are you stuck in the Magic Kingdom and not thrilled with your dinner options? Don't put up with that—*leave!*

That's right, leave! Leave the park, hop on a monorail, and visit any of the great resort restaurants at the Grand Floridian, the Polynesian, or the Contemporary resorts. Or hop on a boat and visit the Wilderness Lodge or Fort Wilderness. All of these have great choices, and even though most really require reservations, some do not—and others might have an opening. When you're done, take that quick trip back, reenter the park, and continue to have a good time. Give it a try, and don't settle for less!

Disney's Grand Floridian Resort

Prepare for the widest range of dining choices of any resort in the Walt Disney World universe. From high-end cuisine all the way to take-it-and-go food, you have it all here!

Victoria & Albert's

Cuisine Type: American
Serving Style: Prix fixe
Breakfast: Not open
Lunch: Not open
Dinner: $ $ $ $ (actually a whole lot more!)
D: No
Rating: ★ ★ ★ ★ ★

Be prepared to spend a minimum of $120 per person in this most exclusive and elegant of all dining at Walt Disney World. The food is different every day, motivated by the produce available. The menu is also affected by your particular needs. If you're diabetic or have other special dietary needs, they'll accommodate you in delicious fashion, as long as you tell them in advance. The food is truly exquisite, and the ambiance is the height of formal elegance. Coat and tie for men is required, the only restaurant at Walt Disney World with that stipulation. Reservations are required, and it isn't part of the Disney Dining Plan, as you might have guessed. Also note that only guests age 10 and older are allowed in. No little ones, I'm afraid.

It's impossible to suggest what you should eat because the menu is constantly changing and everything is excellent. However, for extra-special occasions, you might try to request the Chef's Table, nestled in the kitchen area. You get special one-on-one treatment, with the chef serving you personally and providing commentary on the meal along the way.

Citricos

Cuisine Type: Mediterranean
Serving Style: À la carte
Breakfast: Not open
Lunch: Not open
Dinner: $ $ $ $
D: Yes—2
Rating: ★ ★ ★ ★ ☆

Well-executed Mediterranean cuisine and a contemporary setting make for one of the higher-end restaurant offerings at the Grand Floridian Resort. Several fish and select meats accent the menu with entrées that rarely go below the $30 mark. I can't say that any one Mediterranean nation's cuisine style is more prevalent here, although it seems to approach a modernized coastal Italian that is in no way reminiscent of big bowls of pasta with a heavy red sauce. Certainly, you're safe with any of the selections, although the seafood seems like the best choice.

The setting is beautiful, and this restaurant is one of the more over-looked fine dining destinations.

1900 Park Fare

Cuisine Type: American
Serving Style: Buffet
Breakfast: ♛ $ $
Lunch: Not open
Dinner: ♛ $ $
D: Yes
Rating: ★ ★ ★ ★ ☆

This restaurant is *the* place for character meals in the Grand Floridian Resort. It has a beautifully detailed Victorian charm to it, and the characters appearing here match that setting. Your breakfast host is Mary Poppins, who is just perfect for this restaurant. Many other characters frequent this meal as well, including Alice in Wonderland, and often Winnie the Pooh. The American buffet breakfast offers no surprises, but the quality is excellent. At dinner you are visited by Cinderella and her wicked step-sisters, and the room is swamped with Princess-dressed little girls who are in heaven! The buffet, again, is predictable but very good.

Garden View Lounge

Cuisine Type: Afternoon tea
Serving Style: Prix fixe
Breakfast: Not open
Lunch: Not open
High Tea: $ $
Dinner: Not open
D: No
Rating: ★ ★ ★ ★ ☆

Open only for afternoon tea, here you'll find a variety of tea services and light food options as you celebrate the true art of high tea. Sure, tea in the afternoon is simply not an American standard, but it's a wonderfully elegant and refined way to relax and enjoy one another's company. This is certainly not a place for younger, more excitable children, but it can be a wonderful retreat for some adults, as well as children who are prepared for a touch of genteel refinement.

To those who have experienced a true afternoon tea in London, this is far more like that kind of affair than the character experience one listed in the Hidden Magic note here.

But if you're not looking for something like this already, you should probably pass it up. This is just not everyone's cup of tea (sorry, but you can't blame me for that pun—it's just too easy!).

HIDDEN MAGIC!

A very special, and very expensive, character experience is also available at the Grand Floridian's Garden View Lounge. Several days a week they hold the My Disney Girl's Perfectly Princess Tea. At a cost of $250 for a parent and a child (an added adult guest will run you another $100, another child adds $150 to the bill), your princess can have a tea party with Sleeping Beauty.

Lots of goodies come along with that, including a special doll and tiara (bear and crown for boys). Food includes little PB&J sandwiches, fruit, and kid-friendly drinks as well.

You can reserve it like any other dining reservation, though you certainly will be paying far more for this one than most meals!

Narcoossee's

Cuisine Type: Seafood
Serving Style: À la carte
Breakfast: Not open
Lunch: Not open
Dinner: $ $ $ $
D: Yes—2
Rating: ★ ★ ★ ☆

The views and the seafood are fantastic here, but, then again, so are the prices. Prepare to drop $50 per person minimum, when you dine at this glass-enclosed pavilion. The views of the Seven Seas Lagoon are amazing, and if you can get a view of the Magic Kingdom, you are really in for a treat. The seafood is also an excellent treat, with limited but well-prepared choices.

This is a great dinner choice if you would like to take kids to a finer dining establishment but don't think they can endure the staid atmosphere of a Victoria & Albert's. They will find the views to be a great distraction, and the kid's menu has more than just chicken fingers and fries as a choice.

Grand Floridian Café

Cuisine Type: American
Serving Style: À la carte
Breakfast: $
Lunch: $ $
Dinner: $ $ $
D: Yes
Rating: ★ ★ ☆ ☆ ☆

This more casual table-service restaurant is more of a sandwich-and-burger place at lunch, because even guests with no budgetary worries don't want a white-tablecloth dinner every night. This is a good breakfast destination if you don't want a distracting character experience but also don't want a meal in a sack. For lunch, it's one of the few table-service restaurants open in a resort.

The food and service has been inconsistent at best. I would suggest that it is good for resort guests needing a breakfast, but otherwise other destinations might be more satisfying.

Disney's Polynesian Resort

Entertainment dining is king in this island retreat. The resort has become a dining destination, even for those not staying here.

'Ohana

Cuisine Type: American
Serving Style: Family style
Breakfast: 👑 $ $
Lunch: Not open

Dinner: $ $
D: Yes
Rating: ★ ★ ★ ★ ☆

Enter this Hawaiian-themed room located off the lobby and enjoy family-style dining. Breakfast is mostly American breakfast foods, all served family style for you to share at the table, while hosts Lilo, Stitch, and Mickey Mouse do the usual meet-and-greet. Dinner is even more special, as a Polynesian entertainer serenades with his ukulele and leads kids through the limbo, hula dancing, and more. The selection may not be as broad as in an à la carte restaurant, but the side dishes are ideal for large groups, and the service is excellent. Many have complained about the menu here changing for the worse, but it's a good family dining venue for both entertainment, food quality, and value.

Make sure you ask for a seat in the main room, to enjoy as much of the fun (and views) as possible.

Disney's *Spirit of Aloha* Show

Cuisine Type: Polynesian
Serving Style: Family style
Breakfast: Not open
Lunch: Not open
Dinner: $ $ $ $
D: Yes—2 (for Category 2 or 3 seating)
Rating: ★ ★ ★ ☆ ☆

Prepare for a show that is light on plot and food that is average at best at this long-popular dinner show that brings a touch of Hawaii to Florida. Food is brought family style to your table, with salads and appetizers followed by ribs and chicken. Cocktails are not included but are available. The show is very entertaining, for both the cultural factor and the corny humor element. They've stepped up the audience-participation element and have kids get into the act at the end of the show, letting them do a little hula dancing.

Depending upon where you sit, you'll pay $50 to $60 per adult and $25 to $30 per child. Although Category 1 seating is obviously the best for viewing, choosing Category 2 to save some money still will afford you a great view of the show, especially if you're in the second tier of tables in the center. Make sure you arrive 40 minutes early because they seat the entire restaurant at once. There are usually shows at 5 and 8 P.M. most nights, so you can go to this with younger children and still hit something resembling a real bedtime.

Kona Café

Cuisine Type: American
Serving Style: À la carte
Breakfast: $
Lunch: $
Dinner: $ $
D: Yes
Rating: ★ ★ ★ ★ ☆

This catch-all restaurant is nestled into a wing of the upper floor of the lobby in the Grand Ceremonial Hall. It serves a pretty predictable range of American entrée selections, most with deceptive Hawaiian names. The dining area is very noisy and open to the crowds that tend to congregate in the lobby, so it isn't a great place if you want a quiet meal. The food is really quite good, and it has a cult following, especially for their signature Tonga Toast (banana-stuffed sourdough French toast). If you are there for breakfast it's a great choice. Some might not consider it a destination, but with the ease of getting from there to the Magic Kingdom and Epcot, it is not a bad place to start or end your day.

Disney's Wilderness Lodge

The Lodge is a warm and inviting place, with restaurants to match. Dining with kids, or just the adults, it doesn't matter—there's something here for every group.

Artist Point

Cuisine Type: American
Serving Style: À la carte
Breakfast: Not open
Lunch: Not open
Dinner: $ $ $ $
D: Yes—2
Rating: ★ ★ ★ ★ ☆

While this is an excellent fine dining restaurant with a great ambiance, you will probably only go to it if you are staying in an area resort. That is not a slam on the restaurant; it's just that there are other good selections that are easier to get to, such as the California Grill in the Contemporary Resort. The rustic elegance of the dining room is ideally matched to a nice array of buffalo, halibut, and other beef and game. The food is excellent, prepared with an eye to the theme of the restaurant, with food pairings that have a fun, American-frontier feel to them. The Tillamook Mac and Cheese sounds like it should be on the kid's menu but is perfect when paired with the Hatfield Pork Chop.

Whispering Canyon Café

Cuisine Type: American
Serving Style: À la carte
Breakfast: $
Lunch: $
Dinner: $ $
D: Yes
Rating: ★ ★ ★ ★ ☆

This restaurant is filled with fun, and I defy you not to join in! The festive chuck wagon ambiance is executed so well that even the antisocial cynics in your group will want to join in, as kids and adults alike get a vibe off the positive buzz at this casual eatery. Located off the lodge lobby, it gets so noisy that it makes it hard to sleep in the hotel rooms that overlook it!

With a general sassiness that's executed perfectly, the servers start you off on a fun meal. Later kids are gathered for such activities as a pony race around the dining area (on broom-handle ponies), sing-a-longs, and other brief activities that get them back to their meal quickly. It's just the right dose of fun.

The food won't disappoint you, either. At all the meals, you can order à la carte or select the family-style, all-you-can-eat selection. The Canyon Skillet is the best choice, containing an appetizer and several entrées, but no dessert. The items in the skillet focus on the best food items from the restaurant, like the smoked ribs and the roasted chicken. If you decide to go with the entrées, several great breakfast choices are not so standard and all very good. Lunch entrées are good, too, but I think the Canyon Skillet is preferable.

Dinner brings more appropriate selections, like the New York strip or the grilled chicken pasta, but I still prefer the skillet.

I highly recommend this as a destination dining experience for any group with children.

Walt Disney World Dolphin

The Dolphin brings some of the biggest names in high-end entertaining and dining to your doorstep. From big steaks to the best clubbing in the area, any adult will enjoy the dining part of this stay.

Shula's Steak House

Cuisine Type: Steakhouse
Serving Style: À la carte
Breakfast: Not open
Lunch: Not open
Dinner: $ $ $ $
D: No
Rating: ★ ★ ★ ★ ☆

This national chain of high-end steakhouses has found a home at the Dolphin. They serve arguably the best steak in all of Walt Disney World, with entrée prices that start at $35 and go higher, especially when you add sides. There's not much else to say, except that the ambiance is that clubby, dark-mahogany vibe that has become the hallmark of most national high-end steakhouse chains. This is a great place to close a business deal and is a popular destination for those on property for a convention who can rely on their expense accounts to pick up the tab (which is sure to start around $75 per person and rise quickly). If steak is your thing and cost isn't an issue, there's no better place to go.

Todd English's bluezoo

Cuisine Type: Seafood
Serving Style: À la carte
Breakfast: Not open
Lunch: Not open
Dinner: $ $ $
D: No
Rating: ★ ★ ★ ★ ☆

Excellent seafood and ultrachic decor accented with a European techno-beat soundtrack make this perhaps the most stylish of all restaurants in Walt Disney World. The bar is a cool blue sight to see, ruined only by the requisite television that spoils the ambiance. The show kitchen makes for good viewing as the entrées come out with that touch of showmanship and presentation flair that made celebrity restaurateur Todd English's Las Vegas spots such a hit.

Yes, they have a kid's menu, but I hardly think this is what kids look forward to when visiting the Magic Kingdom. This is a place that is probably best reserved for adult-only parties, especially those at the start of an evening of clubbing.

Cabana Bar & Beach Club

Cuisine Type: American
Serving Style: À la carte
Breakfast: Not open
Lunch: $
Dinner: $
D: No
Rating: ★ ★ ☆ ☆ ☆

This poolside bar with seating is not really much of a restaurant, but it offers a broader and better selection of food than most of the poolside restaurants found at the other resorts. With burgers and some good sandwich and wrap choices, you'll get better-than-average poolside fare.

The Fountain

Cuisine Type: American
Serving Style: À la carte
Breakfast: Not open
Lunch: $
Dinner: $
D: No
Rating: ★ ★ ☆ ☆ ☆

Salads and burgers constitute the bulk of the menu at The Fountain. This casual dining establishment is an ideal stop for families staying at the hotel that are on a budget and don't have the energy to go searching for a restaurant. This is basic fare in a noisy environment, but it's fine for adults and perfect for kids.

Fresh Mediterranean Market

Cuisine Type: Mediterranean
Serving Style: Buffet, à la carte
Breakfast: $
Lunch: $ $
Dinner: Not open
D: No
Rating: ★ ★ ★ ☆ ☆

The breakfast is really more American than Mediterranean, though there are some regional influences. You can either go through the buffet, organized by stations, or order à la carte. Lunch is à la carte, with good paninis and much more of a true Mediterranean influence to the food. The setting is a bit more serene than at The Fountain, and the room is quieter than you might expect, due to the glass enclosures.

Walt Disney World Swan

A more subdued ambiance makes a fine home for a cozy Italian trattoria and other dining options.

Garden Grove Café

Cuisine Type: American
Serving Style: Buffet, à la carte (B, L, D)
Breakfast: 👑 $
Lunch: $ $
Dinner: 👑 $ $ $
D: No
Rating: ★ ⯪ ☆ ☆ ☆

You can pull off breakfast here for under $15, with a choice of buffet or à la carte dining. On the weekends, it becomes a character buffet breakfast (not à la carte), with Goofy, Pluto, and others. This isn't the best character breakfast, in terms of food or entertainment, but it's improving and affordable, at $16.95 for adults and $8.50 for kids.

Lunch is still affordable, with a broad selection. Dinner converts the restaurant into Gulliver's, a buffet character meal again, that lures with low prices rather than exceptional entertainment. Basically, this restaurant serves as the Swan's catch-all dining establishment for families, spiced up with some character interaction. I used to list this as a place to avoid, but it's improving.

Il Mulino New York Trattoria

Cuisine Type: Italian
Serving Style: À la carte
Breakfast: Not open
Lunch: Not open
Dinner: $ $ $ $
D: No
Rating: ★ ★ ★ ★ ☆

The posh and modern elegance of the long bar area is a great place for appetizers and cocktails. Dining on the Abruzzi-region-inspired Italian food has come up with mostly positive reviews, with the occasional disappointment. All things said, I liked the menu for its broad selection and have never had a bad meal here. A good choice, and worth traveling to if you want Italian and are in the Epcot resorts area, though perhaps not the most kid-focused environment.

Kimonos

Cuisine Type: Sushi
Serving Style: À la carte
Breakfast: Not open
Lunch: Not open
Dinner: $ $
D: No
Rating: ★ ★ ★ ☆ ☆

The sushi is quite good, though not as good as the appetizer sushi at the California Grill. The decor, artistic kimonos hanging on the walls, sets the stage for an elegant but not too foreign dining venue. It also can be fun when the karaoke breaks out. I recommend it highly, especially if you want to get away from so many of the child-heavy dining environments elsewhere.

Disney's Fort Wilderness Resort and Campground

This rustic outpost is home to two of the most popular entertainment dining choices. Don't overlook them just because they are not in traditional hotels.

Hoop Dee Doo Musical Review

Cuisine Type: American
Serving Style: Family style
Breakfast: Not open
Lunch: Not open
Dinner: $ $ $ $
D: Yes—2 (for Category 2 or 3 seating)
Rating: ★ ★ ★ ☆

This is one of the longest-running dinner shows at Walt Disney World—and one of the more popular ones as well. With shows at 5, 7, and 9:30 P.M., you have a lot of times to choose from, but be sure to make your reservations early, as it books quickly. The cost is $51 to $60 per adult and $26 to $31 per child, and most will tell you that it's worth it. The price range represents the difference in three classes of seating. Higher cost means seats closer to the show. I definitely think that the $9 extra per person to move to the front of the room is worth it.

The Western-themed entertainment is funny, enthusiastic, occasionally corny, and G-rated. The food is hearty and plentiful, focused on fried chicken and barbecue ribs. If you have a group, especially one with lots of kids, this is a top destination to consider for a rollicking good time at dinner. Consider it also if you have a multiple-family group that plans on only one or two meals together; this is the place to meet and recount your travels. How fun could it be? Well, this is one of the two things my wife remembers from her first trip to Walt Disney World when she was 6, and she is now, well, older. Such longstanding memories say something special.

Mickey's Backyard BBQ

Cuisine Type: American
Serving Style: Buffet
Breakfast: Not open
Lunch: Not open
Dinner: 🏕 $ $ $ $
D: Yes—2
Rating: ★ ★ ★ ☆ ☆

This entertainment dinner really is the best of both worlds. With visits from Mickey, Minnie, and other friends, you get a character meal. With the on-stage acts, you get a dinner show. You get barbecue chicken and ribs, burgers, hot dogs, mac and cheese, corn on the cob, watermelon, and more picnic fare.

Seating is in an outdoor pavilion, so weather plays a factor. Shows are only held on Thursdays and Saturdays, so be sure you check for availability when you make a reservation. The food is better than you might expect, but it's harder for your kids to really get to the characters, and signing autograph books is not part of the experience. This is great with a large group, but diminishes as your party size does.

Trail's End Restaurant

Cuisine Type: American
Serving Style: Buffet (B, D), à la carte (L)
Breakfast: $
Lunch: $
Dinner: $
D: Yes
Rating: ★ ★ ★ ☆ ☆

With only the dinner buffet even getting close to $20 for an adult, this is one of the more affordable buffets at Walt Disney World. Disney is testing moving some meals to à la carte, but either way you will find basic American choices, with a lot of barbecue and fried chicken. The decor is country inn, complete with old pots and pans lining the walls. It's an old-fashioned country chic that matches the resort ambiance. Don't think of this as a cheap choice, but as a fortunately inexpensive one.

Disney's Saratoga Springs Resort

The dining efforts are certainly improving, with a couple of selections designed for the whole family.

The Turf Club

Cuisine Type: American
Serving Style: À la carte
Breakfast: Not open
Lunch: $ $
Dinner: $ $
D: Yes
Rating: ★ ★ ☆ ☆ ☆

The Turf Club has brought more dining options to Saratoga Springs. The limited but appealing selection of entrées is a bit of a step up from The Artist's Palette, though remember that it's just a quick trip to Downtown Disney and all of its interesting eateries. The ambiance is a very clubby one that is child-friendly.

Disney's Old Key West Resort

Basic dining is served up to match your vacation needs. It's always nice knowing you don't have to go somewhere for every meal!

Olivia's Café

Cuisine Type: American
Serving Style: À la carte
Breakfast: $
Lunch: $ $
Dinner: $ $
D: Yes
Rating: ★ ★ ✭ ☆ ☆

A nice table-service destination, it has limited seafood choices, with good options in chicken and beef. The ambiance is light and pleasant, and is very kid-friendly.

Dining at Moderate Resorts

Moderate resorts certainly do not have all the innovative and entertaining dining options that the Deluxe resorts do, but they have very accommodating food courts that serve many of your dining needs. Many of these resorts are also a quick trip away from Downtown Disney, giving you a nice array of other dining choices.

Disney's Caribbean Beach Resort

This island-themed resort has enough dining options to keep most families happy.

Shutters at Old Port Royale

Cuisine Type: American
Serving Style: À la carte
Breakfast: Not open
Lunch: Not open
Dinner: $ $
D: Yes
Rating: ★ ★ ⯪ ☆ ☆

The entrées are definitely intended for a big dinner, with big steaks and chicken selections. The ribs are the only ones with much of a Caribbean flair, so you might try those. The menu really doesn't have as much to offer kids as you might like, so if you're dining with your family, you should consider going elsewhere.

Disney's Coronado Springs Resort

The heavy convention traffic will keep the restaurants here busy, but it's still a great place to grab several of your meals during your vacation.

Maya Grill

Cuisine Type: American
Serving Style: Buffet (B)/ à la carte (D)
Breakfast: $
Lunch: Not open
Dinner: $ $ $
D: Yes
Rating: ★ ★ ★ ☆ ☆

Significant improvements to the menu make this a good choice. Still, I would only visit if I were staying here, and would not make it a destination otherwise. Mexican-inspired selections are now your best bet, but traditional American entrées are offered, too.

Disney's Port Orleans Resort

While some of the dining may be a bit of a hike from your room, this may be one of the best Moderate resort choices, especially when you can also boat over to the restaurants of Downtown Disney.

Boatwright's Dining Hall

Cuisine Type: American/Southern
Serving Style: À la carte
Breakfast: $
Lunch: Not open
Dinner: $ $
D: Yes
Rating: ★ ★ ★ ☆ ☆

You can get a good breakfast for right at $10 and a dinner for just over $20. Each has some American standards, as well as some fun Southern-inspired dishes like jambalaya. A great table-service restaurant, this is the best one available at a Moderate resort.

Dining at Value Resorts

The food courts at the Value resorts are all basically the same, all decorated to celebrate the themes of their respective resorts. Seating is in one long hall that can get noisy at mealtimes, but it's a fun and vibrant environment. The food is offered from a series of cafeteria counters formed into a semicircle, with options including burgers, sandwiches, salads, wraps, desserts, and many packaged foods. Pizza can be ordered from a separate window, and there are small bars with beer, wine, and spirits for sale that also are open to the nearby resort pools.

> **DID YOU KNOW?**
>
> You might consider using your Disney Dining Plan **D** snack credits for some carry-out food from your resort food court. This can serve as a breakfast on the go and can help you stretch your food dollar.

These courts are certainly not elegant, but they serve the needs of most families, with an adequate range of choices and the convenience of being in the resort and near the pools. These courts all accept the Disney Dining Plan:

- End Zone Food Court (All-Star Sports Resort)
- Intermission Food Court (All-Star Music Resort)
- World Premiere Food Court (All-Star Movies Resort)

- Landscape of Flavors (Art of Animation Resort)
- Everything Pop Shopping and Dining (Pop Century Resort)

HIDDEN MAGIC!

What are my favorites in the resorts? Here are a few to consider:

- **Best resort fine dining:** California Grill
- **Best resort character meal:** Chef Mickey's
- **Best counter-service meal:** Mara
- **Best fireworks dinner setting:** California Grill
- **Best dinner show:** *Hoop Dee Doo Musical Review*
- **Most over-the-top cocktails:** Tambu Lounge at the Polynesian Resort
- **Most fun dining at a resort:** Whispering Canyon Café
- **Best steakhouse:** The Yachtsman
- **Best trendy dining:** Jiko—The Cooking Place
- **Best noncharacter buffet:** Boma—Flavors of Africa

Summary

Dining in the resorts ranges from convenience to celebration, as the full gamut of needs seems to be matched. You now know that whatever Disney resort may be your home during your visit, you at least have a food court that will fill your basic daily food needs. And there are so many more dining experiences to be had, if you're looking for that!

Dining in the Parks

In This Chapter

- Find out what you can get other than stale popcorn and over-priced sodas
- Select dining experiences that will enhance your park experience
- Figure out how to keep your food budget under some control

Why would I dedicate a chapter of the book to theme park restaurants? Surely it's all popcorn, burgers, and fries, right? Actually, the Walt Disney World theme parks provide many American families with some ventures into never-before-experienced foreign cuisines. And the dining can be fun, too! Character visits, entertaining service, high-quality meals, and scenic dining vistas can contribute to an enjoyable vacation.

Of course, a series of uninspired, overpriced meals can also ruin a vacation quickly. Cost has long been an issue here. Just as you wonder why a soda in the movie theater costs $5, here you will flinch when you see some of the menu prices. However, if you plan well, you can keep your expenses down while still enjoying quality food, entertaining venues, and memorable experiences. Read on—I walk you through the myriad of choices before you arrive at the theme parks, park by park.

Table-Service Dining in the Magic Kingdom

Take it from me—dining at the Magic Kingdom isn't that bad. It's just that, with Epcot's broad array of world cuisines just a monorail ride away, it's hard to compete. The food you'll find here is usually well prepared, if not very creative or adventurous. Families will find no problem filling the kids' bellies quickly before moving on to the next ride. Consider this a park where you keep your food budget down by having more counter-service meals. That being said, there are some fun character meals as well, so don't overlook them. Let's start by looking at the table-service restaurants.

HIDDEN MAGIC!

What are the *Must Do!* dining options in the Magic Kingdom? That's easy!

- **Character Meal :** The Crystal Palace
  Pooh beats Cinderella for character frequency, food selection, and overall value.
- **Table Service:** Liberty Tree Tavern
  New choices opening up in the Fantasyland expansion might unseat this choice.
- **Counter Service:** Pecos Bill's Tall Tale Café
  We're talking about a fixin's bar that turns your burger into a four-course meal!
- **Snack:** The Dole Whip in Adventureland
  The tasty array of pineapple-flavored desserts is an easy choice.
- **Honorable Mention:** Hot dogs at Casey's

Cinderella's Royal Table

Cuisine Type: American
Serving Style: À la carte
Breakfast: $ $ $ Prix fixe
Lunch: $ $ $ Prix fixe
Dinner: $ $ $ $ Prix fixe
D: Yes—2
Location: Fantasyland
Rating: ★ ★ ★ ☆

Breakfast here has perennially been the hardest seat to get in all of Walt Disney World—not for the cuisine, but for the setting (the throne room within the castle in the Magic Kingdom) and the company (Cinderella makes the rounds). Lunch and dinner are now character meals as well, although that and the addition of other Princess-themed meals have not done much to alleviate the pressure for a table; you'll still have to make your reservation at the earliest possible date if you hope to get a table here.

The food used to be just okay, but has gotten quite a bit better of late. The morning features an all-you-can-eat meal of American breakfast standards. Lunch and dinner offer only a few entrée choices, with basically a single pasta, seafood, beef, pork, and poultry choice per meal.

The experience with Cinderella and the other princesses (typically Belle, Ariel, Snow White, and Aurora) is a must-do for anyone with a little girl in tow. However, while it's still a hard-to-beat experience, you may actually prefer the Princess meals at Restaurant Akershus in Epcot, where you get the same princesses and marginally better food all at a lower cost. If you can't get in here—don't consider it settling if Akershus is where you end up.

The Crystal Palace

Cuisine Type: American
Serving Style: Buffet
Breakfast: $ Prix fixe
Lunch: $ $ Prix fixe
Dinner: $ $ Prix fixe
D: Yes
Location: Main Street, U.S.A.
Rating: ★ ★ ★ ☆ ☆

Located just past the end of Main Street, U.S.A., this bright, cheerful dining room is hosted by Winnie the Pooh and his friends. The American buffet has lots of the standards your kids will want, with just enough variety to keep most adults happy. It is not a huge buffet, but the locale makes it a great choice. Certainly, it's a more affordable alternative to Cinderella's Royal Table, and if your kids are Pooh fans, it should be considered a *Must Do!* meal for you and your family.

Liberty Tree Tavern

Cuisine Type: American
Serving Style: À la carte (L), family style (D)
Breakfast: Not open
Lunch: $
Dinner: $ $ Prix fixe
D: Yes
Location: Liberty Square
Rating: ★ ★ ★ ☆ ☆

American comfort food has a home at the Magic Kingdom. Lunch has some interesting selections, including a decent stab at a vegetarian entrée, but sticking to Thanksgiving-style foods is always a best bet here. Dinner used to be a character meal hosted by Minnie and her friends, however, that ended in 2009. The dinner here, a family-style bounty of roasted meats and strictly Turkey Day–themed sides, might be the best noncharacter table service available in the Magic Kingdom now. The cozy New England restaurant interior provides a charm that goes well with the food in front of you.

The Plaza Restaurant

Cuisine Type: American
Serving Style: À la carte
Breakfast: Not open
Lunch: $
Dinner: $
D: Yes
Location: Main Street, U.S.A.
Rating: ★ ★ ☆ ☆ ☆

Sandwich platters provide a fast lunch or dinner in this Main Street, U.S.A., setting. There's nothing bad here, but nothing to go out of your way for, either. This is a good choice for lunch, especially because of the central location, price, and quiet atmosphere. The grilled sandwiches are the best items on the menu.

Tony's Town Square

Cuisine Type: Italian
Serving Style: À la carte
Breakfast: Not open
Lunch: $
Dinner: $ $
D: Yes
Location: Main Street, U.S.A.
Rating: ★ ★ ☆ ☆ ☆

Taking its inspiration from *Lady and the Tramp*, this Italian eatery is a disappointment for someone looking for a good Italian meal. Part of the disappointment, too, is that the theming to the movie could have been far more fun and filled with atmosphere, but ends up being a dull experience. Stick to the traditional red sauce–based pastas at dinner and the classic Italian sandwiches at lunch. You might find yourself a bit disappointed with the value for price here, but it will do in a pinch.

Be Our Guest Restaurant (Opening Holidays 2012)

Cuisine Type: TBD
Serving Style: Quick service (L), à la carte (D)
Breakfast: Not open
Lunch: Quick-service dining
Dinner: Table-service dining
D: Yes
Location: Fantasyland
Rating: TBD

Themed to *Beauty and the Beast*, guests will be transported to the great dining hall of the Beast's Castle for a regal meal. Some dining rooms recreate other scenes from the movie, and it is anticipated that the dinner will also be a character experience, though that may still be under testing. It is certain that for all of 2013 this restaurant, both at lunch and dinner, will be very crowded. If you can't get an Advanced Dining Reservation, you should definitely try to get in by walking up and asking. It is likely that throughout 2013 it will be in a launch phase, meaning that full reservations may not be taken, so you have a chance!

Counter-Service Dining and Snacks in the Magic Kingdom

Counter service is a good choice in the Magic Kingdom, because table-service restaurants are notable only if they're character meals. Take advantage of those that have fixin's bars to make an ordinary burger a bit more of a special lunch.

Aloha Island

This Dole-sponsored stand is a great source for pineapple-based snacks, both healthful and otherwise. The Dole Whip is famous among Disney fanatics and is a great way to cool off in the summer sun.

Casey's Corner D

Great hot dogs ($5) and a good fixin's bar are just the start. A small stadium-themed seating area shows old black-and-white sports-themed Goofy cartoons.

Columbia Harbour House D

Fried fish and a few sandwich choices highlight this Liberty Square eatery, most for around $7. If you have a burger eater in the group, you're out of luck.

Cosmic Ray's Starlight Café D

The selection here is the broadest in the park for service counters, with burgers, barbecue, chicken, salads, and sandwiches. Kosher items are on the menu as well. It's a bit of a hassle to order here, as you have to get in one line for burgers, another for chicken, and another for salads. There's a fixin's bar and a lot of indoor dining space, including a futuristic lounge singer/robot that will entertain the kids.

Gaston's Tavern

Opening in early 2013, Gaston's Tavern will be a quick-service location in the Fantasyland expansion themed to the raucous pub in *Beauty and the Beast*.

The Lunching Pad D

Really just a food stand stuck under a Tomorrowland ride, it does offer the popular turkey legs.

Main Street Bakery D

This is a great place for treats, but not the best for a full lunch. The cafeteria selection is okay, but there are simply better places to eat. If you have a sweet tooth, this is your place. A variety of sweets are available, some even made on the spot. I like the crispy rice squares, but the caramel apples seem to be a big favorite—and who am I to argue with that?

Pecos Bill's Tall Tale Inn and Café D

This is my favorite counter-service restaurant in the Magic Kingdom for the fixin's bar. The bar has a bit broader selection than others, including nacho cheese, and the burgers are pretty good. You won't find a lot of other selections (barbecue sandwich and a decent turkey wrap), but if burgers ($6) are on your mind, I recommend that you mosey on in. Seating includes indoor and outdoor tables.

The Pinocchio Village Haus D

Pizzas and salads for around $7 highlight this Italian-inspired fast-food restaurant that's much better than in past years, but still not the best choice in the park.

El Pirata y El Perico Restaurante D

This Mexican food–themed counter is often closed seasonally, so don't count on it being open when you visit.

The Tomorrowland Terrace Noodle Station D

Also open seasonally, this Asian-inspired menu has several different meal bowls ($7) available. Seating is outdoor but covered.

Table-Service Dining in Epcot

I can honestly say that there have been times when I was in the Orlando area on business and considered paying $80+ for a park pass to Epcot just to have dinner in one of the many exotic and fun restaurants there. I didn't do it, but the food there can be *just that good*. Cuisine from literally around the world makes visits to the park even more memorable for the meals you have. They don't have to be expensive; counter-service and snack-stand foods are often as well made as the ones served in their table-service sister restaurants.

That being said, if you have any interest in trying new foods, make sure you plan your time at Epcot well. Be sure you get to one of the table-service restaurants in the World Showcase sometime during your visit. With the great fireworks show there, it's well worth your time to schedule more than one dinner at Epcot.

Restaurant Akershus 🏰

Cuisine Type: Norwegian/American
Serving Style: Varied
Breakfast: 👑 $ $ $ Prix fixe
Lunch: 👑 $ $ $ Prix fixe
Dinner: 👑 $ $ $ Prix fixe
D: Yes
Location: Norway Pavilion
Rating: ★ ★ ★ ★ ☆

One word for you: Princesspalooza! Although they're not all there at the same time, the meals are hosted by a bevy of Princesses, including Snow White, Belle, Jasmine, Ariel, Aurora, and Cinderella. Occasionally, Mulan and others come by as well.

The Nordic castle setting is fit for a Princess, and the food is very good. I loved it back when this was a standard Norwegian dining experience, but few people ever scream, "Hey, let's go get some Norwegian food!" so it's probably all for the best.

Breakfast is a family-style all-you-can-eat meal with mostly American staples. Lunch and dinner bring out the Norwegian *koldtbord* (cold table buffet of primarily meats and cheeses) and then à la carte entrées, followed by family-style desserts. The entrées include several Norwegian specialties in the selection. I won't lie to you: finicky kids may not be crazy about all the food choices, but I think when you can get them to look past the menu, they'll find more than several great choices. You really can consider it a mostly American menu at all meals, even if some choices are exotic.

I strongly recommend this to anyone wanting a premier Princess character experience, as it is by far the best one in all of Walt Disney World.

Biergarten Restaurant

Cuisine Type: German
Serving Style: Buffet
Breakfast: Not open
Lunch: $ $ Prix fixe
Dinner: $ $ Prix fixe
D: Yes
Location: Germany Pavilion
Rating: ★ ★ ★ ☆ ☆

This is a fun way to try German cuisine. The buffet line has a good selection, though some German fare you would expect isn't here. There are also some Americanized choices for kids who refuse to try new things. The dinner-time beer-hall atmosphere—complete with an oom-pah-pah band and the family-style seating—makes for a noisy but festive and social environment. This isn't a romantic dining destination, but it's great for families and adult groups who want to have a good time. Seating is family style at tables of eight, so you might get put in with another group.

Often I recommend eating at World Showcase table-service restaurants at lunch to save money while getting the same meal. But in this case, dinner is far preferable, basically because of the entertainment and the way it makes the atmosphere more festive. Oh, did I mention that their beer (extra charge) is not too bad, either?

Bistro de Paris

Cuisine Type: French
Serving Style: À la carte
Breakfast: Not open
Lunch: Not open
Dinner: $ $ $ $
D: Yes
Location: France Pavilion
Rating: ★ ★ ★ ★ ★

This isn't exactly the dining one expects in a theme park, so this high-end eatery may not be what you want on a busy day—the quality of the food and service seem out of place. The cuisine is creative, and the selection is quite nice. It is certainly one of the finer meals I have had in all of Walt Disney World. There's a four-course tasting menu, with a wine-pairing menu to go with it as well. Just because you can get an appetizer and an entrée for under $50, don't expect to get out for less than $75 per person.

Le Cellier Steakhouse

Cuisine Type: Steak
Serving Style: À la carte
Breakfast: Not open
Lunch: $ $ $
Dinner: $ $ $
D: Yes: (L: 1, D: 2)
Location: Canada Pavilion
Rating: ★ ★ ★ ★ ☆

The steaks are served in a cellar dining area that can be a cool and dark escape from the hot and bright Orlando summer. Lunchtime sandwiches are not bad, but the steaks are obviously the draw here. I'm not crazy about steak for lunch, but I would crawl the length of the park for a bowl of their Canadian Cheddar Cheese Soup.

An important note is that this is one of the smaller restaurants around. That, paired with a massive cult following, makes it one of the three hardest restaurants to get into. Reservations are an absolute must!

Les Chefs de France

Cuisine Type: French
Serving Style: À la carte
Breakfast: Not open
Lunch: $ $
Dinner: $ $ $
D: Yes
Location: France Pavilion
Rating: ★ ★ ★ ☆ ☆

This airy dining space provides a great view of the World Showcase walkway immediately outside. The atmosphere is very reminiscent of Parisian street-side cafés, and the food is good. While the steak *au poivre vert* sounds nice, I prefer the Croque Monsieur and side salad for a lighter lunch. Dinner entrées are good, too, but I like to hit this restaurant for lunch, largely for the daytime scenery and people watching, as well as to save some money while still getting what I want.

Why such a high rating when fancier French fare can be found upstairs? Well, no doubt the food is more haute cuisine at Bistro de Paris, but this setting and menu are both more appropriate in the World Showcase, and that counts for a great deal. Also, at lunch you can occasionally be visited by Remy, the star of the Disney Pixar movie *Ratatouille*.

Coral Reef Restaurant

Cuisine Type: Seafood
Serving Style: À la carte
Breakfast: Not open
Lunch: $ $
Dinner: $ $ $
D: Yes
Location: The Seas with Nemo & Friends Pavilion
Rating: ★ ★ ★ ☆ ☆

The view in this restaurant is fantastic. All the tables face huge windows that look into the pavilion's aquarium. It is one of the best scenic options in all dining at Walt Disney World. The seafood is also good. After that, however, the restaurant starts to lose points. First of all, come here *only* if you want seafood. And, although there are only a few seafood selections, that's what they do well. They do have a decent selection of nonseafood entrées, but nothing is very special. The room has a cold and sterile decor. Frankly, if you want seafood (and price is not an object), you're better off walking to the Flying Fish at the nearby BoardWalk.

The Garden Grill Restaurant

Cuisine Type: American
Serving Style: Family style
Breakfast: Not open
Lunch: Not open
Dinner: 🍽 $ $ Prix fixe
D: Yes
Location: The Land Pavilion
Rating: ★ ★ ★ ☆ ☆

The hearty meals, compliments of Chip and Dale, are served at tables in the rotating restaurant that overlooks parts of the Living with the Land attraction. The food is good (flank steak, fried catfish, and pork loin), and some of it is actually raised in the pavilion. This is one of the more affordable character meals, so it's a pretty good value in that category. Make sure to request a seat on the lower level for a better view.

La Hacienda de San Angel

Cuisine Type: Mexican
Serving Style: À la carte
Breakfast: Not open
Lunch: $ $
Dinner: $ $
D: Yes
Location: Mexico Pavilion
Rating: ★ ★ ★ ☆ ☆

A nice middle ground between authentic Mexican cuisine and Americanized flavors that are approachable to most visitors sets the stage for a great new addition to the Epcot dining world. The entrée portions are noticeably small, which can be a bit perturbing when you see that you are certainly not getting off light in the pocketbook. But the food is very good, both from an execution and flavor profile.

This restaurant also has added some much sought after waterside seating that is good for the *IllumiNations* fireworks show. As such, dinners are popular, so get reservations if you can.

Restaurant Marrakesh

Cuisine Type: Moroccan
Serving Style: À la carte
Breakfast: Not open
Lunch: $ $
Dinner: $ $ $
D: Yes
Location: Morocco Pavilion
Rating: ★ ★ ★ ★ ☆

Rock the Kasbah! The setting is very authentic in this Moroccan government–sponsored pavilion. The king of Morocco even sent over artisans to make sure it looked just right. The food is exceptionally authentic as well. That means it may not be the most kid-friendly menu, but the entertainment (Moroccan trio accompanying a dancer) can draw their attention easily. Stick to the lamb and the kebabs, simply because they're so good. Also consider this as a lunch destination to save some dirham (I checked—that's what they use for money). Remember that this is one of those meals that you might not be able to get back home, so why not experiment a little?

Nine Dragons Restaurant

Cuisine Type: Chinese
Serving Style: À la carte
Breakfast: Not open
Lunch: $ $
Dinner: $ $
D: Yes
Location: China Pavilion
Rating: ★ ★ ★ ☆ ☆

This restaurant has recently undergone a massive redesign that has made it a much better choice than in the past, both for the improved food and the more refined atmosphere. Often this restaurant is overlooked because we all know that there are Chinese restaurants back home. Nevertheless, the food is good, and while most of the entrées are pretty standard fare, they're made well.

Tutto Gusto Wine Cellar

Cuisine Type: Italian
Serving Style: TBD
Breakfast: Not open
Lunch: TBD
Dinner: TBD
D: No
Location: Italy Pavilion
Rating: TBD

This newest addition to the Italy Pavilion is a wonderful departure from traditional dining at Walt Disney World. While it has traditional entrées, it is more about smaller plates and it really captures the essence of some of Italy's true dining. Sample cheeses, enjoy some cavatappi, share great but simple food. Perhaps more adult-friendly than kid-friendly, I still think it should have a broad appeal to anyone with an adventurous spirit.

Tutto Italia

Cuisine Type: Italian
Serving Style: À la carte
Breakfast: Not open
Lunch: $ $ $
Dinner: $ $ $ $
D: Yes
Location: Italy Pavilion
Rating: ★ ★ ★ ⯪ ☆

This new restaurant makes semi-upscale dining a bit more fun than the restaurant it replaced in the same location. The cuisine covers several Italian regional flavors, with many of the expected entrées and appetizers. It's a great place to have lunch as opposed to dinner to save some money without losing any of the experience.

HIDDEN MAGIC!

Staffers at the different restaurants are almost exclusively native to that particular nation, here on an academic program. Strike up a conversation with them. They are energetic ambassadors of their countries, and you can walk away with a really positive experience.

Rose & Crown Dining Room

Cuisine Type: English
Serving Style: À la carte
Breakfast: Not open
Lunch: $
Dinner: $ $
D: Yes
Location: United Kingdom Pavilion
Rating: ★ ★ ★ ⯪ ☆

Why is this such a popular dining establishment? After all, everyone makes fun of the British for their food. Well, to start, the outdoor courtyard seating is an idyllic location for watching the *IllumiNations* fireworks show after dinner, if you can get one of the tables. The food is quite good, too, if you stick to the classics. Bangers and mash, fish and chips, or one of the pies is a sure way to a filling and tasty meal. If you just want a quick meal, you can grab the fish and chips from their counter-service window to the side, but I like dining here for the atmosphere.

San Angel Inn

Cuisine Type: Mexican
Serving Style: À la carte
Breakfast: Not open
Lunch: $
Dinner: $ $
D: Yes
Location: Mexico Pavilion
Rating: ★ ★ ★ ☆ ☆

This is *not* Tex-Mex food. The people running this restaurant are from one of the finest restaurant families in Mexico. Selections are very authentic and rich with flavor. However, this is one of the few restaurants where I do not recommend going for lunch instead of dinner to eat basically the same meal for less. The dinner menu here has a much better selection than at lunch, including perhaps the finest mole sauce (rich, chocolate based) I have ever put in my mouth. The setting is also ideal for romantic dinners. While it is located inside the pyramid, the setting is a romantic Mexican plaza at twilight with a volcano and pyramid off in the distance.

With the ascent of the Hacienda de San Angel, this dark restaurant inside the pyramid of the Mexico Pavilion may be doomed. Even after a refresh of the menu, it seems to lag behind its more visible, more up-tempo sister establishment.

Teppan Edo

Cuisine Type: Japanese
Serving Style: À la carte, teppanyaki
Breakfast: Not open
Lunch: $ $
Dinner: $ $
D: Yes
Location: Japan Pavilion
Rating: ★ ★ ★ ☆ ☆

Many know this style of dining from the popular Benihana chain. Seated at a hot grill, often with strangers at the other end of the table, you get to watch a chef swing sharp knives and spice shakers as he grills up your meal. It's entertaining and the food is good, if not particularly exotic. This is a favorite for families with older kids.

Tokyo Dining

Cuisine Type: Japanese
Serving Style: À la carte
Breakfast: Not open
Lunch: $ $
Dinner: $ $
D: Yes
Location: Japan Pavilion
Rating: ★ ★ ★ ☆ ☆

This restaurant has really spruced up and has a great look and feel
to it, with a blend between traditional Japanese architecture and a
cool, modern, and chic ambiance. The menu welcomes you to the
land of Japanese fried foods, as well as a few other choices, including
bento boxes and grilled entrées. Heavily leaning on fried shrimp and
scallops, this dining experience can be a fun one, though maybe too
exotic for some kids. Also, the view overlooking the World Showcase
Lagoon is a nice plus, especially if you can get a window seat. Few
even know that some of these tables have a view of the *IllumiNations*
fireworks show, so you might catch a break!

Via Napoli

Cuisine Type: Italian
Serving Style: À la carte
Breakfast: Not open
Lunch: $ $
Dinner: $ $
D: Yes
Location: Italy Pavilion
Rating: ★ ★ ★ ★ ☆

A new pizzeria that brings the first truly good pizza to Walt Disney
World! The airy central room with high ceilings and a modern
touch to the decor makes for a nice setting; however, the noise levels
can get high during peak meal times. But it's well worth it to try the
Neapolitan–style pizza that features paper-thin crusts charred from
the three wood-fired ovens. Appetizers were a bit disappointing,
but the Italian sodas are a nice treat, and you should be saving room
for the pies anyway.

Counter-Service Dining and Snacks in Epcot

The snack selection is more varied than in any other park, so try something new. This is a great place to get the most value for your counter-service credits if you're on a Disney Dining Plan.

Boulangerie Patisserie D

This is a great place for delicious French pastries and croissants. Some sandwiches are available, but this is a better venue for desserts. It's just too bad it's not open for breakfast.

This counter service location is so popular it will be undergoing a massive expansion in 2013, so it might be closed at times.

La Cantina de San Angel D

Unlike the restaurant inside, this stand is mostly Tex-Mex fast food, with meals available. There are margaritas around the corner as well, for a nice afternoon drink and snack break.

Electric Umbrella Restaurant D

One of the few places to eat in the Future World side of Epcot, this is also one of the few breakfast places in the park. Lunch and dinner are mostly burgers and wraps.

Katsura Grill D

Formerly the Yakitori House, this quick-service dining location has been remade. The grounds are nicer, and the menu is improved, which was badly needed. Still focus on sushi and udon here.

Kringla Bakeri Og Kafe D

The open-face sandwich combo comes with soup and a dessert. All three are Norwegian dishes, so it can be a quick, affordable way to try out this rarely experienced cuisine. Otherwise, stop by for one of the unique desserts.

Liberty Inn D

If your kids (or other traveling partners) just don't care to experiment with foreign cuisines, this is where you need to take them. Grilled chicken and burger meals will fuel them up.

Lotus Blossom Café D

Rice bowls and other Chinese specialties are pretty run-of-the-mill fare.

Sommerfest D

Bratwurst, frankfurters, and pretzels provide portable but expensive lunches.

Sunshine Season Food Fair D

The display kitchens create fresh, flavorful meals that improve upon and redefine fast food. Located in the lower level of The Land Pavilion, the seating area is open to the upper floors, creating a bright, vibrant space that is fun for kids, although a bit noisy. It's all indoors, so enjoying air-conditioning and avoiding the rain are side benefits to dining here. Open for breakfast, but with a very limited menu, things get much better later in the day. Choices include sandwiches, salads, grilled meat entrées, and some Asian-inspired selections.

Tangierine Cafe D

Perhaps the best counter-service restaurant in the World Showcase, this is also the most expensive. *Shawarma* (gyros) sandwich platters go for $12 to $14. They may be expensive, but they are excellent, and are a good value despite the high cost. Good vegetarian options also are available, as well as standard American kids fare, but both are also more expensive than usual. Still, the quality makes up for the extra few dollars, at least for me.

Yorkshire County Fish Shop D

Fish and chips are the specialty here, and they make a decent walking lunch. You can also enjoy a quiet lunch or dinner by taking them down to the nearby patios that overlook the lagoon. Most of my British friends think the fish and chips here are awful, but I have to admit that I like it, so don't come if you are looking for authentic (or healthy) food.

HIDDEN MAGIC!

What is Snackapalooza? Well, if you really want to try some of the great cuisine at the World Showcase, all you have to do is walk the world. Walk around the 11 pavilions of the World Showcase and sample some of the foods available at the stands in each country. If you can share with friends, all the better! You can visit each country and share a bite at each. What do I recommend? Most good selections seem to lean to sweets, but I have picked a few heartier entrée-style choices so you could make a meal of it.

- **Mexico:** Churros (fried dough with cinnamon)
- **Norway:** *Lefse* (potato dough bread rolled with butter and cinnamon)
- **China:** Egg rolls (they come in twos, so easier to share!)
- **Germany:** Bratwurst
- **Italy:** Cannoli
- **American Adventure:** Funnel cake
- **Japan:** Sushi tokyo roll or kagi age udon, for the sushi-wary
- **Morocco:** Lamb *shawarma* (gyros) or a walnut, cinnamon, and peanut baklava
- **France:** *Crêpes au chocolat*
- **United Kingdom:** Fish and chips
- **Canada:** Nothing! Can you believe it? On my last visit, all they had was popcorn. And it was Indiana popcorn. Last I checked, Indiana was still in the United States, not a province in Canada. But that's okay—by now, you should be completely stuffed!

Table-Service Dining in Hollywood Studios

While Epcot may lead the way with international cuisine, the Hollywood Studios eateries bring entertainment to the table in new and innovative ways. They do have character meals, but the greater hits are the fun, kitschy dining options that either lend some Hollywood glamour or take you back to a simpler time. The counter-service meals are no exception, also providing some of the better dining atmospheres in all the parks.

50's Prime Time Café

Cuisine Type: American
Serving Style: À la carte
Breakfast: Not open
Lunch: $ $
Dinner: $ $
D: Yes
Location: Echo Lake
Rating: ★ ★ ★ ★ ☆

One of my favorite restaurants in all of Walt Disney World, this is a *Must Do!* dining experience. Sit at your family's kitchen nook table, complete with black-and-white TVs showing old clips. "Mom," your server, makes sure you clean your plate and brings low-key entertainment to a pleasant level. Their fare of American classics (I recommend the fried chicken or meatloaf) is well prepared, and with the tongue-in-cheek sassy service, you can't miss. This is a nice alternative to a character meal if you want fun but are tired of having Chip and Dale interrupt your meal every five minutes. Come only if you're up for fun and can take a joke.

The Hollywood Brown Derby

Cuisine Type: American
Serving Style: À la carte
Breakfast: Not open
Lunch: $ $
Dinner: $ $ $
D: Yes—2
Location: Hollywood Boulevard (naturally!)
Rating: ★ ★ ★ ★ ☆

While the selection in this re-created Hollywood power-player dining spot is very good and everything seems to be made well, there's little reason not to go with the classic Cobb salad. It was invented at the original Hollywood Brown Derby restaurant, and they make an excellent one here, too. The decor, complete with caricatures of the stars, is very swish and cool, so it can be a nice date restaurant as well. I have never been disappointed here.

Hollywood & Vine

Cuisine Type: American
Serving Style: Buffet
Breakfast: ♙ $ $
Lunch: ♙ $ $
Dinner: $ $
D: Yes
Location: Hollywood Boulevard
Rating: ★ ★ ★ ⯪ ☆

Disney channel characters play host for breakfast and lunch at this buffet eatery. The setting is Art Deco Hollywood. Breakfast is a standard American buffet, while the lunch and dinner buffets focus on barbecue, salmon, and other meat-centered entrées. At dinner, they add flank steak, mussels, and peel-and-eat shrimp to the buffet, and it's usually busier because there are no characters present.

Mama Melrose's Ristorante Italiano

Cuisine Type: Italian
Serving Style: À la carte
Breakfast: Not open
Lunch: $
Dinner: $ $
D: Yes
Location: Studio Backlot
Rating: ★ ★ ★ ☆ ☆

I expected to find a predictable Italian menu, filled with red sauce–covered pastas and garlic bread as far as the eye could see. Instead, I was treated to some light entrées and tangy appetizers that were filling but not heavy. The atmosphere is cheesy and there's no entertainment, but the food is good, the service excellent, and the value reasonable for the price paid. Recommended appetizers include the spicy calamari or the mozzarella-and-tomato salad. For entrées, you can't go wrong with any of the selection of flatbread pizzas or the chicken Parmesan, if you want a little taste of old Italy.

Sci-Fi Dine-In Theater

Cuisine Type: American
Serving Style: À la carte
Breakfast: Not open
Lunch: $
Dinner: $ $
D: Yes
Location: Studio Backlot
Rating: ★ ★ ✬ ☆ ☆

You may not initially realize it when you enter the restaurant, but you are supposed to feel like you're backstage of a show set. When you enter the dining area, you realize that you are being transported to a drive-in movie lot where it's constantly night. Under a starry sky (or so the ceiling is painted to appear), you sit at tables that resemble '50s-era automobiles, with two rows (front seats and back seats of the car) of seating that can handle three little ones or two adults per row comfortably. Stick to the standard burger fare, which is somewhat superior to the counter-service variety. The real treat here, however, is getting a milkshake for dessert. This is a really fun dining experience for kids, though most adults find it to be a disappointment when they see what they paid for a burger meal.

Counter-Service Dining and Snacks in Hollywood Studios

The best choices are the ABC Commissary and the Sunset Ranch Market, for ambiance, food selection, and quality.

ABC Commissary **D**

As counter-service areas go, this is the best indoor seating choice. This dining hall is made to look like an actual movie-lot cafeteria. The interior is more upscale than most counter-service eateries, and the formerly diverse menu selection still packs some international zing added to the burgers and fries, with a Cuban sandwich, a noodle dish, and a curry entrée. It is also a place to get a real breakfast.

Backlot Express D

This is just another basic burger place in a less-than-remarkable atmosphere. The food is fine, but you have better choices elsewhere.

Dinosaur Gertie's Ice Cream of Extinction

Ice cream sold from the belly of a dinosaur makes this a popular stop on hot Florida afternoons.

Studios Catering Co. Flatbread Grill

This covered, open-air dining area has some good Mediterranean choices, like gyros and some Indian entrées, but the highlight is its proximity to the *Honey, I Shrunk the Kids* movie set playground. The food is okay and a nice distraction from more burgers, and it's nice to let the kids loose on the playground after lunch or during a parent soda break.

Starring Rolls Cafe D

While this is a fine place to grab a light sandwich, it shines more as a popular breakfast destination for its coffee and pastries. Try some extravagant cupcakes and muffins for a special treat.

Sunset Ranch Market D

This outdoor food court is not a single restaurant, but several that have an array of choices, including burgers and fries, Toluca turkey legs, pizza, sandwiches, fresh fruit, and more. The picnic tables (some covered, some not) make for a nice al fresco dining spot. People watching on Sunset Boulevard is fun, and the location is great if you want lunch or a snack while you wait for your FASTPASS at the Hollywood Tower of Terror or Rock 'n' Roller Coaster to come due.

If you're on the Disney Dining Plan, the following counter-service restaurants listed on the plan are part of the market: Catalina Eddy's, Fairfax Fare, and Rosie's All American Café.

Toluca Legs Turkey Co. D

These monstrous smoked turkey legs are full meals for most people. You'll see lots of guests walking around with these gigantic drumsticks, and it's hard not to want one. They're so popular that they have made their way to other parks, but Hollywood Studios is where they find their true home. They're messy, tasty, fun, and probably not that good for you, but who really diets on vacation?

Toy Story Pizza Planet

The pizza here simply is not that good. Seating is very limited and all outdoors. The only plus here is the adjacent arcade, but did you spend $80+ on a park ticket for the kids to play video games?

> **HIDDEN MAGIC!**
>
> Where will you be discovered dining at Hollywood Studios? There are so many choices! Here are my favorites:
>
> - **Character Meal:** Hollywood & Vine
>   This is perhaps the best character meal for the very youngest of guests, and it has good food, to boot.
>
> - **Table Service:** 50's Prime Time Café
>   This is one of my five favorite meals in *all* of Walt Disney World. It's fun and comfortably filling.
>
> - **Counter Service:** Sunset Ranch Market
>   The people watching and the variety of food options make it a great fair-weather choice.
>
> - **Snack:** Toluca Turkey Leg
>   This is a meal in itself. Who cares what you look like lumbering down the street with a big stick of meat in hand?

Table-Service Dining in Animal Kingdom

Dining at this newest of the parks is limited but growing. With still only two table-service restaurants, most of your choices are of the fast-food variety. But where they may lack in these options, they make up for it by having some of the best counter-service dining in all the parks.

Rainforest Café

Cuisine Type: American
Serving Style: À la carte
Breakfast: Not open
Lunch: $
Dinner: $ $
D: No

Location: Park entrance
Rating: ★ ★ ✬ ☆ ☆

One of two Rainforest Café restaurants in Walt Disney World, this one matches the decor and food offered at all stops of the national chain. Certainly appropriate due to the park setting, it serves up standard fare with a distracting atmosphere custom-tailored to families.

Yak and Yeti

Cuisine Type: Asian (varied)
Serving Style: À la carte
Breakfast: $ $
Lunch: $ $
Dinner: $ $
D: Yes
Location: Asia
Rating: ★ ★ ★ ✬ ☆

Opened in late 2007, Yak and Yeti's cuisine brings a selection of foods from several different Asian nations. Grilled selections, wok stir-fries, noodle bowls, and specialties that include duck and seafood bring a fantastic array of choices that are well executed in a scenic setting. A bar seating area is great for adult-only couples who want to get in and out quickly.

Tusker House

Cuisine Type: American
Serving Style: Buffet
Breakfast: **$ $**
Lunch: **$ $**
Dinner: $ $
D: Yes
Location: Africa
Rating: ★ ★ ★ ★ ☆

This former counter-service dining area has been converted to a buffet restaurant, complete with a character breakfast. Donald's Dining Safari at both breakfast and lunch feature Donald and his friends in safari costumes. Food at all three meals has both basic American along with a good array of interesting, flavorful, and healthy alternatives that are African- and Indian-inspired.

Counter-Service Dining and Snacks in Animal Kingdom

The Animal Kingdom started out small, but the dining options are growing, and it has some of the more innovative meal options. Look here for some of the best Asian cuisine and some truly good barbecue.

Dawa Bar

Okay, it's not a snack, but if you need a cocktail to make the day go by more easily, this is your one stop. They have a full bar. (I recommend the Rum Runner.)

Flame Tree Barbeque D ■

This is perhaps the top counter-service meal in all of Walt Disney World, for two reasons. First, the barbecue is really quite good, with ribs, chicken, and pulled-pork sandwiches that are better than any fast-food barbecue I have ever had. Second, there are the scenic outdoor seating areas. There's a web of outdoor verandas, each surrounded by jungle-like growth, providing some seclusion, shade from the sun, and great river views. After sitting in packed, loud dining halls for the better part of your trip, isn't it nice to get seating with a view that's worthy of a far more expensive meal?

HIDDEN MAGIC!

With not a lot of choices in Animal Kingdom, what should you do?

- **Character Meal:** Donald's Dining Safari (Tusker House)
  Safe buffet foods for kids, but some more adventurous choices for the adults make this a great family compromise.

- **Table Service:** Yak and Yeti
  Finer dining in an exotic atmosphere just helps you feel like you are still in a far off world.

- **Counter Service:** Flame Tree Barbeque
  The outdoor seating is the backdrop to memories that you won't forget easily. The Yak and Yeti counter service is a close second, so choose based on what you want to eat.

- **Snack:** Kusafiri Coffee Shop
  This can be one of the nicer, light breakfasts that you have in a vacation filled with overeating.

Harambe Fruit Market

Fruit here seems always to be of the best quality, both the freshly cut fruit salad varieties as well as bananas, apples, and oranges.

Yak and Yeti Counter

While the sit-down restaurant attached to this is exceptional, the counter has some very good and exotic choices that break the monotony of burgers and fries. Served in the iconic Chinese restaurant takeout containers, they used to be infamous here for filling containers almost entirely with rice and just a touch of the entrée selection. Servings are much more generous of late, making it a great choice for a quick (and portable) lunch.

Kusafiri Coffee Shop

Here you can order coffee and a pastry at the window.

Pizzafari **D**

The pizza is standard, but some indoor seating could make this a good lunch choice on a hot day.

Restaurantosaurus **D**

Simply blah burgers and fries in a busy setting. But the dig-site camp decor of the dining area is kind of fun, although noisy.

Dining at the Water Parks

Dining here is strictly available to fill a need. You don't want to have to make the hour-long round-trip by bus to your resort just to eat at a food court, so they have the bare basics here. Adult beverages can be had as well, but at a rather steep price.

Summary

So there it is, dining in the parks in a nutshell. Quite a large shell, isn't it? The key is to remember that with the few exceptions of destination dining that you may want to try, let your location drive where you dine. Have a few favorite dining options picked out for the parks you're visiting, but schedule ahead for a few of those special dining experiences that might well make the vacation more memorable than you ever imagined.

Other Dining Options at Walt Disney World

In This Chapter

- Taste the choices at the BoardWalk
- Get a sampling of the food at Downtown Disney
- Figure out what is good for kids

You now know about the food in the parks, as well as the restaurants at the resorts. But sometimes you're hungry, are bored with the choices in your hotel, and don't feel like trudging to the parks for a meal. A little nightlife couldn't hurt, could it?

Not a problem. Disney has some remedies for your nighttime blues, and they go by the name of BoardWalk and Downtown Disney. These largely nighttime diversions run the gamut of whatever shopping and dining needs you may have, as you will see in Chapter 22. But what food is really available here? Let's dig in!

Dining at Downtown Disney

Downtown Disney has a lot of restaurants, from good national chains to unique one-off restaurants, where you can get a nice range of foods. Certainly if you're planning to hit the shopping of the Westside or going to see Cirque du Soleil, you should think of having dinner at any one of the fine area establishments.

DID YOU KNOW?

Most of the restaurants in Downtown Disney now finally accept the Disney Dining Plan (only a few used to). Check the Disney Dining Plan brochure online, or check each restaurant's page at www.disneyworld. com.

Bongos Cuban Café

Cuisine Type: Cuban
Serving Style: À la carte
Breakfast: Not open
Lunch: $ $
Dinner: $ $ $
D: Yes
Rating: ★ ★ ★ ✯ ☆

This large whitewashed restaurant does a good job of combining a nightclub atmosphere with a higher-end restaurant. The Miami Beach–styled suave atmosphere makes for a great romantic or adult group setting in this Gloria Estefan–owned restaurant. The food is authentic Cuban fare, and if you're in a *Miami Vice* mood, the bar can be a great starting point for a night on the town. For lunch, I recommend the Club Cubano sandwich, and at dinner, all of the chicken selections are quite good, especially the Chicharrones de Pollo.

Cap'n Jack's Restaurant

Cuisine Type: American
Serving Style: À la carte
Breakfast: Not open
Lunch: $ $
Dinner: $ $ $
D: Yes
Rating: ★ ✯ ☆ ☆ ☆

This restaurant has been here forever, dating back to the days of Lake Buena Vista Village (what they called it when there was little here but convenience shopping). The menu is American, but not seafood, as the name might make you think.

You can barely get out of here for under $20 for lunch and $30 for dinner. For that, you could get a more interesting meal elsewhere just a walk away, so I'm not a big fan. It's not that they don't serve perfectly good food; it's just that you can get more with your money at many of the nearby choices. Consider this a good choice for a family that wants to stick to more traditional American dining.

It is sad, really, as many longtime Walt Disney World visitors have fond memories of this stalwart. But great memories of old don't make for good meals of today.

Fulton's Crab House

Cuisine Type: Seafood
Serving Style: À la carte
Breakfast: Not open
Lunch: $ $
Dinner: $ $ $ $
D: Yes (2)
Rating: ★ ★ ★ ☆

It doesn't matter that over the last several decades this restaurant, on a steamboat, has never budged an inch; kids will love dining here. Crab is obviously the main choice, and although it's plentiful and well prepared, something is missing. For the cost, it seems as if you should get a more upscale dining experience. Again, the food was perfectly good; I just didn't like the experience. So if crab is what you want, come here and be prepared to leave quickly; otherwise, you might want to seek out other choices.

House of Blues

Cuisine Type: American/Southern
Serving Style: Buffet (B), à la carte (L, D)
Breakfast: $ $ $ Prix fixe
Lunch: $ $ $
Dinner: $ $ $
D: Yes
Rating: ★ ★ ★ ☆

This national chain offers live music and food in a fashion that is both unique and filled with life like no other place I can imagine. The menu is the same for lunch and dinner, accented with genuine Southern cuisine. Creole, Cajun, and just down-home cooking influences serve up spicy and flavor-rich entrées and remarkable appetizers. Jambalaya, shrimp, grits—they're all good. So if you're okay with a little spice to your meal, try something here.

The Sunday Gospel Brunch is also a special and fun show. While you enjoy the live gospel singing, you can stuff yourself on the excellent buffet. It combines breakfast standards prepared in Southern fashion with lunch items that showcase the cuisine of the restaurant. That meal alone is what bumps this to a 4-star choice. Can you say "cheesy grits"?

Paradiso 37

Cuisine Type: South and Central American
Serving Style: À la carte
Breakfast: Not open
Lunch: $ $
Dinner: $ $
D: Yes
Rating: ★ ★ ★ ⯪ ☆

Located in the center of the Downtown Disney area, this often overlooked restaurant brings a nice array of Central and South American flavors to their menu.

They do a good job in all phases of the menu of including authentic regional choices, Tex-Mex and Americanized versions of Latin foods, and then some straightforward American classics.

The warm ambiance is often peppered with live musical entertainment, and of course there are select seats that offer good water views for more romantic encounters.

As the Hyperion Wharf expansion grows, more will discover this hidden gem of Downtown Disney.

Planet Hollywood

Cuisine Type: American
Serving Style: À la carte
Breakfast: Not open
Lunch: Not open
Dinner: $ $
D: Yes
Rating: ★ ★ ☆ ☆ ☆

This place used to rely on the movie-themed decor to keep you from noticing that the food was boring and overpriced. Now it's there just to keep you from noticing that the food is just boring. Although the prices have not risen at the same rate as at the joints that surround it, the bill is more about the view than the food.

The food is fine, but it's nothing you can't get back home, and with so many other interesting choices in the area, you should come here only if you have a group that doesn't want anything but standard U.S.–chain restaurant fare.

Portobello

Cuisine Type: Italian
Serving Style: À la carte
Breakfast: Not open
Lunch: $ $
Dinner: $ $ $
D: Yes
Rating: ★ ★ ★ ☆ ☆

This eatery has its menu focused squarely on the Italian peninsula, and it does so very well. Recently updated menus and redesigned dining areas have made it a more interesting venue, both for what you put in your mouth and what you have as scenery. The meatball bar is an oddly conceived menu addition, so only try it out if you are looking for bar food, not a full meal. If you want a romantic dinner setting and Italian, it's preferable to the Italian Pavilion restaurant in the Epcot World Showcase, for both food and the lovely water views.

Raglan Road Irish Pub and Restaurant ▟

Cuisine Type: Irish
Serving Style: À la carte
Breakfast: Not open
Lunch: $
Dinner: $ $ $
D: Yes
Rating: ★ ★ ★ ★ ☆

This exceptional addition to the Downtown Disney restaurant scene brings both traditional Irish cuisine and more modern takes on the national standards. The food is good, the drinks are fantastic, and the entertainment and ambiance should win awards. From the incomparable house band to the Irish dancers, you will find a lively time here. If you can get a seat in the main room, you'll find conversation hard, as the energetic entertainment keeps the room humming into the wee hours. This is truly a destination for parties looking for a good time at night.

Many of the entrées are exceptional, and the sides are good, too. The *colcannon* is a wonderful vinegary potato dish that you will probably not find in your local pub, and you won't go wrong with the lamb, the pork, or the bangers (sausages).

The Cookes of Dublin storefront is located around the corner and is a walk-up stand for some evening sweets. Perhaps more fun is the nearby Raglan Road outdoor bar courtyard, if you're old enough to enjoy.

HIDDEN MAGIC!

What are the dining choices at Downtown Disney and the BoardWalk that shouldn't be missed? That's easy!

- **Raglan Road Irish Pub and Restaurant:** Whether for dinner or drinks, this pub oozes ambiance and fun
- **Seashore Sweets:** Stop by for an evening dessert as you stroll along the BoardWalk

Rainforest Café

Cuisine Type: American
Serving Style: À la carte
Breakfast: Not open
Lunch: $
Dinner: $ $
D: Yes
Rating: ★ ★ ✭ ☆ ☆

The busier of the two Rainforest Cafés in Walt Disney World, this one has the same decor and food offered at all stops of the national chain. It's a good choice for families because of the kid-friendly menu and because so many Downtown Disney eateries have prominent bars that may turn some families off. But if you like this experience, you would probably prefer the newer T-REX that is run by the same company.

T-REX Café

Cuisine Type: American
Serving Style: À la carte
Breakfast: Not open
Lunch: $
Dinner: $ $
D: Yes
Rating: ★ ★ ✭ ☆ ☆

One of the newest additions to the Downtown Disney area, this Landry's-managed table-service restaurant combines a well-varied menu with an entertaining prehistoric setting. Think of it as a Rainforest Café set in the Jurassic period. Burgers, sandwiches, build-it pizzas, and even seafood provide a lot of choices, all named cutely after our extinct brethren. The food isn't great, but the attraction is the entertainment and decor, not the cuisine.

Their kid's menu is more varied than most Disney-run restaurants, making it a good choice for families, as long as the dino-hosts won't scare the tykes. The ice age room is visually stunning as you are bathed in a blue glow. Fun, but it can be annoying by the end of a long dinner, so only request the room if you are in for lunch or quick dinner.

There is also a dino version of the Build-A-Bear concept in the lobby, if your kids like that.

Wolfgang Puck Café

Cuisine Type: Italian
Serving Style: À la carte
Breakfast: Not open
Lunch: $ $
Dinner: $ $ $
D: Yes (2 credits for the upstairs dining room)
Rating: ★ ★ ★ ☆ ☆

The restaurant is described as having California cuisine, but the pasta- and pizza-heavy menu will make you think Italian. While the modern and colorful dining space can get loud, I think it's a great place. The food has always been superb, the busy service has always been adequately attentive, and the overall experience has always been good. You can get out of here for under $20 a person, but without an appetizer.

There's also an upstairs room for special (and expensive) occasions. You can order à la carte, but the prix fixe menu runs about $75 per person, giving you an idea of what you might be getting yourself into.

This restaurant proves that Wolfgang is a notch above most other gourmet restaurateurs, executing good food not just in the lands of the well-heeled, but in a setting fit for the masses as well. Kudos.

HIDDEN MAGIC!

If you have a fun group and want to go somewhere a bit bohemian where you can really interact over good food, Café Tu Tu Tango is the place for you. Located nearby on International Drive, the lobby has local artists at work, and the walls are covered with an eclectic mix of art and curios. The dining is tapas style (sharing appetizer-style dishes around the table), which really sparks the conversation. The food is excellent, and the variety of tapas selections can suit just about anyone. For more information, visit www.cafetututango.com/orlando.

Earl of Sandwich

Serving Style: Counter service
D: Yes

This fast-food sandwich shop brings roast beef and horseradish to several of the selections of hot and cold sandwiches. The best counter service choice in Downtown Disney, and better than some of the table service choices, too! VERY BUSY!

Ghirardelli Soda Fountain & Chocolate Shop

Serving Style: Counter service
D: No

I gained 10 pounds just walking by this decadent shrine to chocolate and ice cream. They even put it into coffee; you'll enjoy every last drop. This San Francisco–based confectioner has a broad selection of ice-cream-sundae concoctions, and it can be a great place to take kids for a special dessert.

Wetzel's Pretzels

Serving Style: Counter service
D: Yes

Hot dogs, pretzels, and lemonade. Blah.

Wolfgang Puck Express

Serving Style: Counter service
D: Yes

This recently upgraded venue is a *huge* improvement over its embarrassing past. Swing by here for trendy sandwiches and salads to go, as well as some fun culinary shopping.

Dining at the BoardWalk

The second and smaller of the two nightlife areas, the BoardWalk has a decidedly toned-down atmosphere compared to Downtown Disney. The dining, though limited in the number of venues, does offer a surprising amount of variety. In addition to being an entertainment destination unto itself, the restaurants here serve as the food choices for guests of the BoardWalk Inn and Villas, so they always seem to have a buzz. Let's look at what is here.

Big River Grille & Brewing Works

Cuisine Type: American
Serving Style: À la carte
Breakfast: Not open
Lunch: $ $
Dinner: $ $
D: Yes
Rating: ★ ★ ★ ☆ ☆

This brewpub elicits none of the typical beer-making smells of a hometown microbrewery. It's up to you whether that's a good thing. The cool tones in the hip, modern interior are far less appealing than the tables located outside on the deck. This is where you should take your sandwich, burger, or entrée dinner. Lunch and dinner menus are typically identical, and the prices seem a bit high, making it an expensive Disney lunch but a moderately priced dinner.

ESPN Club

Cuisine Type: American
Serving Style: À la carte
Breakfast: Not open
Lunch: $
Dinner: $
D: Yes
Rating: ★ ★ ☆ ☆ ☆

You can keep a meal to under $20 per person here, and although it's not haute cuisine, it's decent pub food. The atmosphere is like that of a sports bar that has been cleaned up and had the lights turned on. TVs are everywhere the eye can see, and the typical BoardWalk crowd ensures that it's an okay place to take the kids without them picking up some new vocabulary. Sandwiches are the fare; don't go too far from that if you want to be happy.

If you have kids who are video game enthusiasts, there are some tables where they can provide you with gaming systems while you dine, and of course there is the adjacent ESPN Yard, an arcade with many sports-themed video games.

Flying Fish Café

Cuisine Type: Seafood
Serving Style: À la carte
Breakfast: Not open
Lunch: Not open
Dinner: $ $ $ $
D: Yes—2
Rating: ★ ★ ★ ★ ☆

The cool ambiance, excellent service, and exceptional food make Flying Fish—with by far the best seafood in all of Walt Disney World—a top pick. With entrées in the $30 range, meals rarely fall under $50 per person. The seafood selections are diverse and all well prepared, and there are a few well made nonseafood alternatives for the land-lubbers among you. If you really crave quality seafood or have an expense account that you can drop this bill on, I highly recommend a stop here.

Kouzzina

Cuisine Type: Mediterranean
Serving Style: À la carte
Breakfast: $
Lunch: Not open
Dinner: $ $ $
D: Yes
Rating: ★ ★ ★ ☆ ☆

Formerly known as Spoodles, Kouzzina was created by Iron Chef favorite Cat Cora. The cuisine is inspired by the many storied cultures of the Mediterranean, with a particular leaning on Cat's Greek background.

Breakfast has many American standards, as well as some Greek-inspired entrées as well. It is at dinner when Cat really turns on the Mediterranean influences. I would consider this a good choice for most groups, though reviews are mixed, as this venue seems to be inconsistent in its performance. This restaurant is both safe for families in the morning but also provides a much-needed zing of variety and flavor at dinner to this area.

Seashore Sweets ▰

Serving Style: Counter service
D: No

This small storefront is a great dessert place in the evening. Watch your kids' eyes come to life in this temple dedicated to their sweet tooth. Although there's a nice range of candies and other goodies, the big draw is the ice-cream counter.

BoardWalk Bakery

Serving Style: Counter service
D: Yes

Coffee and pastries, particularly of value to area resort guests needing a jolt before they get on their way to their day's activities.

BoardWalk Pizza Window

Serving Style: Counter service
D: Yes

A full pizza runs $18. They are decent and, while expensive, can be a great carry-out to your area resort room for a quieter night "at home" with your party.

Summary

Of course, there are a great deal more dining options throughout the Orlando area, but these nearby choices should keep most of your taste buds happy! After you've selected the BoardWalk and Downtown Disney dining options, you should be pretty full!

Bring on the Entertainment: The Theme Parks

It's time to get to the reason why we are all here—the theme parks! In Part 4, I review the four major theme parks. I tell you what different attractions you'll find in the Magic Kingdom, Epcot, Hollywood Studios, and Animal Kingdom. You get to walk through the rides, the shows, and the attractions, reviewing ratings for each based on different age groups. Now you can get an idea of where you'll want to go and what you'll want to avoid. Bon voyage!

The Disney Theme Park Primer

In This Chapter

- Learn about what you can expect at a Disney theme park
- Understand the special services that make your visit even more fun
- Discover the facilities that you can rely on for your visit

Walt Disney World theme parks are the best. Any question to the truth in this statement? Well, these four theme parks regularly rank in the top 10 most-visited theme parks in North America and, for that matter, in the world. Usually, they have three of the top four every year, with the Magic Kingdom always at the top of the heap. So you could say that if guests vote with their wallets, these are the parks that win every year.

While the parks are all about being transported to magical places and out-of-this-world entertainment, Disney works to make sure that your real-world needs are easily met so that you can keep your imagination focused on those fantasies. In this chapter, I give you some basics to keep in mind that apply to all the parks, and to help plan your trip before we get into the actual park chapters.

General Park Information

The parks may seem like fantastical dream worlds, but behind each well-orchestrated facade is an extremely efficient and intricately detailed workplace. Disney and its cast-member employees have their work down to a science. They also try to extend this efficiency to you so that you can make the most of your trip. Here's some information on the general park operation system, as well as some specific programs that will make your visit even better.

Park Operating Hours

The hours of operation for each park change throughout the year; the parks remain open longer during the busier seasons and shorter during the slow times. Always check ahead on the Walt Disney World website, where they post times for the current month and the next six months. Here's how to do so:

- Highlight the "Parks" section at the top of the Walt Disney World website.

- When the drop down menu appears, simply select the park for which you want to check for operating times ("Magic Kingdom" for instance).

- Once you are on that park's main page, just select "Calendar" from the left column choices.

- Once the calendar shows, you can adjust to whatever month you are planning to visit by clicking on the menu to the upper right of the calendar.

- You will now see the park hours, by day, for the whole month. If you click on an actual date, it will even show you the schedule for major show and event times for that day.

DISNEY DON'T

Don't just assume that having a ticket will get you into a park. As with anything else in life, there's a maximum capacity to each park. When the park reaches that number, they won't allow anyone else in, even if they have a valid ticket.

This doesn't happen all that often, but on super busy days, like Christmas Day and New Year's Eve Day, you'll want to ensure you arrive early and don't leave the park.

Extra Magic Hours

Available in both mornings and evenings, this program gives Disney resort guests exclusive access to the parks before or after normal operating hours. For the morning Extra Magic Hours, a park opens an hour earlier than usual, but only to guests of Disney-owned resorts, as well as to guests from the Shades of Green hotel, the Swan and Dolphin hotels, and the Hilton located on Hotel Plaza Boulevard. The evening version of Extra Magic Hours keeps a park open up to an extra three hours after normal closing times. Not all attractions are open at these times, but most of the popular ones are, so it's well worth getting in early or staying late to avoid some of the crowds. The daily schedules show what parks open early or stay open late and they change throughout the year.

HIDDEN MAGIC!

If you're planning to arrive at the parks at opening time, make sure you get a good view of the opening show. "Rope Drop" shows, as they are known, help keep the crowd entertained until opening time, and they also assist in getting you excited for the day to come. The show at the Magic Kingdom is outside the park, at the foot of the rail station, the Animal Kingdom one is on Discovery Island, Epcot's is in the center of Future World, and the one at Hollywood Studios is at the end of Hollywood Boulevard.

FASTPASS Ticket System

The FASTPASS is Disney's way of accelerating your fun! The FASTPASS service is available at the most popular rides, which are marked in this book with the **FP** icon. With this service, you can get a ticket for an assigned time later in the day to ride the attraction. The line you'll get into is shorter than the traditional line and, in the meantime, allows you to go do other things in the park.

How It Works

When you approach an attraction that has FASTPASS, you'll see the traditional line, with a clock that estimates your wait. Off to the side will be the FASTPASS kiosks. Simply insert your park tickets into one of the many kiosks, and you'll get a voucher with a specific return time. Make sure you insert every ticket and get a FASTPASS for every member of your group. Go experience something else in the park, and then when the time printed on your FASTPASS voucher comes around, just hop into the FASTPASS line, and away you go. This line will be significantly shorter than the standard line, thus the appeal of the FASTPASS system.

Consider some important facts about the FASTPASS system:

- You can have only one FASTPASS voucher at a time for any ride.

- Everyone can use the FASTPASS system; it's not a special perk that you have to pay extra for.

- Some FASTPASS kiosks are open only on select days, usually during the busy season.

- The available FASTPASS vouchers for many rides will "run out" early in the day, meaning that they've handed out times until closing. So get yours early if a ride is a must-do for your group.

- When loading a ride, the cast members at Disney will load anywhere from 10 to as many as 25 people from the FASTPASS line for every one in the standard line, so you can imagine how much faster it is to have a FASTPASS!

- Disney DOES enforce the return times. They have always insisted you can't enter the line BEFORE your FASTPASS start time, but as of 2012 they stopped letting people in line if their FASTPASS end time has expired.

> **DISNEY DON'T**
>
> Don't forget to grab your park tickets out of the FASTPASS kiosk. Leaving these behind can really be a hassle on your vacation!

Rider Switch

It's supposed to be a fun vacation for everyone. Why should your kids have all the fun, while you just trail around behind them? Is there a thrill ride that you really want to try, but your child is too short to meet the height requirement? Not a problem. You can still enjoy any attraction that has a height requirement, as well as some of the others, by using the Rider Switch feature.

With this feature, you get a pass from the attraction attendant by the standby entrance. The first parent goes on the ride, via the standard line. When they are done, the second parent uses the Rider Switch pass, getting in the FASTPASS line, regardless of time of day. This way both adults get a chance to try some of the thrill rides and roller coasters. I cannot stress enough how important it is that adults enjoy their vacation, too. Please, please, please make sure that you use this feature to get on some of the rides that you really want to try. If you're having a good vacation, your mood will help make it a better one for your kids, too.

> **DID YOU KNOW?**
>
> Disney is testing a new FASTPASS+ system that will allow guests to reserve FASTPASS times for select attractions from home before they leave on their vacation. Expect to see more in 2013 on this new feature.

General Park Services

What support facilities can you expect to find at the parks? Well, Disney has made sure that you're well taken care of in your daily needs so that you enjoy your visit. After all, they want you to come back!

The following sections discuss some of those park facilities that you can count on.

> **DID YOU KNOW?**
>
> Rides in this book are rated by five age groups. You can find these ratings at the end of the ride description, and they can help you decide if the ride is right for your party. The age groups are:
>
> - Tots (infants age up to 6 years old)
> - Young Children (kids age 7–12)
> - Teens (older children age 13–19)
> - Young Adults (adults, age 20–50)
> - Mature Adults (seniors, age 50 and older)
>
> These ratings range from 0 (worst) to 5 (best). Remember that some 50-year-olds are far more daring than some 20-somethings, and there are 30-year-olds who grow excited over thrills a 7-year-old wouldn't even blink at. So take no offense at the age generalizations—pick the group that best symbolizes your attraction interest, and choose your rides!

Tots	Young Children	Teens	Young Adults	Mature Adults

Baby Care Centers

These centers, currently sponsored by Nestlé, are a paradise for parents of toddlers. The centers, found in each park, have numerous resources to help you out. The facilities are free to use, but don't think of them as just being for emergencies. Use of the "cool down" room can give your youngster some quiet time to nap or just get a break from the frantic pace. Use their changing tables whenever you're in the area for a calmer time than you would get in a park bathroom. Feed your toddler in a proper chair rather than balanced on your knee in a busy restaurant. Basically, I think it's a great idea to plan to use the centers frequently so you can enjoy more of your visit. The centers include these useful resources:

- Changing tables

- Private nursing rooms

- Feeding high chairs

- A play room with a TV, toys, and comfortable seating

- A small sales counter with baby essentials (diapers, formula, etc.)

The supplies come at a charge, and they're there for your convenience, in smaller portions. The staff has always been friendly, informative, and supportive. I suspect that underneath their calm and soothing demeanors are nerves of steel!

So where are these centers? In the major parks, they're at the following locations:

- **Magic Kingdom:** Just next to the Crystal Palace restaurant entrance

- **Epcot:** The Odyssey Center, behind the Test Track

- **Hollywood Studios:** Immediately to your left as you enter the park

- **Animal Kingdom:** On Discovery Island, as you head toward the Africa land and near the Pizzafari restaurant

Strollers

Disney strollers are a popular rental, and on a busy day you'll see them literally everywhere. Renting a stroller is a good idea even with children that don't use strollers at home anymore because they can get tired and can use the break. Strollers also serve as a place to store your stuff, as long as you remember not to leave valuables in them.

DISNEY DON'T

Don't assume that there's an endless supply of strollers. True, they seem to have more strollers than would ever be needed, but if you arrive at a park on a busier day, you may not be able to get one.

A one-day rental is $15 for a single-seater and $31 for a double. If you're visiting a second park in the same day, get a receipt when you turn in your stroller as you leave the first park. Then get a stroller at the next park without having to rent again.

At any of these locations, or as part of your vacation package, you also can get a stroller "length-of-stay" rental. With this, you pay as little as $13 (single) or $27 (double) per day. It's well worth it if you know you're going to use a stroller each day. You can rent the strollers at the following locations:

- **Magic Kingdom:** Inside and to the left as you enter the park

- **Epcot:** Inside and to the right as you enter the park, or at the International Gateway

- **Hollywood Studios:** Inside and to the right as you enter the park, in the gas station

- **Animal Kingdom:** Inside and to the right as you enter the park

ATMs

You'll find several ATMs per park, operated by Chase Bank.

Wheelchairs

Wheelchairs are also available for rent, at $10 per day.

Electronic Controlled Vehicles (ECVs)

More of these electronic wheelchairlike vehicles are showing up in the parks. Rentals are $50 per day. If that seems steep, know that Orlando-area companies will rent you one for the length of your stay. A standard one (good for up to 300 pounds), and heavier-duty models are available from Scootarama (www.scootarama.com). You can make reservations online at their website, which is recommended, and they'll deliver them to area hotels.

The Disney buses, boats, and monorails all have ECV and wheelchair ramp systems.

Lockers

Lockers can really make your day in a park more enjoyable. If you can stick a backpack in a locker, you unburden yourself of one more concern. You avoid having crushed snacks or punctured juice boxes, and you can store extra clothes to change into after a wet ride or as the evening gets cooler. Each park is a bit different when it comes to locker location, but rentals are all $7, with a $2 return. As with a stroller, if you show your locker receipt from one park, you get a free rental the same day at another park.

Park Tours

I'm one of those people who do not want to see how they make the special effects in a movie because, for me, it spoils the fantasy. But for those who love to know how the magic is made, a number of back-stage tours can provide special insight on the operation, creation, and history of Walt Disney World.

Several are specific to particular interests, like gardening, scuba diving, and trains, and they can be a ton of fun; at least check them out. Others provide special access to attractions for once-in-a-lifetime experiences. Many of them are listed here. You can book most by calling 407-WDW-TOUR (407-939-8687).

- Steam Trains Tour
- Disney's Family Magic Tour

- Disney's Keys to the Kingdom Tour
- Mickey's Magical Milestones Tour
- Behind the Seeds at Epcot
- Backstage Magic
- The UnDISCOVERed Future World
- Seas Aqua Tour
- Dolphins in Depth
- Around the World at Epcot
- Backstage Safari
- Wild by Design
- Wild Africa Trek

HIDDEN MAGIC!

Put your focus on family, frolic, and fun when Disney's VIP Tour Services customize a vacation experience that maximizes the magic! This isn't a tour, but a personal travel guide service that can add that extra luxurious touch to your vacation. Your guide can help get you dinner reservations and primo parade seats, and provide you with interesting facts and details all the while. The cost is $125 to $150 per hour, with a six-hour minimum.

Summary

So now you have some of the basics of the Disney theme parks. Now that you know when they're open and how they work, you can get started looking into what the parks really have to offer. In the next four chapters, you get to the real meat of Walt Disney World, so enjoy reading about all the great attractions waiting for you!

The Magic Kingdom

In This Chapter

- Familiarize yourself with the park layout
- Pick the attractions that will make you the prince or princess of the kingdom
- Discover little-known park features to make your visit more magical
- Learn about the major changes to Fantasyland!

The Magic Kingdom is where it all started—at least in Florida. The park was established in 1971, but everything looks fresh and new as you enter the storied Main Street, U.S.A. With crews that do nothing else but paint the buildings here, it always has a fresh coat, and the cast members always have a smile for you. Many of the attractions are new and exciting additions from just the last few years. In particular, the ever-popular Fantasyland section of the Magic Kingdom is undergoing a massive expansion that adds attractions, dining options, and even more princess-themed magic than ever before. This park's rides do tend to be a bit more child-focused than those at the other parks, but there's still plenty of entertainment for guests of all ages. This is the epitome of Walt Disney World. Enjoy.

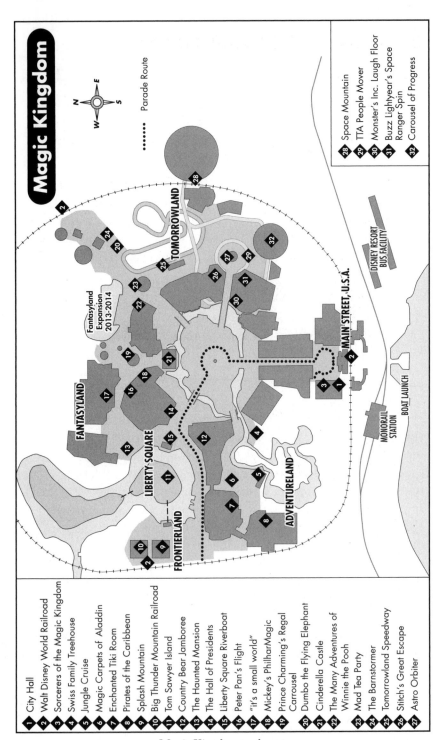

Magic Kingdom

N
W — E
S

•••••• Parade Route

TOMORROWLAND

FANTASYLAND

Fantasyland Expansion 2013-2014

LIBERTY SQUARE

FRONTIERLAND

ADVENTURELAND

MAIN STREET, U.S.A.

DISNEY RESORT BUS FACILITY

MONORAIL STATION

BOAT LAUNCH

1 City Hall
2 Walt Disney World Railroad
3 Sorcerers of the Magic Kingdom
4 Swiss Family Treehouse
5 Jungle Cruise
6 Magic Carpets of Aladdin
7 Enchanted Tiki Room
8 Pirates of the Caribbean
9 Splash Mountain
10 Big Thunder Mountain Railroad
11 Tom Sawyer Island
12 Country Bear Jamboree
13 The Haunted Mansion
14 The Hall of Presidents
15 Liberty Square Riverboat
16 Peter Pan's Flight
17 "it's a small world"
18 Mickey's PhilharMagic
19 Prince Charming's Regal Carrousel
20 Dumbo the Flying Elephant
21 Cinderella Castle
22 The Many Adventures of Winnie the Pooh
23 Mad Tea Party
24 The Barnstormer
25 Tomorrowland Speedway
26 Stitch's Great Escape
27 Astro Orbiter
28 Space Mountain
29 TTA People Mover
30 Monster's Inc. Laugh Floor
31 Buzz Lightyear's Space Ranger Spin
32 Carousel of Progress

Magic Kingdom park map.

General Park Information

Park Layout

The Magic Kingdom is made up of six themed lands, arranged in what is described as a hub-and-spoke style. This means that they all basically surround the central, circular plaza in front of Cinderella Castle.

All guests enter the park by going under the Railroad Station and emerging onto the cozy town square of Main Street, U.S.A. After traveling down "the street," they pour into a round, central plaza that serves as the heart of the park. From this vantage point, the lands are in the following order as you go clockwise from your left:

- Adventureland
- Frontierland
- Liberty Square
- Fantasyland
- Tomorrowland
- Main Street, U.S.A.

You may wonder, "What happened to Mickey's Toontown Fair?" This land, which used to be nestled behind Fantasyland and Tomorrowland and served as a cartoon home to Mickey, Minnie, Donald, and Goofy, is no more. This space is being used for the ongoing Fantasyland expansion, and only one element of the land continues to exist, The Barnstormer. But we will cover that in depth later.

Park Operating Hours

The Magic Kingdom typically opens at 9 A.M. and closes at 9 P.M. Closing times can vary from as early as 7 P.M. to as late as 2 A.M. due to a variety of reasons, so be sure to check the operation calendars ahead of time at www.disneyworld.com.

Must Do! Rides 📝

The *Must Do!* attractions and activities at the Magic Kingdom are:

- *Wishes Nighttime Spectacular*
- *SpectroMagic Parade/Main Street Electrical Parade*
- Space Mountain
- Buzz Lightyear's Space Ranger Spin
- Peter Pan's Flight
- *Mickey's PhilharMagic*
- "it's a small world"
- Buying your Mickey ears hat at Le Chapeau
- Walking through and around Cinderella Castle
- *Monsters, Inc. Laugh Floor Comedy Club*

Dining Summary

Dining in the Magic Kingdom has greatly expanded in the last year. What was once a disappointing range of choices has now been improved as the Fantasyland expansion brings more venues to the table.

You'll find a few great character meals, including the single most popular one in all of Walt Disney World, breakfast at Cinderella's Royal Table. Then, at the other extreme, are numerous counter-service restaurants located in nearly every land. But in the middle is where the park comes up woefully short for moderately priced table-service restaurants without entertainment.

Don't sweat it, though. The two extremes should do the trick. For the best in character meals, try the Crystal Palace, with Winnie the Pooh and friends. For the best counter-service meals, go to Pecos Bill's Tall Tale Inn and Café. Visit the Dole-sponsored Aloha Island for pineapple treats. And if you want to try the new choices, there are *Beauty and the Beast*–themed choices in the Be Our Guest Restaurant and Gaston's Tavern.

Tip Board Location

The tip board that displays attraction show times, waiting times, and closures is located at the end of Main Street, U.S.A. It's near the central hub, on the left side, outside the entrances to Casey's and the Crystal Palace.

Shopping at the Park

Shopping at the Magic Kingdom is almost exclusively focused on Disney-themed merchandise, and the selection is quite good. Only the Downtown Disney area has a greater array. Most of this shopping is concentrated on Main Street, U.S.A., although several stores in each land sell attraction-related merchandise as well. Some highlights include these:

- Personalized Mickey ears hats are available at Le Chapeau, located to your right on the square as you enter the park. Getting a pair of Mickey ears with your name embroidered on them is a *Must Do!* tradition that nobody should pass up.

- Main Street, U.S.A., stores on the left side of the street as you enter the park also have a wide array of Disney-emblazoned items. The other side of the street has some retail shopping, too, but it's mostly food and snacks.

- The second location of the Bibbidi Bobbidi Boutique store/salon is located within Cinderella Castle. Read more about this store in the chapter on Downtown Disney.

Child Care at the Park

The Baby Care Center is located by the Crystal Palace, right off the central hub of the park. The center features changing tables, nursing rooms, high chairs, and a play room with a TV and comfy seating—all complimentary. A limited selection of baby items is available for sale.

Park Touring Strategies

The park is usually crowded. Surprise! That being said, you can certainly navigate through the maze of people to find the rides you want to enjoy. Consider the following basic plans.

- FASTPASS your way to happiness. Use these passes to secure seating later in the day for a ride that your group simply can't miss.

- If Space Mountain, Splash Mountain, or Big Thunder Mountain Railroad are high on your list, pick up a FASTPASS early, before they run out.

- Most traffic early in the day flows back to Fantasyland, especially with all the new sights to see. Visiting that area in the mid- to late-afternoon might serve you well, although FASTPASS vouchers for select rides might be gone by then. Consider sending one adult to gather vouchers and then join the rest of the group in another land.

- Split your visit to the Magic Kingdom into two or more days if your party includes small children. This will help you pace yourselves, and you can FASTPASS different rides each day.

DID YOU KNOW?

Magic Kingdom FASTPASS rides include:

- Space Mountain
- Buzz Lightyear's Space Ranger Spin
- The Many Adventures of Winnie the Pooh
- Peter Pan's Flight
- *Mickey's PhilharMagic*
- Splash Mountain
- Big Thunder Mountain Railroad
- Jungle Cruise
- Stitch's Great Escape!

Transportation to/from the Park

If you're staying at a Disney resort hotel, you'll take a bus, boat, or monorail to get here.

By Monorail or Boat:

- Contemporary Resort
- Grand Floridian Resort
- Polynesian Resort

By Boat:

- Wilderness Lodge and Villas Resorts
- Fort Wilderness Campgrounds

By Bus:

- All other Disney resorts

Parking for guests driving to the park costs $14.

Main Street, U.S.A.

This idyllic first land in the Magic Kingdom is based on Walt Disney's childhood home of Marceline, Missouri. This walk through an America of our past has colorfully painted storefronts brimming with bright lights and filled with Disney-themed products all ready for your purchase. But there's more to do here than just spend money. Some of your best memories will take place right here, from parades to your first pair of Mickey ears, to the first time you saw Cinderella Castle.

HIDDEN MAGIC!

A lot of fun things to do on Main Street, U.S.A., don't officially qualify as an attraction:

- Buy your own set of personalized Mickey ears at Le Chapeau, a store located to the right as you enter the park. Now you can build custom ones, even choosing the ears and other parts that you want to have on your hat. Nobody should leave the Magic Kingdom without their own set of ears—nobody!

- Get a haircut at the Barber Shop on the left of the square as you enter the park. It runs just under $20, and you can include some particularly magical highlights. And how cool is it to say that you got your hair cut in the Magic Kingdom?

- Mail a postcard from City Hall. They'll stamp it as coming from the Magic Kingdom before posting it, if you ask.

- Check out the horses. The stables are located to the left as you enter, and often one of the Main Street Vehicles horses is there with a handler.

Main Street Vehicles

Attraction Type: Carnival attraction

A wide array of vehicles can transport guests up and down Main Street. Some are horse drawn, others are powered, but all are slow. These wonderful diversions are here not for moving people, but for adding to the ambiance. They are a pleasantly relaxing way to see the street and catch some quiet moments with your traveling partners. Note that they're not always available, especially around parade times.

Tots	Young Children	Teens	Young Adults	Mature Adults

SpectroMagic Parade/Main Street Electrical Parade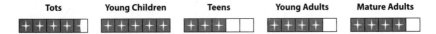

Attraction Type: Parade/fireworks

All the Disney parades are good, but the evening ones are the best. The historic *Main Street Electrical Parade* recently returned to the Magic Kingdom, reportedly only as a seasonal replacement for the *SpectroMagic Parade*. Regardless of which of these is the parade running the evenings you are there, you are sure to enjoy either one. The extensively lit parade cars and characters (covered head to toe with bright white lights) make these nighttime shows ones that light up the eyes of kids as much as the parade route. All the classic characters are included, along with many of the newer ones. On select nights, a parade is run more than once. The first one is typically overcrowded, but I think the second showing can seem anticlimactic, so I like to brave the larger crowd. As a final note, when the parade is over, the rush of humans making for the exit is more than annoying; it's downright scary. Make sure you have a hold on your kids, and consider doing some window shopping while you let the crowds clear out ahead of you.

Tots	Young Children	Teens	Young Adults	Mature Adults

Celebrate a Dream Come True Parade

Attraction Type: Parade/fireworks

The Magic Kingdom's daytime parade is a great show with a variety of classic and new characters. Well worth the time for the little ones, it's a great way to take a break in the day without having to totally stop "seeing things." This is not as special as the *SpectroMagic Parade*, but it's a great parade nevertheless.

And, of course, if you are not interested in parades, it provides a great diversion that shortens lines at attractions, so go hit the rides while the crowds line the parade route!

Tots	Young Children	Teens	Young Adults	Mature Adults
+ + + + + +	+ + + + + +	+ + +	+ +	+ + +

Move It, Shake It, Celebrate It Parade

Attraction Type: Parade/fireworks

This daytime parade is another move by Disney to make things more interactive. The parade, comprised of float-sized gift boxes manned by different Disney movie characters, stops periodically for an impromptu street party. During these parties, most notably in the hub area in front of Cinderella Castle, the gift boxes open up for more surprises, and characters draw members of the audience into the party. Very fun, if your kids are comfortable with characters.

Tots	Young Children	Teens	Young Adults	Mature Adults
+ + + + +	+ + + + + +	+ + +	+ + +	+ +

Wishes Nighttime Spectacular 🏳

Attraction Type: Parade/fireworks

This nighttime extravaganza uses the castle as a central prop to a show that is rife with photo opportunities. The fireworks, projected lights, and coordinated music combine for a show that's hard to beat. While it's best to see the show from inside the park, also consider watching it from sites outside, like the California Grill at the top of the Contemporary Resort, the beaches of the Polynesian Resort, or the public areas behind the Grand Floridian Resort.

Tots	Young Children	Teens	Young Adults	Mature Adults

HIDDEN MAGIC!

Where should you watch the fireworks and parades? While many will tell you that the best place to see the parades is in Frontierland or Adventureland because the crowds are smaller, I think it's well worth the time to have someone stake out a spot on Main Street. This could be one of your most iconic memories of your trip, and the setting makes watching the parade worth the 30 minutes (perhaps an hour during the busy season) that someone has to sit there and people watch. For the fireworks, being in the central hub in front of the castle is essential to enjoying the spirit of the crowd and seeing the show the way it was intended. It can get crowded, so keep an eye on the little ones.

Walt Disney World Railroad

Attraction Type: Carnival attraction

Walt Disney was an avid railroad enthusiast. That's why this and many other railroad lines play such a pivotal and noticeable role in the park. This one takes guests around the park in a slow, scenic, and relaxing ride that stops at the park's entrance, as well as in Frontierland. This train can also be an enjoyable treat if you find yourself finishing your day back by one of the other stops and can take the train back to the front of the park rather than having to hike out.

Tots	Young Children	Teens	Young Adults	Mature Adults

Sorcerers of the Magic Kingdom

Attraction Type: Experience area/playground

This new interactive role-playing game uses technology, collector cards, and storytelling to create a new kind of park experience. You pick up cards as you enter, then you explore different lands in the park while using the cards to get technology pods. These pods direct you on what to do next and tell you more of the story.

Tots	Young Children	Teens	Young Adults	Mature Adults
+	+ + +	+ + + + +	+ +	+

Adventureland

Welcome to the land of pirates and jungle adventure, home to two of the oldest and still most popular rides at the Magic Kingdom. Recent upgrades to long-standing classics have done a good job of freshening up the Adventureland experience while staying true to the original kitschy, exotic environment. The fun here is of the kind that's not too scary for little kids but with plenty of adult fun factor, too. This can be the best land to hit first because it sets your imagination going, though thrill-ride fans will flock this way to get onto the two mountains early.

Disney has really spiced up the atmosphere in Adventureland with a pirate training camp. A pirate with a cart of swords and other swashbuckling attire will set up an impromptu training camp somewhere in the streets of Adventureland for would-be pirates. Ask a cast member when the next one will be held.

DID YOU KNOW?

Opened in the Summer of 2009, kids can get a pirate makeover in a decidedly boy-themed answer to Bibbidi Bobbidi Boutique at the Pirate's League. There are boy- and girl-themed makeovers, making this a great place to inspire the little buccaneer in your family.

Pirates of the Caribbean

Attraction Type: Theme ride

The ride has been updated to add the Captain Jack Sparrow character from the recent *Pirates of the Caribbean* movies. It remains a great, somewhat politically incorrect show, with *audio-animatronic* pirates looting and pillaging a Caribbean port town. Consider this boat ride a loud but air-conditioned *Must Do!* when you visit the Magic Kingdom, if only because you have to say you rode it! Warning: Some with very small children don't like it for the noise factor.

Tots	Young Children	Teens	Young Adults	Mature Adults
+ + + +	+ + + + +	+ + + +	+ + + +	+ + + +

> **MICKEY-SPEAK**
>
> **Audio-animatronics** refers to robotic characters in numerous attractions throughout the Disney parks. These figures, originally conceived by Walt Disney, are more than mannequins being moved by a small engine; they're intricate robotic characters that mimic many of the mannerisms and movements of the living characters they imitate. They can be so lifelike that some guests actually think they're actors on stage.

The Magic Carpets of Aladdin

Attraction Type: Carnival attraction

This is the first of many Dumbo-style rides around all of the parks where you ride in circles while going up and down. In this one you ride a magic carpet, and the nearby bazaar-themed stores really make kids feel like they are in Arabia. Keep an eye out for the spitting camel!

Tots	Young Children	Teens	Young Adults	Mature Adults
+ + + + + +	+ + + + +	+ + +	+ +	+ +

The Enchanted Tiki Room AC ⊙⊙

Attraction Type: Theater/movie/show

This classic Disney attraction is a personal *Must Do!*. Sit in a small Hawaiian chamber filled with audio-animatronic birds on perches that sing and swing to the music. Some special effects, a great deal of humor, and some catchy songs make this a fun sit-down theater experience that offers fairly short lines. Some smaller children may be a bit frightened by a simulated storm, but for the most part, it's a charming show.

Tots	Young Children	Teens	Young Adults	Mature Adults
+ + +	+ + + +	+ + +	+ +	+ + +

Jungle Cruise

Attraction Type: Theme ride

This was one of the first rides built at the park, and it remains over-whelmingly popular to this day. Jump aboard a jungle river steamer that takes you past audio-animatronic animals, natives, and other jungle sights. Corny gags and stale humor don't seem to miss the mark, and while you may think that you won't enjoy the ride, you'll still find yourself disembarking with a chuckle.

Tots	Young Children	Teens	Young Adults	Mature Adults
+ + + +	+ + + + +	+ + + +	+ + +	+ + + +

Jungle Cruise.
Photo © Disney.

Swiss Family Treehouse

Attraction Type: Experience area/playground

This attraction might have inspired the StairMaster exercise machines. Explore the tree home of the Robinsons, climbing from landing to landing as you make it around the tree complex. I prefer Tom Sawyer Island for exploring, but this is a great place to wear out kids who have a bit more energy than you can handle.

Tots	Young Children	Teens	Young Adults	Mature Adults
+ + +	+ +	+	+	

Frontierland

The worlds of foreign adventure merge very easily into the Old West. More adult-targeted thrill rides, with a coaster and a log ride, help make the fun more evenly distributed across all age groups. Grab a FASTPASS for either attraction early; they get booked up quickly.

Big Thunder Mountain Railroad 🄵🄿 👥

Attraction Type: Thrill ride

This roller coaster takes you on a rickety set of mining tracks in and out of a series of Southwestern mesas. As a roller coaster, it's moderately tame, but the setting is fun and it's not a kiddie roller coaster by any means. Thrill-seeking teens will find it too tame, but it's still popular. Guests must be 40 inches tall to enjoy this ride.

Tots	Young Children	Teens	Young Adults	Mature Adults
	+ + +	+ + + +	+ + + + +	+ + + +

Splash Mountain 🄵🄿 👥

Attraction Type: Thrill ride

This traditional log flume ride is themed to the story of Brer Rabbit. There are brief moments of darkness, but nothing too scary. The wet factor at the end isn't too bad, so although you will want to protect valuables, you don't have to waterproof yourself completely before taking the plunge. Guests must be 40 inches tall to enjoy this ride.

Tots	Young Children	Teens	Young Adults	Mature Adults
+	+ + +	+ + + + +	+ + + +	+ + +

Country Bear Jamboree 🄰🄲

Attraction Type: Theater/movie/show

Audio-animatronic bears tell jokes, sing songs, and entertain the crowd in an Old West saloon theater. This show remains popular because it provides G-rated entertainment and air-conditioning.

If you saw the movie based on this attraction, I'm sorry, but please don't use that as an excuse not to see this show.

Tots	Young Children	Teens	Young Adults	Mature Adults

Frontierland Shootin' Arcade

Attraction Type: Carnival attraction

This is one of the few pay-as-you-go attractions remaining in the parks. All it takes is a little loose change, and you'll be shooting a rifle at a Western scene filled with humorous targets. Hit any of the targets, and your reward is some kind of show, like making a snake's tail rattle or causing wolves to bay at the moon. The rifles fire light, not bullets, at the targets, so they're completely safe.

Tots	Young Children	Teens	Young Adults	Mature Adults

> **HIDDEN MAGIC!**
>
> Shrunken Net's Junior Jungle Boats gives you a chance to steer your own miniature boat by flaming torches, stone temples, and other boats in this Adventureland locale. You have to pay to play, much like with the Frontierland Shootin' Arcade, but it can be a nice distraction.

Tom Sawyer Island 👀

Attraction Type: Exploration area/playground

Take the pontoon boats across to this two-island play area and let the kids loose! These islands provide rustic exploration trails complete with caves, a fort, barrel bridges, and other surprises, all themed to the tales of Mark Twain. Fort Langhorne on the far island has rifles that you can actually fire (sound only) at passing steamboats, and it also has a fun escape route. Be careful with little ones; the caves are very dark, narrow, and can be both disorienting and scary.

Tots	Young Children	Teens	Young Adults	Mature Adults

Liberty Square

The world of the American frontier gives way to a Revolutionary War–era East Coast city that mixes in the out-of-context fun of a haunted house and a riverboat. It just doesn't seem to matter that the decades get mixed, and open-air entertainment such as the fife and drum corps makes it a lively land.

Liberty Square Riverboat

Attraction Type: Carnival attraction

Hop aboard a steam-powered riverboat and tour the Frontierland and Liberty Square lands via waterway. This is by no means a thriller, but it's a relaxing 20-minute ride. Be aware that there are no restrooms on the riverboat. Overall, this is a pretty sleepy experience, but if you needed sleep, you would have gone back to your hotel room, right?

Tots	Young Children	Teens	Young Adults	Mature Adults
+				+

The Hall of Presidents AC

Attraction Type: Theater/movie/show

This is one of the original attractions at the Magic Kingdom, and it's regularly updated whenever we elect a new president. The stage is filled with an audio-animatronic figure of every president. Although few have speaking parts, they all move independently, and they certainly have fooled many over the years into thinking they were live actors. The show is brief and a bit dry for kids, but it's undoubtedly patriotic. For me, it is a personal *Must Do!* attraction, but not everyone agrees, so it all depends on your interest.

Tots	Young Children	Teens	Young Adults	Mature Adults
+	+++	++++	++++	++++

The Haunted Mansion 🆎 👓

Attraction Type: Theme ride

This perennial favorite is a great ride for almost everyone in your family. While it borders on being a thrill ride (it can be scary for some kids), the cars move on a straight track and it is in no way a roller coaster. The ride takes you through various scenes of a haunted house, trying to portray ghosts and goblins as more funny than frightening. A fun twist at the end puts a ghost in your seat, and a recent refurbishment makes it really come to life.

I will say that most kids are more scared by the thought of a haunted mansion than by the ride itself.

Tots	Young Children	Teens	Young Adults	Mature Adults
+ +	+ + +	+ + + +	+ + + + +	+ + + + +

Fantasyland

When kids think of the Magic Kingdom, this is what they have in mind. Princesses, castles, Peter Pan, Dumbo—all the classics. Playing on that popularity, Disney is in the midst of a massive Fantasyland expansion that will grow the area significantly. It has several rides that may be designed for kids but that most adults also find worth the wait. When you see the little ones' faces, even if they're not your own, it will make your day.

Because you may be visiting at a time when the expansion is still underway, make sure to explore the area beyond just the marquee attractions that you might have read about before your trip.

Consider this a land where you'll spend a great deal of time if you're traveling with younger children. You may be rewarded if you visit more than once, even if it's at the expense of another land in the Magic Kingdom or even another park. Just make sure you hit everything the kids want and the fun will be shared by all. This is the place where magic really does happen, and you don't want to short yourself in that department.

Cinderella Castle

Attraction Type: Experience area/playground

The centerpiece of the entire Magic Kingdom is a child's paradise in sights to be seen. While often the interior is blocked off as a staging area for performances shown in front of the castle, if you can get inside to see the tiled murals telling Cinderella's story, it's well worth it. There is a Bibbidi Bobbidi Boutique store/salon and the entrance to a restaurant on the ground floor, but the real use of the castle is as a backdrop for shows and fireworks. Let a child explore the grounds around the castle and you'll be richly rewarded. Of particular note, take time in the winding garden paths, visit the wishing well, and just take it all in.

For more about the Bibbidi Bobbidi Boutique store, see the Downtown Disney/BoardWalk Chapter.

Tots	Young Children	Teens	Young Adults	Mature Adults
+ + + + + ◼	+ + + + + +	+ + + ▢ ▢	+ + + ▢ ▢	+ + + ▢ ▢

> **HIDDEN MAGIC!**
>
> When it was originally conceived, Cinderella Castle was allegedly going to have an apartment inside for Walt Disney and his family. Walt unfortunately passed before Walt Disney World was built, and the room never happened. But in 2007 a hotel suite was completed that is worthy of a princess.
>
> I have visited the suite, and I can say that if you are offered the opportunity to stay in it, take that chance. It is truly a once-in-a-lifetime experience!

Dream Along with Mickey

Attraction Type: Theater/movie/show

A stage show held in front of Cinderella Castle several times during the day, this song-and-dance number is a great way for kids to get another dose of Mickey and friends without waiting in line.

Tots	Young Children	Teens	Young Adults	Mature Adults
+ + + + + ◼	+ + + + + ◼	+ ▢ ▢ ▢ ▢	+ ▢ ▢ ▢ ▢	+ ◼ ▢ ▢ ▢

Mad Tea Party

Attraction Type: Carnival attraction

Hop into a tea cup that spins around madly in multiple directions. This is another Disney classic ride that's an almost required photo opportunity. It isn't exciting for adults, but even the most tech-savvy youngster will lose his mind enjoying the spinning. And remember the old adage: the family that spins together, laughs together.

Tots	Young Children	Teens	Young Adults	Mature Adults
+ + +	+ + + +	+ + +	+ +	+

The Many Adventures of Winnie the Pooh

FP AC OO

Attraction Type: Theme ride

This is one of three important character-themed *dark rides* in Fantasyland. Make sure you go to all of the ones in which your kids care for the characters. In this one, you hop aboard a honey pot and dive into the world of Winnie the Pooh, Tigger, Piglet, and the rest of the childhood friends of Christopher Robin. The queue line, complete with Pooh's tree-trunk home and interactive elements, makes the wait bearable.

Tots	Young Children	Teens	Young Adults	Mature Adults
+ + + + +	+ + + +	+ +	+	+

MICKEY-SPEAK

Dark rides are attractions in which you ride in a car through a dark indoor set, visiting a series of scenes. Why is this important? Some kids, no matter how benign the subject matter, will have a melt down in the dark. Good to know if you have one of those kids with you, don't you think?

"it's a small world" 🔲 AC

Attraction Type: Theme ride

Another Disney classic that has been recently refurbished, this boat ride lets you visit the children of the world country by country. The song is infectious, and the scenery, while a bit 1960s, hits a high note in the nostalgia category. It's a *Must Do!* for all ages, simply because you have to say you rode this when you show pictures of your vacation when you return home. Also, the recently retrofitted queue line includes Disney's most recent advancements in character greeting technology, so don't miss it!

Tots	Young Children	Teens	Young Adults	Mature Adults
+ + + +	+ + + +	+	+ +	+ +

Dumbo the Flying Elephant

Attraction Type: Carnival attraction

Dumbo is still in Fantasyland, but in early 2012 he was moved over to the Storybook Circus section that sits where Toontown used to be. The real perk is not just that they have renovated the ride, but they doubled it! There are now two rides, helping keep the lines from getting too long. The waiting area is more fun, too.

Tots	Young Children	Teens	Young Adults	Mature Adults
+ + + + +	+ + + + +	+ +	+ + +	+ + +

Prince Charming Regal Carrousel

Attraction Type: Carnival attraction

This is a beautiful carousel by anyone's standard. It's easy to understand why most guests pass it by, feeling that it's nothing special you couldn't find elsewhere. But if you have young children or are a romantic at heart, you should take a ride and appreciate the amazing craftsmanship that went into building this piece of moving art.

Tots	Young Children	Teens	Young Adults	Mature Adults
+ + + +	+ + +	+	+	+

Mickey's PhilharMagic 🔲 FP AC

Attraction Type: Theater/movie/show

This is the best 3-D movie in all of Walt Disney World—and my wife's favorite attraction anywhere. Join Donald as he bumbles through the world of music trying to regain control of Mickey's sorcerer's hat while characters from several Disney movies try to help. The music is powerful and catchy, the 3-D effects are impressive, and the in-theater effects are perfectly balanced. Some kids will be scared by 3-D effects but with the glasses off will enjoy the music and show.

Tots	Young Children	Teens	Young Adults	Mature Adults
+ + + + +	+ + + + + +	+ + + + +	+ + + + +	+ + + + +

Peter Pan's Flight 🔲 FP AC ∞

Attraction Type: Theme ride

The second of the three Fantasyland character-themed dark rides, this one takes you over the streets of London and the islands of Neverland in a pirate ship. Follow the heroic exploits of Peter Pan and the evil plotting of Hook in what is probably the most popular ride in Fantasyland. Really, if tales of Pan are even just of occasional interest to your kids, you need to ride this to make a classic come to life for them again.

Tots	Young Children	Teens	Young Adults	Mature Adults
+ + + + +	+ + + + +	+ +	+ +	+ +

The Barnstormer 🛗

Attraction Type: Thrill ride

This roller coaster is designed for the younger set, but it still has a height restriction. The slow turns and dips make this one of the more ideal rides where an adult and a child truly can share the experience. So many rides are designed for one or the other, but this is really fun for both. Guests must be 35 inches to enjoy this ride.

Tots	Young Children	Teens	Young Adults	Mature Adults
+ + + +	+ + + + + +	+ +	+ + +	+ + +

Casey Jr. Splash 'N' Soak Station

Attraction Type: Experience area/Playground

This new addition to the Magic Kingdom is in the Storybook Circus area, providing a great place for kids to run around and cool off.

Tots	Young Children	Teens	Young Adults	Mature Adults
+ + + + +	+ + + ☐ ☐	☐ ☐ ☐ ☐ ☐	☐ ☐ ☐ ☐ ☐	☐ ☐ ☐ ☐ ☐

Under the Sea: Journey of the Little Mermaid

Attraction Type: Theme ride

Hop into a clamshell and enjoy a ride through the tale of Ariel. Feel as if you have been transported into the ocean on this partially dark ride, based inside Prince Eric's Castle, and enjoy the sights and soundtrack.

Tots	Young Children	Teens	Young Adults	Mature Adults
+ + + + +	+ + + + +	+ + + ☐ ☐	+ + + ☐ ☐	+ + ☐ ☐ ☐

Enchanted Tales with Belle

Attraction Type: Character experience

Relive the story of *Beauty and the Beast* with Belle as the host and director. This is more than a line-up-and-get-an-autograph experience, with children getting to be more interactive with the experience.

Tots	Young Children	Teens	Young Adults	Mature Adults
+ + + + +	+ + + + +	☐ ☐ ☐ ☐ ☐	☐ ☐ ☐ ☐ ☐	☐ ☐ ☐ ☐ ☐

Ariel's Grotto

Attraction Type: Character experience

Meet the actual Ariel in her grotto, returned to the park after all the Fantasyland expansion growth.

Tots	Young Children	Teens	Young Adults	Mature Adults
+ + + + +	+ + + + +	+ ☐ ☐ ☐ ☐	☐ ☐ ☐ ☐ ☐	☐ ☐ ☐ ☐ ☐

DID YOU KNOW?

The Fantasyland expansion, still underway at the time of this writing, still has more to offer. Still to come in 2014 will be a landmark attraction, the Seven Dwarfs Mine Train. Themed to Snow White, this thrill ride should become one of the featured attractions in the park.

Tomorrowland

This land is supposed to be a look back at how we envisioned the future. Confused? Well rather than say, "This is what the future will look like," only to be constantly looking dated as our technology evolves in real time, they instead paint a picture of what people thought the future would look like back in the 1950s movies of spaceships and travels to the moon, Mars, and beyond. Anchored by the iconic Space Mountain roller coaster, the land has become a fun area for all ages.

Tomorrowland Speedway 👤

Attraction Type: Theme ride

I used to hate this ride. It was slow, boring, noisy, and ugly. That's when the team from the Indianapolis Motor Speedway (IMS) stepped in, and it's a world better now. While it is no longer branded to the Indy 500, it's still a fun diversion. It's also definitely a ride more for kids than adults, but what did you expect here? Drive a car (yes, a real car, with a real engine—not some electronic track-pulled prop!) around the looping course. A single rail keeps the cars from veering off, and the new refurbishment brings banked turns that make kids really feel like they're in the big race. Guests have to be 54 inches tall to ride alone; otherwise, they can ride with an adult and be way shorter!

Tots	Young Children	Teens	Young Adults	Mature Adults
+ + + +	+ + + + +	+ + +	+ +	+

Stitch's Great Escape! 🅵🅿 🆎 ⚙ 👬

Attraction Type: Thrill ride

Formerly known as the *Extra TERRORestrial Alien Encounter*, this attraction was softened a bit because the earlier version was just too scary for most. The attraction now puts you on the security detail watching Stitch, who, naturally, escapes and causes mayhem and havoc. While the effects are more fun, it's still far too scary for most kids. Prolonged dark periods and some realistic effects will definitely scare them. Guests must be 40 inches tall to enjoy this attraction.

Tots	Young Children	Teens	Young Adults	Mature Adults
	+ +	+ + + + +	+ + + +	+ +

Space Mountain ▨ 🅵🅿 🆎 ⚙ 👬

Attraction Type: Thrill ride

This is still the best-known roller coaster at Walt Disney World, and it still thrills. The dark interior, lit only by stars, makes the twists and turns a surprise no matter how many times you've been on this classic. This thrill ride is a *Must Do!*, not only because it's a trademark ride at the park, but because it's a great ride that still pulls in roller-coaster enthusiasts from around the world. Guests must be 44 inches tall to enjoy this attraction.

Tots	Young Children	Teens	Young Adults	Mature Adults
	+ + +	+ + + + +	+ + + + +	+ + + + +

Buzz Lightyear's Space Ranger Spin ▨ 🅵🅿 🆎

Attraction Type: Theme ride

You've been enlisted by the Space Rangers to help Buzz fight power-hoarding bad guys. Emperor Zurg (the bad guy) needs to be stopped, and you are just the ranger to do it! Hop into a two-person car equipped with laser guns for shooting at targets throughout the ride. The guns actually score points based on whatever targets you hit along the way, so you even get to compete with your party.

This is one of the better new rides in the Magic Kingdom. You can encourage your kids to shoot things without worrying about sending the wrong message, because they're just shooting targets to sap the batteries of their power. Kids also enjoy seeing what rank of ranger their score earns them at the end of the ride—and seeing if they beat Mom or Dad!

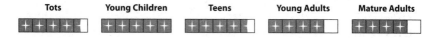

Tots	Young Children	Teens	Young Adults	Mature Adults

Tomorrowland Transit Authority PeopleMover

Attraction Type: Theme ride

This ride is impressive, in that it's run by magnetic power and technically has no moving parts but the cars themselves. You get an above-ground view of Tomorrowland, gliding around the park and even inside Space Mountain. It's not very exciting, but it's a relaxing ride if you need a cool-down period after a meal or before your next FASTPASS is valid.

Tots	Young Children	Teens	Young Adults	Mature Adults

Astro Orbiter

Attraction Type: Carnival attraction

This modern take on the traditional carnival ride (replace Dumbo with a rocket) has you circling on spaceships that rise up and down. Located in the middle of the courtyard in the center of Tomorrowland, it's a pretty simple ride with few surprises, but the height above ground level (about three stories up) can be a problem for some kids, so consider that first before riding.

Tots	Young Children	Teens	Young Adults	Mature Adults

DID YOU KNOW?

Tomorrowland has a talking trash can. Usually found around the restrooms near the Astro Orbiter, this moving, chatting can is a big surprise to most and a surprisingly pleasant conversationalist. See if you can get him to scare Mom when she comes out of the restroom. Priceless.

Walt Disney's Carousel of Progress 🄰🄲

Attraction Type: Theme ride

I'm sorry—I really want to like this ride, due to its history: Walt Disney actually created it for the 1964 World's Fair. But it really needs either an upgrade or a replacement. In this attraction, you sit in a theater that goes around to a series of stages with audio-animatronic action figures that walk you through the technology advancements from the early 1900s to today. It's always reputed to be closing or being refurbished, but neither seems to be true. There are rumors that Walt demanded that it *never* be closed down. There are also websites dedicated to the ride's preservation, but you should simply consider it an uncomfortable air-conditioned rest from the Orlando humidity. Otherwise, you may want to pass it by. Let's hope that this is updated soon, keeping Walt's dream alive!

Tots	Young Children	Teens	Young Adults	Mature Adults
☐☐☐☐☐	☐☐☐☐☐	☐☐☐☐☐	◀☐☐☐☐	➕☐☐☐☐

Monsters, Inc. Laugh Floor Comedy Club 🄰🄲

Attraction Type: Theater/movie/show

Disney has created a new technology that allows for an interactive cartoon show, originally debuting in *Turtle Talk with Crush* in Epcot. This sets the ideal stage for kids, where they can *really* interact with the stars of the movies that they've grown to love. In this attraction, you are part of the crowd in a comedy club located in the mythical town of Monstropolis depicted in *Monsters, Inc.* Mike (the one-eyed green creature originally voiced by Billy Crystal) is trying to power the city with your laughter, so he pulls out many of his friends to help.

A really innovative feature of the attraction is that you can use your cell phone to text-message a joke to them while you are waiting in line to enter the show. They'll even text you back to let you know if they're going to use it.

This is a *Must Do!* attraction because the humor works for all, and the technology used is what we should all dream of. It enhances the show, but we don't spend time figuring it out—we just enjoy it!

Tots	Young Children	Teens	Young Adults	Mature Adults
+ + + +	+ + + + +	+ + + +	+ + +	+ + +

Summary

The Magic Kingdom is the true heart of Walt Disney World. The long list of attractions should tell you that they've crammed as much fun into the park as they can, and they've tried to find something for everyone. As you plan your trip, make sure that you recognize this and that you plan your time accordingly. Whereas other parks may get a day of your time, the Magic Kingdom can take two days and still have you heading home without having seen it all. Don't let that be a negative—that just means you'll always have something to come back to see. For kids, that can mean everything.

Epcot

In This Chapter

- Learn about the secrets of the future (Future World)
- Travel the world, or at least the World Showcase
- Decide how best to enjoy the attractions, shopping, and dining of the two parks that make up Epcot

Epcot stands for the *Experimental Prototype City of Tomorrow*, and it was conceived by Walt Disney himself. While it is vastly different than his original plans, the Disney Imagineers created a park that is essentially two parks made into one. Roughly organized like a figure eight, this park conveys the excitement of the future and manages to combine it with an idyllic view of the rest of the world.

Nothing is more fun on your first visit to Epcot than to enter by way of the monorail as it circles Spaceship Earth. This large geodesic globe is the symbol of Epcot and it sits near the center of Future World, which celebrates different aspects of technology, nature, and mankind through a series of pavilions. These pavilions, which form a circle around Spaceship Earth, take you on journeys that explore these worlds and show how they will change as we, our technology, and our planet change. This forward-looking approach makes it interesting and fun, and explains why they call it Future World.

I hear you groaning, "Oh, no, not *learning* on a vacation!" Don't worry; this is a fun park that just happens to have some learning hidden here and there. It has some of the fastest thrill rides (Test Track and Mission: SPACE), a 5-million-plus-gallon aquarium, and a whole lot more.

Then there's the World Showcase. This circle of pavilions brings different corners of the globe to central Florida. Kind of like a permanent World's Expo, the 11 national pavilions put you squarely in front of the Eiffel Tower, in the shadow of an Aztec pyramid, and in the heart of a Moroccan bazaar. Staffed by students native to the many countries represented here, the World Showcase lets you feel as though you're globe-trotting. This part of Epcot brings some unique shopping, exceptional food, and impressive views. While it may not have traditional theme park rides, the World Showcase is an experience not to be missed, especially around fireworks or mealtimes. It has been listed by many as a perennial favorite simply for the great atmosphere.

So you have the whole world—and the world of the future—right at your feet. What are you going to do now? This chapter helps you choose which of the Epcot pavilions you'll visit and takes you on a tour of the rides and attractions available in each. This chapter also gives you an insider's guide to the best shopping sites available at Epcot right now—no need to wait for the future to enjoy this place!

Park Introduction

Let's consider Epcot in two parts. We will start with Future World and then move on to the national pavilions that make up the World Showcase.

General Park Information

What are the ABCs of visiting Epcot? Let's look at some of the basics of the park that you need to know.

Park Layout

As mentioned earlier, the park is basically two separate parks connected to form a figure eight. The first part, Future World, is made of pavilions that surround a central hub, Innoventions Plaza. As you enter the park, you pass under Spaceship Earth to arrive at that central plaza. Immediately surrounding the plaza are stores and restaurants, as well as the two sides of the Innoventions attraction. Beyond those areas are the pavilions. As you go clockwise from the left of the central plaza you'll find the Universe of Energy, Mission: SPACE, and Test Track pavilions on your left. As you continue around on the right you will find the Imagination!, The Land, and The Seas with Nemo & Friends pavilions. There are several walkways to the World Showcase located between the Test Track and Imagination! pavilions.

World Showcase is more easily navigated, as the 11 national pavilions are all located on the walkway that goes around the World Showcase Lagoon. Starting at the pavilion to your left as you enter from Future World, you pass Mexico, Norway, China, Germany, Italy, American Adventure, Japan, Morocco, France, the United Kingdom, and Canada. There's a "back door" to Epcot, the International Gateway, which is a separate entrance to the park. It's located between the France and United Kingdom pavilions, and it leads by boat and walkways to the BoardWalk, Hollywood Studios, the Yacht and Beach Club resorts, the BoardWalk Inn and Villa resorts, and the Swan and Dolphin hotels.

Park Operating Hours

The park is unique in that the two parts carry different operating times. Future World is traditionally open from 9 A.M. to 7 P.M., while the World Showcase is usually open from 11 A.M. to 9 P.M. Be sure to check the operational calendars ahead of time at www.disneyworld.com.

Must Do! Sights

- Mission: SPACE
- Test Track
- Soarin'
- *Turtle Talk with Crush*
- *The American Adventure*
- *IllumiNations*
- Agent P's World Showcase Adventure

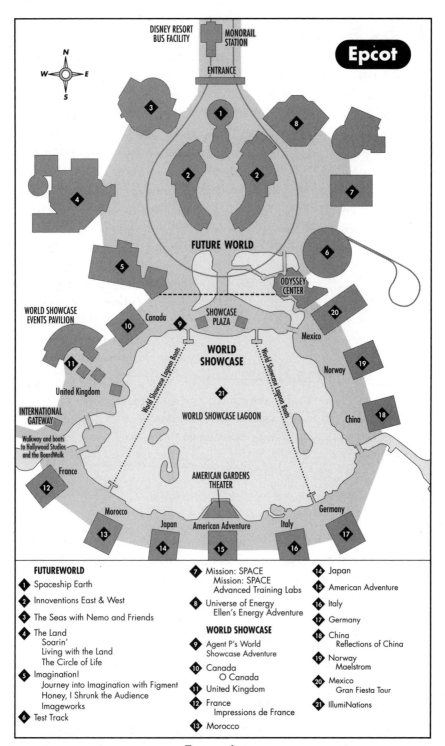

Epcot park map.

Dining Summary

Epcot brings the cuisines of the world to Orlando, and it's one of the biggest draws to this park. The World Showcase pavilions all sport table-service restaurants that serve their nation's traditional cuisine, and the product is almost uniformly high quality. The ambiance also makes dining here a special experience, so I recommend that any visit to the park be paired with some planned dining. You can find out more about the individual restaurants in the park in Chapter 14, but for now, I just give you an overview of the offerings.

Table Service—The table-service restaurants in the World Showcase side of the park are not just Americanized versions of the respective national cuisine. Influential culinary luminaries from Mexico and France played a role in their respective restaurants, and the other nations all have something great to offer. A popular princess character meal is also here, in the Norway Pavilion, and other restaurants are prized not only for their food, but for the views that their tables afford of the *IllumiNations* fireworks show. The real problem with the dining here is choosing from the many great options.

That's not to say that all the food is on the World Showcase Lagoon. Seafood at The Seas with Nemo & Friends is a good choice, and the character meal at The Land combines an enjoyable character experience with food grown right there in the pavilion.

Counter Service—The counter stands at the national pavilions offer a great way to sample smaller bites of different countries, and the Sunshine Season Food Fair in The Land Pavilion offers a broad array of well-prepared foods in a comfortable setting.

Snacks—The bites you can get in the World Showcase make it hard to go back to the standard snacks. Why not choose a *crêpe au chocolate* over the standard ice-cream bar, or replace fries with an authentic German pretzel?

Tip Board Location

The tip board is located in the central hub of Innoventions Plaza.

Shopping at the Park

Starting in Future World, you can find one of the best in-park general merchandise stores located in Innoventions Plaza. Mouse Gears has a broad array of products, with a particular emphasis on a good selection of clothes.

From there, you enter the mecca of international shopping. The pavilions of the World Showcase feature extensive shopping from the respective nations and have products ranging from inexpensive knick-knacks to extremely high-priced luxuries. The following sections discuss some of the highlights included.

Mexico

Inside the pyramid is a nice courtyard store with an inexpensive selection of sombreros, artwork, pepper sauces, and clothing.

Norway

While there's a range of luxuries like perfume and jewelry, the real appeal here are the plastic Viking helmets for kids and the expensive but beautiful Nordic sweaters in the back of the store.

China

An entire department store is located here, featuring furniture, clothing, decorations, and other luxuries from China. This is a *very* impressive array of shopping for a theme park, but the product quality is not quite up to the similar-scope store in the Japan Pavilion.

Germany

Crystal, wine, Hummels, caramels and other sweets are plentiful here, but the Christmas ornaments and nutcrackers are the best takeaways for most guests.

Italy

Although there are wines, fine glass, and perfumes available here, the best (and somewhat affordable) purchase is the selection of Venetian festival masks.

American Adventure

This is perhaps the least impressive store in the World Showcase. It makes sense, as we're already in the U.S.A. and you can get all that stuff right outside the park doors for far less.

Japan

The large department store that fills most of the Japan Pavilion is run by one of the large store chains back in Japan. This is probably the best store in the whole park, with a great array of toys, including some harder-to-find Hello Kitty and Pokemon merchandise. There are high-end luxuries, clothing, foods, sakes, bonsai trees, and sushi sets. Please don't miss this store, if for no other reason than to look at the bags of dried fish and crabs that pass as snack food.

Morocco

The stores here are smaller than those in China and Japan, but they make do, bringing a nice array of metal and leather products. Some clothing choices are also nice to consider, especially as attire for the summer months.

France

Perfume and wine are better than expected, but the trinkets store has some fun choices including miniature Eiffel Towers and products featuring the art of many famed French painters.

United Kingdom

Several stores populate this pavilion, and they're not all connected, so make sure you don't miss any. Twinings tea has a large presence, and there's also a heraldry booth. My favorites, however, are the toys and soccer gear.

Canada

Unfortunately, many of the stores in this pavilion have closed, but there's still a good selection of Roots sportswear, maple syrup, and some cute stuffed animals.

Child Care at the Park

The Baby Care Center is located in the Odyssey Center, which is behind and to the right of the Test Track Pavilion. The center features changing tables, nursing rooms, high chairs, and a play room with a TV and comfy seating, all complimentary. A limited selection of baby items is available for sale.

Transportation to/from the Park

If you're staying at a Disney resort hotel, you can walk or take a boat, bus, or monorail to get to Epcot.

By Foot or Boat (to the International Gateway entrance):

- Yacht and Beach Club resorts
- Swan and Dolphin resorts
- BoardWalk Inn and Villas

By Monorail (changing to the Epcot monorail at the TTC):

- Contemporary Resort
- Grand Floridian Resort
- Polynesian Resort

By Bus:

- All other Disney resorts

You can also get to Epcot from Hollywood Studios and the BoardWalk via boat, and from the Magic Kingdom via monorail.

Park Touring Strategies

All the rides people would fight over are located in the Future World side, so your first goal is to go after FASTPASS vouchers for attractions there that you're interested in trying out. Some good ideas include:

- Thrill-ride enthusiasts should get a FASTPASS for either Mission: SPACE or Test Track first thing, and then ride the other immediately.
- If thrill rides aren't your thing, go for a Soarin' FASTPASS and then wait in line for *Turtle Talk with Crush*.
- Plan to enjoy rides in The Land Pavilion in the late morning so that you can use the dining area as a stop to relax and reenergize while you wait for your FASTPASS to become valid.

- Use the single-rider line in Test Track to get on in the afternoon if all the FASTPASS vouchers have been given out for the day.

Future World Pavilions and Attractions

Future World is based on pavilions that exhibit different parts of our present and future, including the land, seas, space, and imagination. These pavilions are also air-conditioned, so you can cool down, find some interesting discoveries, and (heaven forbid!) learn something at the same time. Spaceship Earth sits in the center of Future World, surrounded by the two sides of Innoventions. The other pavilions are listed in clockwise order starting to your left as you enter the park.

Spaceship Earth AC OO

Attraction Type: Theme ride

The white geodesic dome of Spaceship Earth is the symbol of Epcot, and all guests are sure to see it as the monorail circles the dome on its way into the park. The slow ride inside Spaceship Earth tells of the history of communication and how it has impacted the overall history of mankind, ending with a nice rosy view of the future. A new sponsorship by Siemens has led to a recent refurbishment that not only updated the ride, but also improved an interactive area at the end called Project Tomorrow that is filled with technology-rich exhibits that kids will love.

The slow-moving cars ascend and descend at steep angles and go backward for the second half of the ride, but none of this is a thrill—just part of the show. The ride has several dark parts, so be aware with small children.

Tots	Young Children	Teens	Young Adults	Mature Adults
+++	+++	+++	+++	+++

Innoventions East & West 🄰🄲

Attraction Type: Experience area/playground

These exploration areas are supposed to show little snippets of the future, and used to suffer from being constantly outdated. Disney has done a great job over the last few years of making sure, with the help of corporate partners, that they do a good job of showing emerging technologies in a way that's interesting to kids. There are interactive, technology-intensive displays that showcase (among other things) recycling, plastics, durability testing, Segway people movers, personal finance, and home fire safety. There is also a place to register for Agent P's World Showcase Adventure. Just across the walkway there is a character-greeting area that has some exclusive greeting times for Chase Disney credit card holders. If you have the Disney credit card, contact Chase about gaining access to this area. Times are limited, so plan accordingly.

Tots	Young Children	Teens	Young Adults	Mature Adults
+++	+++++	++++	+++	+++

Ellen's Energy Adventure 🄰🄲 ⦿⦿

Attraction Type: Theme ride

Located in the Universe of Energy Pavilion, this attraction's roof is covered with solar panels, and from there you know that the story inside will be about energy sources and how they are impacting human life.

Ellen DeGeneres is your tour host, and Bill Nye, the Science Guy, is her knowledgeable sidekick as you learn about energy and the earth's natural resources. Ellen is funny as usual, as she walks you through the different kinds of energy sources, explaining where they come from and where they're going. The ride is not too preachy, and there are even some mild thrills (audio-animatronic dinosaurs) as the show cars lumber through the attraction. I still go on it every now and then; Ellen is funny and the ride is well done.

Some dark areas, as well as the dinosaur scenes, can scare some smaller children. The ride is 45 minutes long, so plan accordingly.

Tots	Young Children	Teens	Young Adults	Mature Adults
+	+++	++++	+++++	+++

DISNEY DON'T

If you're looking at a map, you may see a building between Universe of Energy and Mission: SPACE. That is the Wonders of Life Pavilion. Basically, the pavilion and its three rides (Body Wars, Cranium Command, and The Making of Me) are now extinct.

Mission: SPACE 🏷 FP AC 👬

Attraction Type: Thrill ride

Located in the Mission: SPACE Pavilion, this is one of the most thrilling of the thrill rides. Actual astronauts have reportedly said that it is the closest thing to real space travel that they have ever encountered, and the g-forces certainly seem pretty real to most people.

Using centrifuges and other advanced ride technology, you get to re-create a space trip, complete with take-off, slingshots around the moon, and a rather bumpy landing. Unfortunately, the effectiveness of the technology has led to the ride being more than many can handle.

HIDDEN MAGIC!

Outside the Mission: SPACE Pavilion is a large model of the moon. On the surface of this 10-foot-tall sphere are markers representing where human landings have occurred. It's an interesting diversion to look at while you're waiting for the astronauts in your group to finish their mission inside.

Disney has retooled the attraction, in a fashion, so that it's more fun for most guests. You can still experience the normal version of the ride, but they now offer a milder version, with the centrifuge turned off but the other effects still there. I have ridden both, one immediately after the other. While the wild version is definitely more intense than the milder one, the mild one is still a great thrill ride and well worth taking. As you enter the ride line, you'll be given the opportunity to choose your version.

I've labeled this as a *Must Do!* attraction, as it is an amazing, intense, and thrilling ride. But if you have any reservations about hopping on, pass on it. Guests must be 44 inches or taller to enjoy this attraction.

Tots	Young Children	Teens	Young Adults	Mature Adults
☐☐☐☐☐	✚✚✚☐☐	✚✚✚✚✚	✚✚✚✚✚	✚✚✚✚☐

Mission: SPACE Pavilion.
Photo © Disney.

Mission: SPACE Advanced Training Labs AC

Attraction Type: Experience area/playground

Also located in the Mission: SPACE Pavilion, this computer lab and playground area is really well done, making it a great place to wait for the members of your group who are on the Mission: SPACE ride.

The playground is much like you would find in a fast-food restaurant, complete with climbing nets, tubes, and slides. It's a perfect retreat for the very youngest of guests. The lab area is also really neat. Some individual workstations and photo/video booths let you create your own space video greeting card and send it to an email address. The larger lab space has team contests in which guests work together to accomplish tasks via their computer monitors, working together and competing at the same time.

Tots	Young Children	Teens	Young Adults	Mature Adults
+ + + +	+ + + + +	+ + + + +	+ +	+ +

Test Track 🖋 FP AC 👥

Attraction Type: Thrill ride

This attraction has been re-tooled in 2012. The results are more hands-on interactive areas that let you design your car, a move from an overall GM theme to one focused just on Chevrolet, and a sleeker, modernistic set. But the thrills are just as fast as they were before. It's fun and fast, and the end of the ride is a blast.

Make sure you take advantage of the single-rider line available for this attraction. It can save you as much as an hour of wait time. Guests must be 40 inches or taller to enjoy this ride.

Tots	Young Children	Teens	Young Adults	Mature Adults
☐☐☐☐☐☐	✚✚✚✚☐☐	✚✚✚✚✚✚✚	✚✚✚✚✚✚✚	✚✚✚✚✚✚

Honey, I Shrunk the Audience FP AC

Attraction Type: Theater/movie/show

Located in the Imagination! Pavilion and one of the many 3-D experiences at Walt Disney World, this theater show uses more than visual effects to bring the movie *Honey, I Shrunk the Kids* to life. The seats have water misters, motion simulators, and other devices that coordinate with the movie to make it seem more real, as the 3-D glasses make the action seem to spring from the screen. Although that movie debuted in 1989, this popular 3-D thriller has retained its fun factor over the years, and you don't need to have seen the movie to get it.

All that being said, it's not as good of a 3-D show as *PhilharMagic* at the Magic Kingdom, and it's starting to become a bit dated, but I still think you'll enjoy it. The show lasts for 20 minutes.

Note that since mid-2010 this theater has been used for performances of *Captain EO*. This movie from the 80s, featuring Michael Jackson, is there for a limited but undefined timeframe. So you could find the theater showing the *Honey* film, the *EO* film, being closed, or even perhaps showcasing something new.

Tots	Young Children	Teens	Young Adults	Mature Adults
✚✚✚✚✚☐	✚✚✚✚☐☐	✚✚☐☐☐☐	✚☐☐☐☐☐	✚☐☐☐☐☐

Journey into Imagination with Figment AC

Attraction Type: Theme ride

Located in the Imagination! Pavilion, this is an older ride designed to appeal to the very youngest kids. The attraction explores our human senses and how they play a role in our imagination and creativity. Although this ride is slow and designed for very young children, it has several areas with loud noises and dark spaces that may spook more skittish children. This attraction may be boring for adults, but let's be honest, you mostly came here for the kids, didn't you?

Tots	Young Children	Teens	Young Adults	Mature Adults
+++++	++++	+		

ImageWorks 🅰🄲

Attraction Type: Experience area/playground

Located in the Imagination! Pavilion, these labs, feature hands-on computer stations that let kids explore through some of the fun that the world of cameras can provide, including image manipulation, color effects, and other imaging technologies.

While the postride activities at newer rides are a bit more advanced, these should still captivate younger children and give you a nice place to gather yourselves up before venturing back out into the summer heat.

Tots	Young Children	Teens	Young Adults	Mature Adults
+++	++++	+++	++	++

Soarin' 🄵🄰🄲🄸

Attraction Type: Thrill ride

The Land Pavilion is packed with attractions (three total) as well as a great counter-service dining area. This new attraction is a ride copied from Disneyland in California.

Climb aboard a hang glider that takes you soaring over the vastly different geographic regions of the state of California. The ride swings up so that your toes are dangling in front of a gigantic panoramic screen that curves around you as far as you can see.

Other effects are used to make the trip seem even more real, so much that you can smell the oranges in the groves and feel the mountain lake's water sprinkling your face.

This is an amazing *Must Do!* ride, one not to be missed. It can be a bit intimidating to someone severely afraid of heights, but after that, the height restriction is just because of the seat harnesses, not because of any ride turns or excessive speeds. Also, the line area has been redone to include a lot of enjoyable interactive elements that make it almost an attraction unto itself. Guests must be 40 inches or taller to enjoy this attraction.

Tots	Young Children	Teens	Young Adults	Mature Adults
	+ + + +	+ + + + +	+ + + + +	+ + + +

Living with the Land FP AC

Attraction Type: Theme ride

This ride is located in The Land Pavilion. Hop aboard a slow-moving boat that takes you through the different labs in the back of The Land Pavilion. These labs are raising foods in innovative new ways that conserve energy, natural resources, and space. There are tanks of fish, hydroponic plants, and exhibits of how to grow food in space. The foods raised here are used in the Garden Grill Restaurant upstairs.

Sounds dull, but I've seen kids of all ages enjoy this ride, and I think it's a great attraction for everyone. Seeing plants growing without any soil, as well as their attempts to grow squash in the shape of Mickey ears, is pretty neat.

If you have a 4-H or FFA kid in your group, this is an absolutely necessary stop for your group!

Tots	Young Children	Teens	Young Adults	Mature Adults
+ + +	+ + +	+ + +	+ + +	+ + + +

The Circle of Life AC

Attraction Type: Theater/movie/show

Located in The Land Pavilion, this theater, featuring the cast from *The Lion King*, shows nature's circle of life and how things we do can threaten that circle. This isn't a bad movie, and it's a great show for a child who is a big *Lion King* fan. It's not too preachy, and it's a good diversion.

Tots	Young Children	Teens	Young Adults	Mature Adults
+ + + +	+ + + +	+ +	+	+

The Seas with Nemo & Friends Pavilion 🆎

Attraction Type: Experience area/playground

I list the pavilion itself as an attraction, as the giant aquarium that is the centerpiece of the pavilion is a sight to be seen. Where some other pavilions simply hold a ride, this one has displays, diversions, and the huge tank itself. The variety of sea life is amazing, and the views are breathtaking, as this donut-shaped tank ensures that you are always near some marine life. Rays, a shark, giant grouper, and even the scuba divers make it an interesting view. This, paired with the sea-life exhibits around the pavilion, make it a fun experience.

Tots	Young Children	Teens	Young Adults	Mature Adults
+++	+++	++	+++	+++

The Seas with Nemo & Friends 🆎

Attraction Type: Theme ride

Located in The Seas with Nemo & Friends Pavilion, this attraction revives the old attraction that used to be located here with a new theme from the popular movie. The line area alone is great, as you become aware that you are underwater, complete with the bottom of a fishing boat peeking out from the ceiling. From there you board a clamshell car that takes you on a trip through the ocean, retelling the story of Nemo, Dory, and Marlin. Many of the effects along the way are visually stunning, if not on one occasion a bit scary for little children. But the ride is meant for them, and I think the scary part is short and not too bad.

During the climax of the ride, you pass by the real aquarium and can see the characters from the *Nemo* movie swimming inside. I won't say how they do it, but it's pretty cool.

Tots	Young Children	Teens	Young Adults	Mature Adults
+++++½	+++++	++	+++½	++

Turtle Talk with Crush 🔲 🆎

Attraction Type: Theater/movie/show

Also in The Seas with Nemo & Friends Pavilion, this attraction showcases one of the newest storytelling technologies developed by

Disney. The technology behind this small theater show has already been used at a Magic Kingdom show and will probably be used in several other places.

As you enter the small theater, you will find a carpeted area up front for kids and some bench seating for the parents in the back. This is all facing what looks like a cartoon re-creation of the windows that look into the aquarium tanks elsewhere in the pavilion.

Crush, the Aussie turtle from the *Nemo* movie, arrives on scene and starts a conversation with the children at the front of the room. I mean, he literally talks to them and responds to their questions. The cartoon technology is pretty impressive, and it really helps the characters come to life.

I think this is a *Must Do!* attraction, not for the new technology but because it's fun for the kids—and even the adults—to interact with Crush.

Tots	Young Children	Teens	Young Adults	Mature Adults

Turtle Talk with Crush *is inspired by the Walt Disney Pictures presentation of a Pixar Animation Studios film,* Finding Nemo.
Photo © Disney/Pixar.

World Showcase Pavilions

The World Showcase is a series of 11 international pavilions that encircle a lagoon with a broad walkway going all around. These different lands offer a visually breathtaking tour into their respective countries, with meticulously accurate buildings, temples, and courtyards from around the world. A stroll around the lagoon, taking in all the sights, is an attraction unto itself. While there are some rides and movies that tell more about these nations, the real experience is in the restaurants, the shops, and the architecture.

HIDDEN MAGIC!

Where are the top choice dining destinations?

- **Character Meal:** Restaurant Akershus
- **Table-Service Meal:** Le Cellier
- **Counter-Service Meal:** Tangierine Cafe
- **Honorable Mention:** Counter service at Sunshine Season Food Fair
- **NEW STARS!:** Hacienda de San Angel Inn in Mexico, including fireworks viewing areas, and Via Napoli, for the best pizza in all of Walt Disney World!

The pavilions are a combination of both outdoor street scenes from the different cultures and shops and other indoor venues. Most have an art or cultural display that changes regularly and, unfortunately, is often ignored by the guests. Some of the displays are worth your time, so don't run by them just because they seem like "education" on a vacation. And if you can interact with the cast members, most of whom come from the actual countries, do so. They are enthusiastic ambassadors and can make your experience more interesting, informative, and fun. The pavilions are listed in clockwise order, starting on your left as you enter the World Showcase from Future World.

DID YOU KNOW?

If you want to take a breather, you can cross the lagoon via boat and save some shoe leather. The four-and-a-half-minute trip connects the Showcase Plaza area, where Future World and the World Showcase meet, to points in front of either the Morocco Pavilion or the Germany Pavilion.

I don't rate the pavilions themselves, as they're not attractions as much as exploration areas where stores, restaurants, and some attractions reside. You can judge for yourself whether they're something worth visiting, but for any group that would like a little taste of some different cultures, this should be considered a mandatory visit.

IllumiNations: Reflections of Earth

Attraction Type: Parade/fireworks

Before we get into the different national pavilions, let's talk about the best attraction in the entire World Showcase. Anchored in the center of the lagoon is a globe that comes to life as the show starts. Miniature TV screens project scenes from around the world. From there, the synchronized music, fireworks, lasers, water fountains, and roaring fires make for a stunning visual experience. Lighting on the pavilions themselves is even integrated in what I consider to be the single best fireworks show in all of Walt Disney World. Assuming that you can stay up late enough for the show, this is a definite *Must Do!*. Showings are usually around 9 P.M., but check at your hotel or as you enter the park to be certain.

Tots	Young Children	Teens	Young Adults	Mature Adults
+‌+‌+‌+	+‌+‌+‌+‌+	+‌+‌+‌+‌+	+‌+‌+‌+‌+	+‌+‌+‌+

KidCot Fun Stops

Attraction Type: Experience area/playground

Throughout the park, including a few locations within the Future World side, are craft discovery areas. Each World Showcase pavilion has one as well, where cast members from the different countries help kids work on simple craft projects. These brief stops allow children to relax a bit, interact with the cast members, and create a free keepsake from each country. Cast members will write notes in a foreign language, as well as give passport stamps that make it a truly special experience. Think of it as a passport stop in each country for your kids.

Tots	Young Children	Teens	Young Adults	Mature Adults
+‌+‌+‌+	+‌+‌+‌+			

DISNEY DON'T

Why buy a passport for the KidCot Fun stops when you probably already have an autograph book handy? Use that, save some money, and keep all the kid's memories in one spot!

Agent P's World Showcase Adventure

Attraction Type: Experience area/playground

Disney has really raised the bar across all the parks in moving their entertainment for kids from "watch this" shows to "be a part of this" activities. Matching the needs of more tech-savvy kids of today, this adventure has recently been re-themed to the popular Platypus detective from the Disney Channel hit show *Phineas and Ferb*. Kids pick up interactive devices at Adventure Kiosks, and as they go around the Epcot World Showcase they get clues on how to vanquish the evil Dr. Doofenshmirtz. Seven of the eleven national pavilions have related activities.

Don't worry if you have never seen the cartoon before. It is not necessary. However, if you have some hearing impairment, you will find that hearing the phone speaker in a crowded park can be difficult.

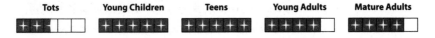

Tots	Young Children	Teens	Young Adults	Mature Adults

Mexico Pavilion

The pyramid that is the centerpiece of the Mexico Pavilion is tucked into lush undergrowth, making you feel as though you came upon it while walking through the jungle. Just inside the pyramid you will find displays of native arts from around Mexico's different regions. Past that, but still inside the pyramid, you enter a courtyard that is permanently set in the evening. In that courtyard are carts selling Mexican crafts, a Tequila bar, the San Angel Inn Restaurant, and the entrance to the Gran Fiesta Tour ride.

Outside is a newly refurbished counter-service restaurant (La Cantina de San Angel), and a new table-service restaurant (La Hacienda de San Angel) with great fireworks views.

Gran Fiesta Tour 🆔 ⚙

Attraction Type: Theme ride

Located in the Mexico Pavilion, this brief boat ride walks you through the history, peoples, and culture of Mexico, as the Three Caballeros (Donald Duck and friends) make their way through the countryside. It's not that great of a ride, but the Dia de los Muertes holiday scenes are interesting, and the recent refurbishment that added in the Disney characters make it a bit more watchable.

Tots	Young Children	Teens	Young Adults	Mature Adults
+++	++++	+++	+++	+++

Norway Pavilion

The Norway Pavilion provides a striking array of visual sights that offer a window into the Scandinavian nation. There is a replica of a stave church with small displays inside, a Nordic castle, and a 10-foot-tall wooden gnome that's a great photo opportunity for kids.

Probably the greatest draw here, though, is the restaurant. Hosting character meals with a bevy of Princesses for breakfast, lunch, and dinner (see Chapter 14), Restaurant Akershus is fast becoming one of the hottest meal reservations in all of Walt Disney World. If you're looking for a smaller bite to eat, try the treats at the bakery by the stave church. They're good, and the shopping in the store is really great, too, though a bit on the expensive side.

Maelstrom 🆕 🆔 ⚙

Attraction Type: Theme ride

Located in the Norway Pavilion, this boat ride and movie appears to have been created by the Norwegian Tourism Bureau, and it ends up feeling like a long advertisement. The ride provides a panoramic view of this beautiful nation. There's a very brief, very mild thrill moment, and some children may find it scary.

Tots	Young Children	Teens	Young Adults	Mature Adults
++	++++	++	+	+

China Pavilion

The most interesting part of the China Pavilion is the perfect re-creation of a famous round temple, as well as the entertainers who perform on the grounds directly in front. There's also a large store inside the pavilion, with a broad variety of goods for sale ranging from the very affordable to the very expensive.

Check on times for the entertainment here, and try to swing by during one of the performances after taking in the sights of the pavilion.

The temple in the China Pavilion.
Photo © Disney.

Reflections of China 🅰🅲

Attraction Type: Theater/movie/show

Located in the China Pavilion, the 360-degree theater provides stunningly beautiful and sweeping views of this vast country that is still a mystery to most. The pictures of the Forbidden City as well as the Great Wall of China are amazing and could well be worth the visit. Of the three pavilions with 360-degree movies (China, France, and Canada), this is my favorite. The film runs for 14 minutes.

Tots	Young Children	Teens	Young Adults	Mature Adults
+	+ +	+ + +	+ + + +	+ + + +

Germany Pavilion

No ride—just shopping, beer, and food. Don't get me wrong; that's a pretty good lineup! This is a great place for dinner if you have a group that wants to have fun, especially at their Oktoberfest-like restaurant complete with a band. This is a dinner reservation that an all-adult group looking for a good, loud time should make. The stores also have a great range of products of interest, even though they're not as big as the ones in China and Japan. A new caramel shop should be considered a required stop for anyone with a sweet tooth!

Italy Pavilion

Again, no ride. This time, however, the shopping is a bit more high end, and the restaurants are improving, with a new general Italian table-service restaurant (Tutto Italia) and the best pizza on property (Via Napoli). While the courtyard in back has some interesting entertainment, this pavilion is a bit less lively than others. The most interesting part of this pavilion is the architecture, making it one of the faster stops for most visiting the World Showcase.

American Adventure Pavilion

The American Adventure Pavilion serves as an anchor for the entire World Showcase. But because the real America is just outside the gates, it's not as much of a showcase of landmarks as the other pavilions are for their respective nations.

This pavilion has a few different features. First is the American Gardens Theater, an open-air theater nestled by the lagoon. It's regularly used for concerts, special events, exhibitions, and other activities. These are often related to special events being held in Epcot, such as the Food and Wine Festival.

In the main building is a small souvenir store, a courtyard for KidCot and other activities, and a counter-service restaurant. But the premier attraction here is *The American Adventure* show.

The American Adventure 🔲 🄰🄲

Attraction Type: Theater/movie/show

Located in the American Adventure Pavilion, this 30-minute theater show is live, but the actors are not. The audio-animatronic cast walks us quickly through the history of the United States, with Benjamin Franklin and Mark Twain as hosts. The different scenes recount major events such as the Civil War and the Great Depression. It also recounts the struggles and actions of important figures in history, including suffragette Susan B. Anthony and inventor Thomas Edison.

The figures are realistic, and the show is moving without being sappy. I think of it as a *Must Do!* because it's a good show and there are few other attractions in the World Showcase. While it uses the same general technology as the *Hall of Presidents* at the Magic Kingdom, this show is far more captivating and entertaining.

Tots	Young Children	Teens	Young Adults	Mature Adults
+ +	+ + +	+ + + +	+ + + + +	+ + + + +

Japan Pavilion

This pavilion captures the architecture and spirit of Japan but is mostly about the eating and the shopping. With no real ride involved, the Japan Pavilion usually offers an interesting display or art exhibit. But the real fun is in the stores, which are managed by a leading Japanese retailer. Complete with bonsai trees, clothing, sake, toys, and even some interesting seafood snacks, the store is really a neat glimpse into modern Japan and a good source for some truly unique gifts.

The street entertainment out front is best of breed when it comes to genuine cultural art from the host nation. The Taiko Drummers are full of energy and are fun to watch. A candy maker has been spotted as well who is surprisingly entertaining, for kids and adults.

Morocco Pavilion

This is perhaps the most exotic pavilion within the World Showcase and one that may rank as the neatest to just roam through. The king of Morocco actually sent over artisans to ensure that the pavilion was accurate down to the last detail. The narrow walkways and bazaar-like shopping surely make you feel like you are actually there. The shopping is unique, if not as broad as that in the Japan Pavilion, with leather goods and metalwork.

The real fun here, though, is the food. The table-service restaurant is an exotic treat, transporting you to North Africa. If you don't have the time or budget for full sit-down dining, grab a snack from the counter-service restaurant—you won't be disappointed.

The pavilion sometimes plays host to the characters from the Disney movie *Aladdin*.

France Pavilion

With the Eiffel Tower looming in the background, the France Pavilion is an active open space that always draws large crowds. The shops and restaurants do an excellent job of re-creating some of the best aspects of Paris, even if you can't sit at an outdoor café and sip coffee or a glass of wine.

Human statues startle and entertain the passing crowd, and the wine and crêpes stands are popular stops. The land is also often host to characters from *The Hunchback of Notre Dame*.

Impressions de France AC

Attraction Type: Theater/movie/show

Located in the France Pavilion, this 20-minute show takes full advantage of the 360-degree film format, bringing beautiful views of the French countryside. It's both beautiful and eye opening.

Tots	Young Children	Teens	Young Adults	Mature Adults
+	+ +	+ + +	+ + + +	+ + +

United Kingdom Pavilion

This seems like one of the larger "lands," complete with a fish-and-chips shop, a pub, and some back streets that have Beatles-imitation bands and marching soldiers.

The shops sell a wide array of items, and any Manchester United (soccer) fan will be thrilled. The food ranges from a real pub to a sit-down restaurant to counter service, with the beer choices being the highlight.

> **DID YOU KNOW?**
>
> Want to visit the BoardWalk? Use the "back door" for Epcot. That's right, the park has an entrance that leads to the BoardWalk, Hollywood Studios, and several hotels in the area. The International Gateway is located between the France and United Kingdom pavilions. You can select from walking paths and boats that are part of the Disney transportation system. If you're going to Hollywood Studios, the boats are the best option; if you're going to the BoardWalk, walking might be a faster option, especially when lines are long for the boats.

Canada Pavilion

The last of the lands as you go around the lagoon, this pavilion goes further back from the main walking paths and can be a bit of a climb to really get around the buildings and stores. But they are worth the walk, and the view onto the rest of the World Showcase is a nice surprise.

Many of the original stores have closed, making the walk to the movie in back seem like you may have taken a wrong turn. But the scenery back there is better than in any other pavilion, and in this cozy back nook, you will feel like you have disappeared into the Great White North.

A bandstand on the World Showcase walkway is often host to Off Kilter, a great Canadian band. They certainly keep guests here when little else is going on.

O Canada!

Attraction Type: Theater/movie/show

This show is located in the Canada Pavilion. The vast expanses of the Canadian landscape are perfectly suited to the 360-degree film format in this 22-minute show. The scenes often are reminiscent of the new Soarin' ride, without the technology to jazz it up. This movie was recently updated, and it is greatly improved. In particular, the stars featured in the movie make it seem more relevant to today's audiences. I often hear someone say "I didn't know he was Canadian!"

Tots	Young Children	Teens	Young Adults	Mature Adults
+	+ +	+ + +	+ + + +	+ + + +

> **HIDDEN MAGIC!**
>
> The World Showcase has a variety of entertaining and colorful performers from around the world. These are just a few of the ones you should check out, if possible. Others are listed in the pavilions where they perform.
>
> - **Canada:** Off Kilter
> - **China:** Dragon Legend Acrobats
> - **Germany:** Oktoberfest Musikanten
> - **Japan:** Taiko Drummers (a.k.a. Matsuriza)
> - **American Adventure:** Spirit of America Fife & Drum Corps
> - **American Adventure:** Voices of Liberty

Summary

Now you know how to see the future—and the world! Epcot has enough rides, food, and fun to keep you and your friends busy for quite some time. You now should have your Epcot cards all checked off and ready for that day at the park, so let's check out what the magic of the movies has in store for you in Hollywood!

In This Chapter

- Discover this land dedicated to the silver screen (and the little TV one, too!)
- Choose the attractions that will make you the star of the vacation
- Learn where to meet and watch all the right characters

Hollywood Studios is a shrine to the worlds of movie and television, places where Walt Disney made his fame. When you visit the park, you will be immersed in 1930s Hollywood, complete with aspiring actors roaming the boulevards, classic deal-making restaurant venues, and vintage cars that truly set the mood.

The park blends some of Walt Disney World's most thrilling rides with live entertainment for kids and grown-ups alike. Hollywood Studios has such a perfect array of attractions that I regard it as the best-balanced park in terms of having something for all ages. Consider this park a perfect destination for whatever kind of group you are bringing to Walt Disney World.

Park Introduction

What does every aspiring movie star need to know about the Hollywood Studios? Let's take a look at the park basics.

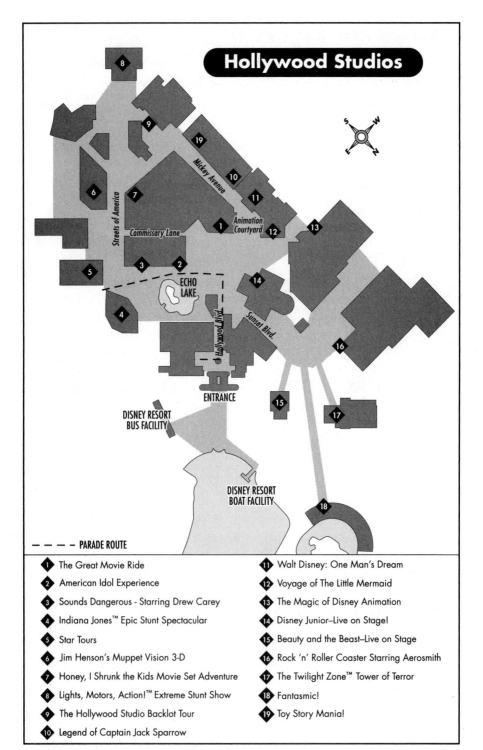

Hollywood Studios park map.

General Park Information

What are the ABCs of visiting Hollywood Studios? Let's look at some of the basics of the park that you need to know.

Park Layout

Unfortunately, Hollywood Studios (known as Disney-MGM Studios until recently) is not laid out as simply as any of the other three parks. Instead of following that simple hub-and-spoke system we find elsewhere, it is instead a series of boulevards that connect here and there. That being said, you're not in a real maze, and because maps are so plentiful at the parks, you shouldn't have any real trouble finding your way around. Here's the basic layout.

As you enter the park, you start out on Hollywood Boulevard. Simple enough. This is basically the same as being on Main Street, U.S.A., at the Magic Kingdom. When you reach the end of the boulevard, you are at what serves as the central hub of the park. They have even added a large sorcerer's hat that towers above most everything else around it so you can't miss it. From there, as you go clockwise from your left, there's the Echo Lake area, the Streets of America, Commissary Lane, Pixar Place, Animation Courtyard, and finally Sunset Boulevard. The Streets of America area is actually reached through either Echo Lake, Commissary Lane, or Pixar Place.

Don't worry if it sounds difficult. The "backlot area" of the Streets of America has a lot of directional signage and is well interconnected, so you won't have any problems.

Park Operating Hours

The park is traditionally open at 9 A.M. and closes at 8 P.M.

Must Do! Sights 🖫

- *The American Idol Experience*
- *Indiana Jones Epic Stunt Spectacular*
- *Jim Henson's Muppet Vision 3-D*
- *Lights, Motors, Action! Extreme Stunt Show*
- Toy Story Mania!

- *Voyage of The Little Mermaid*
- Rock 'n' Roller Coaster Starring Aerosmith
- The Twilight Zone Tower of Terror
- *Beauty and the Beast—Live on Stage*
- *Fantasmic!*

Dining Summary

By far, some of the most entertaining dining is located in Hollywood Studios. Although it's not filled with character meals, you have some great fun, and even some special packages for making your evening experience even more unique. See Chapter 14 for more information on the choices listed here.

Table Service—The table service here is unique. First you have the Hollywood Brown Derby, which serves up a mean Cobb salad and sets the table with a posh atmosphere. Then you have entertaining options like 50's Prime Time Café, Hollywood & Vine, and the Sci-Fi Dine-In Theater. You even have some not-so-traditional Italian at Mama Melrose's that has a subdued impact on the ambiance and the wallet.

Counter Service—Plan well here because there are great places to dine, like the Sunset Ranch Market and the ABC Commissary, and then many that are not so great. Choose wisely and enjoy some of the better counter-service dining when it comes to selection and variety.

Snacks—One of the more popular—and noticeable—snacks in all of Walt Disney World has its true home here. The Toluca Turkey Leg looks like a caveman's club, and you'll find many guests toting it around. Why we call it a snack is beyond me. It's so large that it's a meal on a stick that makes vegetarians shiver. Other great snacks, of the sweet variety, can be found throughout the park, but many of the special ones are found along Sunset Boulevard. The stores there have great crispy rice treats, caramel apples, fresh fruit, and lots more.

Tip Board Location

The tip board is located at the end of Hollywood Boulevard, right in front of the Hollywood Brown Derby Restaurant. This board shows you show times and waiting times, as well as what attractions are open and closed, for around the entire park.

Shopping at the Park

Shopping is really quite good here, with a great deal of merchandise that is not repeated everywhere else at Walt Disney World. There are naturally attraction-related stores, most notably the *Star Wars* store at Star Tours and a small but fun store outside the *Indiana Jones Epic Stunt Spectacular.* But the bulk of the shopping is located along the storefronts of both Hollywood and Sunset boulevards.

Sunset Boulevard has a Planet Hollywood store as well as a great villains-themed store (Villains in Vogue) along its west side. The right (north) side of Hollywood Boulevard has a great toy store (Cinema Storage Toys) and a place for monogramming, while the left (south) side is more for clothes and toys, with Keystone Clothiers having some of the best selection of adult clothing I've ever found.

Child Care at the Park

The Baby Care Center is located just inside the park entrance to the left of the gates. The center features changing tables, nursing rooms, high chairs, and a play room with a TV and comfy seating, all complimentary. A limited selection of baby items is available for sale.

Transportation to/from the Park

If you're staying at a Disney resort hotel, you can take a bus or boat to get here.

By Boat:

- BoardWalk Inn and Villas
- Swan and Dolphin resorts
- Yacht and Beach Club resorts

By Bus:

- All other Disney resorts

You can also get to Hollywood Studios from both Epcot and the BoardWalk via boat.

Park Touring Strategies

Make sure you know what attractions you want to see, and use whatever FASTPASS vouchers are available to ensure you get to them. Here are some good strategies:

- The crowds flow heavily in the morning to Sunset Boulevard for the thrill rides and to Animation Courtyard in the mid-morning for the kid shows. Either make sure you can beat them or go elsewhere.

- A FASTPASS for Toy Story Mania! is a great starting point if you're not a roller coaster enthusiast.

- Sometimes FASTPASS vouchers are available for the *Lights, Motors, Action! Extreme Stunt Show*, so grab these first in the morning to avoid the crowds and be assured of a seat at this great new show.

DID YOU KNOW?

Hollywood Studios FASTPASS attractions include:

- *Indiana Jones Epic Stunt Spectacular*
- Star Tours
- *Voyage of The Little Mermaid*
- Rock 'n' Roller Coaster Starring Aerosmith
- The Twilight Zone Tower of Terror
- *Lights, Motors, Action! Extreme Stunt Show* (sometimes)
- Toy Story Mania!

- Plan dining into your day here at one of the many entertaining and comparatively affordable table-service restaurants.

- If you plan to watch the *Fantasmic!* show, skip the dining package and prepare to wait 45 minutes to $1\frac{1}{2}$ hours for a seat.

- If the Twilight Zone Tower of Terror or the Rock 'n' Roller Coaster are must-do rides for you, get a FASTPASS for either of these as early as possible.

Hollywood Boulevard

Hollywood Boulevard is the Main Street, U.S.A., of Hollywood Studios, and while it may not have the same charm, it does have a sense of style. Lined with stores that evoke the golden age of film, the streets are occasionally beset by random groups of cast members acting out comedic scenes that always involve the park guests. These fun encounters are worth watching and enjoying, as they're great at setting the mood and can put a smile on your face. The street is also home to the park's parade, as well as The Great Movie Ride, which, although not a marquee attraction anymore, is still the grand homage to the movies that the park is all about.

Beyond that, the street really just serves as a merchandising center and park entrance. It houses all the key park amenities, including stroller rental, lockers, and the Baby Care Center, that the park requires.

The Great Movie Ride 🆔 🔤

Attraction Type: Theme ride

Revel in the world of the big screen as this tame but entertaining ride takes you through the history of film. Riding aboard a slow-moving car, you make your way through a giant panorama-screen theater showing highlights of movies from the very beginning of the silent era right up to some recently debuted films. Needless to say, there are more than a few Disney movies tossed in the mix.

As the cars move from there, you go through set re-creations from a variety of film genres that bring some mild excitement and fun to the ride. The darkness here is not particularly scary, but it's mentioned because particularly skittish children might be a bit uncomfortable. Finally, you return to the start of the ride, realizing that you have arrived at the front of a grand and brilliantly lit movie theater ready for a red-carpet premiere.

Kids may not recognize many of the movies shown here, but they do paint a decent history of the progression of movies.

Tots	Young Children	Teens	Young Adults	Mature Adults
+ + +	+ + + +	+ + + +	+ + +	+ + + +

Pixar Pals Countdown to Fun Parade

Attraction Type: Parade/fireworks

This parade features the characters from several of the Pixar movies, including the *Toy Story* franchise; *UP!*; *Bug's Life*; *Monsters, Inc.*; and *The Incredibles*.

This is just one of many ways the Hollywood Studios park is being made over with a heavy influence from the Pixar movies. Kids seem to react very well to this change, as these characters are far more familiar to them than many of the traditional characters you may find in parades in the other parks.

Tots	Young Children	Teens	Young Adults	Mature Adults
+ + + + +	+ + + + +	+ + +	+ + +	+ + + +

Echo Lake

This land within the park does not carry a particular theme to it; instead, it's a collection of unrelated attractions that had to go somewhere. There's no reason to linger in the area to soak up the ambiance, but there are a few decent attractions here, so you'll probably make it through here sometime during your visit.

The American Idol Experience 🄰🄲

Attraction Type: Theater/movie/show

This is hard to categorize as a theater/show attraction, as there is a significant interactive element to this show. Guests who register ahead of time can be selected to get a quick makeover backstage and then perform in front of the live audience. All the day's winners are invited back to an end-of-day final contest to vie for a unique prize. Every day's Grand Finale winner will get a guaranteed reservation for a stadium audition for the actual show.

If you are a fan of the wildly popular television phenomenon, you will want to make sure to catch this show.

Tots	Young Children	Teens	Young Adults	Mature Adults
+ + +	+ + + +	+ + + +	+ + + +	+ + + +

Indiana Jones Epic Stunt Spectacular ⬛ 🄵🄿

Attraction Type: Theater/movie/show

Seated in a well-covered outdoor amphitheater, you can marvel at the skills and secrets of stunt performers as they re-create several of the scenes from the first *Indiana Jones* movie. From the exciting tomb raiding at the start of the show to the exploding vehicles and fistfights later, the action is both live and lively. With cast members explaining some of the activities along the way, this entertaining and exciting show has something for everyone and is easily rated a *Must Do!* attraction.

Some audience volunteers can get into the act, so if you have someone (over 18) who might want to play along, make sure you arrive early and sit up front and near the middle. For the rest of us, this is just a great show to watch and enjoy.

Tots	Young Children	Teens	Young Adults	Mature Adults
+ + +	+ + + +	+ + + +	+ + + + +	+ + + + +

Star Tours 🄵🄿 🄰🄲 👥

Attraction Type: Thrill ride

Recently this ride was completely revamped, bringing in the newest of the new technology, and totally re-theming it to some of the newer *Star Wars* movies. You do not need to know the plot of these movies, or necessarily be a *Star Wars* fanatic to appreciate and enjoy this simulated thrill ride. The large AT-AT fighter that looms large over the entrance is also a great photo opportunity for kids, and during the *Star Wars* Weekends held every summer, there are even more photo ops. Guests must be 40 inches or taller to enjoy this ride.

Tots	Young Children	Teens	Young Adults	Mature Adults
	+ + + +	+ + + +	+ + + +	+ + +

> **HIDDEN MAGIC!**
>
> A great way for a young *Star Wars* fan to have some fun is to join in on the Jedi training classes that are held in the walkways around the Star Tours attraction. Jedis select a dozen or so young volunteers and train them in the basics. Much like the pirate training camp held in the Magic Kingdom, this is one of those moments that can turn a great Walt Disney World vacation into an experience of a lifetime for young guests as they are taught how to wield a light saber.

Sounds Dangerous—Starring Drew Carey 😎 📺

Attraction Type: Theater/movie/show

This small theater show exhibits just how important sound is to telling a story in TV and movies today. You put on a pair of headphones and listen along as Drew Carey plays a bumbling police officer who is miked up for a reality police show. You get to listen, if not watch, as he pursues the criminals. Frankly, this show is likely to go away in the future, whenever they can find a suitable replacement. The show has over eight minutes of total darkness which can bother even the most stalwart of younger kids. The headphones are kind of nasty, and the show only seems to be open seasonally.

Tots	Young Children	Teens	Young Adults	Mature Adults
◼	+	◼+	◼+	+

ATAS Hall of Fame Plaza

Attraction Type: Experience area/playground

This is merely a small courtyard with busts of different celebrities who were honored by the Academy of Television Arts and Sciences. It's not exciting, but it could be worth visiting if you want a picture with Oprah, Bill Cosby, or Walt Disney.

Tots	Young Children	Teens	Young Adults	Mature Adults
			◼	◼

Streets of America

The Streets of America are a great example of old-style set making. The streets re-create parts of New York City, San Francisco, and elsewhere by combining street scene sets and backdrop paintings. The backdrop paintings really make you feel like you're looking off at one of San Francisco's rapidly rising streets, and the sets look like there really could be a store behind the facades they've created. These streets have a few restaurants and some attractions, and are the home to the holiday lights show and to some of the best character greetings areas.

HIDDEN MAGIC!

During the holiday season, you'll find the Streets of America decorated to the hilt with lights as part of the Osborne Family Spectacle of Dancing Lights. The lights are everywhere and are an attraction unto themselves. If you're here from late November through early January, try to come at night to see them in their full glory. You won't regret it.

Jim Henson's Muppet Vision 3-D

Attraction Type: Theater/movie/show

This 3-D movie is a bit older, but just as entertaining as ever. The Muppets make for perfect entertainment that appeals to all ages, and the theater uses a number of real-life effects and characters to really bring the show to life. It's perfect for most anyone. Avoid the front rows, and try to sit in the middle, if you can. The 3-D effects do not work as well if you are too close to the screen.

There are live entertainers involved here, as well as action both from the rear and sides of the theater, so make sure you are prepared to swivel around and see all the fun!

Tots	Young Children	Teens	Young Adults	Mature Adults
+ + + +	+ + + + +	+ + + +	+ + + +	+ + + +

Honey, I Shrunk the Kids Movie Set Adventure

Attraction Type: Experience area/playground

This playground is a perfect escape for kids. As they enter the area, they're surrounded by giant blades of grass, oversized bugs, and lawn trinkets that dwarf them. The surface is a spongy, soft rubber, so bumps and bruises are minimized, and there are tons of places to hide. Also, entry is limited to one way in and out, so there's less chance of a kid wandering off while you think they're hiding somewhere.

Rumors suggest that this may soon be re-themed to the characters from the Pixar movie *Bug's Life*.

Tots	Young Children	Teens	Young Adults	Mature Adults
+ + + + +	+ + + + +	+ +		

Lights, Motors, Action! Extreme Stunt Show

Attraction Type: Theater/movie/show

This outdoor covered theater is the setting for a loud, exciting, and active show. Cars and motorcycles zoom around at high speed through a Mediterranean villa scene, doing stunts, shooting at each other, and making for a lively show. As with the *Indiana Jones* show, the stunt coordinators regularly interject some backstage information on how they do the stunts, and they even invite a young guest to be a volunteer.

The high-octane show at Lights, Motors, Action! Extreme Stunt Show.
Photo © Disney.

Now these are not fake cars on tracks, but real stunt drivers zooming around, bumping each other, and making real jumps. It's a fantastically choreographed show, one that you should definitely not miss.

Try to get a seat in the middle of the auditorium, right above the control booth, to get the best views of all the action.

The show is held only a few times a day, so make sure you try to get one of the rarely available FASTPASS vouchers. Because the 5,000-seat auditorium fills up quickly, these can be a great way to ensure you get in. Noise levels are high, so younger guests may need earplugs or may want to pass it altogether.

Tots	Young Children	Teens	Young Adults	Mature Adults
+ + + +	+ + + +	+ + + + +	+ + + + +	+ + + +

Hollywood Studios Backlot Tour

Attraction Type: Theme ride

The Backlot Tour is an interesting and often-changing view into movie making. The show starts with a performance on how movie makers capture certain kinds of action scenes, particularly ocean-based adventures such as *Pearl Harbor* and *Crimson Tide*. This first stage of the tour requires some volunteers; if you're picked, you may get a little wet, but you'll enjoy the experience. From there, you board a bus that takes you through the backlots of the studio, looking in on costume- and set-making areas, as well as driving through vehicle graveyards that feature planes, cars, and UFOs from a variety of new and old movies.

The climax to the ride is your visit to Catastrophe Canyon, where fire and water combine to give you a quick but safe thrill. This isn't too scary for most kids, but you may want to keep them from sitting on the far left side of the bus bench if you think they may be a bit sensitive to the action.

Yes, this used to be one of the marquee rides here, but it has bottomed off since the arrival of newer, more exciting attractions. But it's still an interesting ride and can be a fun diversion if you're still a bit early for your *Lights, Motors, Action! Extreme Stunt Show* performance time. The Backlot Tour takes 35 minutes.

Tots	Young Children	Teens	Young Adults	Mature Adults
+ +	+ + +	+ + + +	+ + + + +	+ + + +

Pixar Place

Pixar Place is a pretty plain stretch of road sandwiched between show buildings, but the plain decor hides not only a great new attraction, but also many popular character greeting areas.

Toy Story Mania! 🔲 FP AC

Attraction Type: Theme ride

Disney has rolled out several new ride technologies all at once in this hot new attraction. It combines 3-D technology, interactive gaming elements, and the still-popular characters from the *Toy Story* movies. You and your party hop into slow-moving two-seater cars that rotate through the attraction, pointing guns at the action. You shoot a myriad of imaginary projectiles (in 3-D imagery only) at targets that are reminiscent of the games you would find on a boardwalk or a state fair midway. Hitting targets can cause funny different visual gags to occur, as well as add to your score. Much like the scoring in the Buzz Lightyear attraction at the Magic Kingdom, this new inter-activity really makes it more fun for groups, as they can compete with each other.

This new genre of interactive attractions, which enable you to do more than just sit, ride, and watch, are making Disney World more fun, and you really need to go to this show, regardless of your age or love of the *Toy Story* movies.

WARNING: This attraction is so popular that FASTPASS vouchers can often run out before noon, so make sure to get a round of passes first thing in the morning so you don't miss the ride altogether.

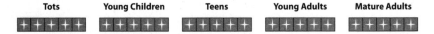

Tots	Young Children	Teens	Young Adults	Mature Adults
+++++	+++++	+++++	+++++	+++++

Legend of Captain Jack Sparrow

Attraction Type: Experience area/playground

At the time of this writing, this area was transitioning from a walking tour showing how the Narnia movies were made, to a Pirates of the Caribbean attraction. Don't think ride, think experience area with great effects. If you are a Pirates movie fan, this should rate a visit.

No ratings available at the time of publication.

Walt Disney: One Man's Dream 🄰🄲

Attraction Type: Experience area/playground

Another display area, this one is dedicated to the life and accomplishments of Walt Disney. The 15-minute self-guided tour starts with a museum-style gallery that recounts his life, with some interesting examples of his work and a display of his actual office. From there, kids will love the billiard table–sized models of different theme park icons that have been dusted off for display. From a model of Castaway Cay (the island used on Disney Cruises) to one of the castles, to the water parks from one of the Asian Disney parks, the models are always a big hit. The tour is then finished with a quick movie about Disney in a comfortable theater. You can skip the theater part if you want, although it's rather short and very informative.

Again, this may not be what you were looking to do on a theme park vacation day, but remember that everything doesn't have to be a roller coaster, and the quiet but enjoyable aspects of the attraction may make for a nice break for kids who might be reaching their breakdown points.

Tots	Young Children	Teens	Young Adults	Mature Adults

Animation Courtyard

This courtyard holds the entrances to many of the most popular attractions in all of Hollywood Studios for the youngest of guests. *Disney Junior—Live on Stage!* and the *Voyage of The Little Mermaid* are so overwhelmingly popular that you'll find yourself spending a great deal of time here.

Disney Junior—Live on Stage! **AC**

Attraction Type: Theater/movie/show

An absolute *Must Do!* for anyone with a toddler! I can't list it as a must-do for everyone because it's so kid-focused, but this is perfect for tots. This indoor theater has no seating—just a large carpeted area so that the tikes can sit, dance, jump, and generally enjoy an unencumbered good time. Stars of this 22-minute show change over time, but the current lineup includes Handy Manny, Jake and the Neverland Pirates, the Little Einsteins, and the gang from the Mickey Mouse Clubhouse.

Parents can sit or stand in the back, and getting to an unhappy child is not too difficult, so make sure you leave the room up front for the younger set.

Tots	Young Children	Teens	Young Adults	Mature Adults
+ + + + + +	+ + + + + +			

Voyage of The Little Mermaid 🧜 **FP** **AC**

Attraction Type: Theater/movie/show

This live theater show is 17 minutes packed with excitement for any budding mermaid. The indoor theater is well decorated to help them realize they are now at the bottom of the ocean, complete with caves and seaweed.

The action is fun, and the music will get even those new to the movie tapping their toes. Part of the performance involves Ursula (the evil octopus), which can be a bit scary for kids, and there are occasionally dark parts, but it's pretty much perfect for almost all kids.

This show is not a FASTPASS attraction by accident. It's not only a good show, it's a *Must Do!* for anyone with a child.

Tots	Young Children	Teens	Young Adults	Mature Adults
+ + + + + +	+ + + + + +	+ + +	+ + +	+ +

The Magic of Disney Animation AC

Attraction Type: Experience area/playground

This interactive attraction is basically a series of presentations and hands-on animation areas that let kids try their hand at creating cartoons. You start in a small theater featuring a video to explain the creative process. Then you move through a series of rooms that include touch-screen computers that cover everything from drawing and coloring to adding voice and action. Exhibits interlaced with these rooms often show clay models and artists' conceptual drawings of recent and future movie characters.

Tots	Young Children	Teens	Young Adults	Mature Adults
+ +	+ + +	+ +	+	+

Sunset Boulevard

Sunset Boulevard may be the walkway to the two most adrenaline-packed attractions in the park, but the road itself is a casual walk down the Californian farm communities that often were the hosts for golden-era movie sets. After you pass the stores that link it to Hollywood Boulevard, you pass the farmers' market stands that serve as the Sunset Ranch Market. This dining area is a great al fresco dining space, and the selection is good for counter-service food.

From there, the road leads to big rides, like the Rock 'n' Roller Coaster and the Tower of Terror, and to big shows, like *Beauty and the Beast* and *Fantasmic!*

HIDDEN MAGIC!

Need some rest? The picnic seating in the Sunset Ranch Market is a great place to take a break. If you packed your own snacks, break them out here and people watch. Also, you can wait for your FASTPASS at the Rock 'n' Roller Coaster or Tower of Terror to come due, or get in line for the next *Beauty and the Beast* show. And if you're really hungry, try the famous turkey legs sold here!

The fast-paced excitement of the Rock 'n' Roller Coaster Starring Aerosmith.
Photo © Disney.

Rock 'n' Roller Coaster Starring Aerosmith

[icons]

Attraction Type: Thrill ride

This all-indoor roller coaster takes you along on the frantic-paced life of rock stars living in the fast lane. Join Aerosmith on their way to the concert in a stretch limo that redefines the "roll" part of rock 'n' roll. The start of the coaster ride is an exhilarating explosion of power as you go from standing still to full speed in just seconds. The coaster is run entirely in the dark, with perfectly choreographed music piped in from the cars themselves. The track is periodically lit with glow-in-the-dark road signs that give you little clue to where the next turn will take you. Do ensure that you check out the pictures as you leave. Most of the waiting line is outdoors. Guests must be 48 inches or taller to enjoy this ride.

Tots	Young Children	Teens	Young Adults	Mature Adults
	+ + +	+ + + + +	+ + + + +	+ + + +

The Twilight Zone Tower of Terror [icons]

Attraction Type: Thrill ride

It's hard to say what's more intimidating. Could it be the tall tower of the hotel looming over you as you near the ride? Maybe more unnerving are the frequent screams from those already on the ride as the doors open to Sunset Boulevard below. Both set the stage for this unique thrill ride even before you enter the waiting line. The decor in the hotel further adds to the mood, as you walk through the lobby of this once-luxurious hotel that has obviously been abandoned. Even the creepy elevator attendants let you know you're in for the ride of your life.

Once you climb aboard your elevator, you're taken up to different floors, viewing scenes that tell the tale of the night that an elevator of guests disappeared when the hotel was hit by lightning. It becomes obvious that they're still here, haunting the premises. All this is told with snippets here and there of Rod Serling, the host from the long-popular show *The Twilight Zone.*

Without ruining the attraction, the elevator makes some unexpected moves, including a series of randomized falls that provide that soundtrack to future riders on Sunset Boulevard below, ensuring that they're properly scared as well. Guests must be 40 inches or taller to enjoy this ride.

Tots	Young Children	Teens	Young Adults	Mature Adults
	+ +	+ + + + +	+ + + + +	+ + + +

Beauty and the Beast—Live on Stage

Attraction Type: Theater/movie/show

This live theater show runs about 30 minutes long and is a great performance that retells the movie's plot with all the energy and toe-tapping music that you would expect. Held in a covered outdoor theater, the mix of humans and costumed characters do great justice to the songs and give you a more Broadway-caliber performance than you might have expected. There aren't that many shows in a day, so make sure you have someone waiting in line to get you seats well in advance of show time.

Tots	Young Children	Teens	Young Adults	Mature Adults
+ + + + +	+ + + + + +	+ + +	+ + +	+ + +

Fantasmic!

Attraction Type: Parade/fireworks

This fireworks show is definitely unique in its presentation and is more a hybrid of a fireworks show, a character parade, and a theater show. The outdoor seating is a bit uncomfortable over a long time, but the show is worth it.

Follow along as Sorcerer Mickey and his entourage of heroes and heroines battle a group of Disney movie villains. The stage is an island, surrounded by a moat that has a constant traffic of boats carrying different movie characters in front of the audience. The plot is a bit thin, but the effects and fireworks—not to mention the character appearances—make for a popular and well-received performance.

Attendance at this show has grown dramatically over the last few years, and with historically only a few performances a week, you must make sure you are in line a good hour in advance of showtime to ensure you get in. In 2012 they resumed a schedule of almost daily performances, and that has helped only a little in diminishing the crowds. The affiliated dining package does not reserve you very good seats, and you still have to wait in line, so skip that and just bite the bullet.

Tots	Young Children	Teens	Young Adults	Mature Adults
+ + + +	+ + + + +	+ + + + +	+ + + +	+ + +

Summary

Hollywood Studios is a park dedicated to the movies and to keeping guests of every age happy. From top-notch thrill rides, to theater shows for kids, to attractions that show how the magic of TV and the movies is made, the park has something for most anyone.

Now you know what attractions you'll want to visit and how to get to as many as possible before the curtain closes on your day here. So have fun, and don't forget the popcorn!

Animal Kingdom

In This Chapter

- Learn where to take your safari to find all the animals
- Select the attractions that will make you the king (or queen) of the jungle with your tribe
- Find a balance between taking thrill rides and seeing animals from around the world

Many who have never been to the Animal Kingdom park at Walt Disney World assume it's a glorified zoo, complete with some Mickey Mouse stickers put here and there for effect. Nothing could be further from the truth! Animal Kingdom is a whole new breed of theme park. Sure, it has traditional park entertainment, including roller coasters, stage shows, and carnival rides. But then it goes further, creating unique attractions that bring us closer to animals from around the world in settings similar to their native habitats.

That's no slam on zoos. Animal Kingdom is not better than your hometown zoo; it's just different. And the atmosphere helps make the visit memorable. Large Main Street–style avenues are replaced by jungle paths that wind through lush tropical plant life and vibrantly painted villages. Walking these paths can make you feel like you're not in a park with tens of thousands of other guests, but out on safari in Africa or Asia. The atmosphere of Animal Kingdom is a truly refreshing experience. Prepare to enjoy the wild world of Animal Kingdom!

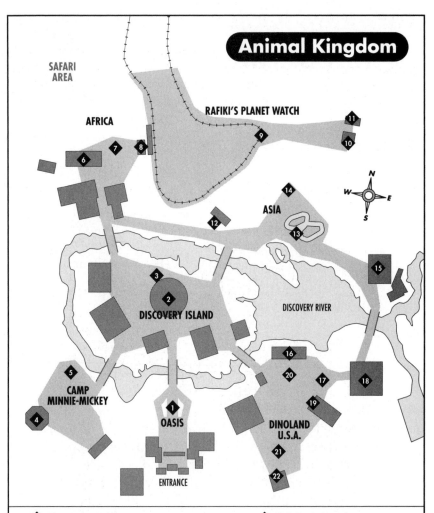

Animal Kingdom

1. The Oasis Exhibits
2. It's Tough to Be a Bug!
3. Discovery Island Trails
4. Festival of the Lion King
5. Greeting Trails
6. Kilimanjaro Safaris
7. Pangani Forest Exploration Trail
8. Wildlife Express Train
9. Habitat Habit!
10. Conservation Station
11. Affection Station
12. Flights of Wonder
13. Kali River Rapids
14. Maharajah Jungle Trek
15. Expedition Everest–Legend of the Forbidden Mountain
16. The Boneyard
17. Fossil Fun Games
18. Finding Nemo–The Musical
19. Primeval Whirl
20. TriceraTop Spin
21. Dino–Sue
22. DINOSAUR

Animal Kingdom park map.

Park Introduction

The Animal Kingdom park is physically double the size of the other parks, so knowing your way around will save you a lot of shoe leather and some sore legs. Let's look at basic park info and some ways to best plan your day.

General Park Information

What do you need to know when you are on safari? Here's a look at the basics of the Animal Kingdom park.

The Tree of Life is the centerpiece of Animal Kingdom.
Photo © Disney.

Park Layout

All guests entering Animal Kingdom start by passing through the Oasis, which combines the park entrance and a series of jungle pathways that lead to Discovery Island. Home to the Tree of Life, the symbol of Animal Kingdom, the Discovery Island area is the central hub of the park. With one exception, all the other lands radiate around this island, with bridges leading to each land. Going clock-wise from the Oasis, there's Camp Minnie-Mickey, Africa, Asia, and then DinoLand, U.S.A. That one exception is Rafiki's Planet Watch, which is reached by taking a train from Africa. Walking paths out-side Discovery Island connect Africa, Asia, and DinoLand, U.S.A., to each other, but not Camp Minnie-Mickey.

Tigers on the Maharajah Jungle Trek.
Photo © Disney.

Park Operating Hours

As with all parks, the operating hours change both seasonally and daily, and I recommend checking the schedules online at www. disneyworld.com before visiting. You can usually count on the park opening at 9 A.M. Closings traditionally fall around 5 P.M., but some-times are as late as 8 P.M.

Must Do! Sights ⬛

- Expedition Everest
- *Festival of the Lion King*
- *It's Tough to Be a Bug!*
- Kilimanjaro Safaris
- Maharajah Jungle Trek
- Pangani Forest Exploration Trail
- *Finding Nemo—The Musical*

Dining Summary

This park has the most limited dining options, largely because it's still the newest of the parks and pulls in the smallest crowds. That being said, there are a few really good choices and some good variety, so you should be able to meet most of your needs. An interesting feature here is that there are no straws or lids for standard fountain sodas, as they could be dangerous if they drifted into animal living areas. See Chapter 14 for more information on the choices listed here.

Table Service—There are now three table-service restaurants in the park, namely Rainforest Café, which is adjacent to the park entrance and can be accessed from both inside and outside the park; Tusker House in Africa; and the new Yak and Yeti in Asia. Yak and Yeti is not only a full-service restaurant, it also has counter service, offering tastes from all over that continent. Yum!

Counter Service—The Flame Tree Barbeque combines scenic seating with better-than-fast-food barbecue. Pizzafari provides standard pizza fare. Restaurantosaurus is a basic burger-and-fries spot, with some chicken options as well. And as mentioned earlier, Yak and Yeti also has counter service with Asian entrées.

Snacks and Other—Snack choices around the park are pretty standard, with some good fresh fruit in Africa. There's also the Dawa Bar, located in Africa, that has a full bar. It seems kind of out of place but can be a welcome relief for some.

Tip Board Location

A tip board is located on Discovery Island as you cross over from the Oasis on your right. There's a smaller tip board in Africa in front of the stores that lists nearby attractions and live entertainment for that land.

Shopping at the Park

The bulk of the shopping opportunities are found on Discovery Island, with a couple of stores in Asia, Africa, and DinoLand, U.S.A. You can find a nice blend of the standard items available elsewhere within Walt Disney World, as well as many Animal Kingdom–themed toys and clothing items. Additionally, some exotic African and Asian trinkets, clothes, and gifts also can be found.

Child Care at the Park

The Baby Care Center is located on Discovery Island, near the bridge to Africa. The center features changing tables, nursing rooms, high chairs, and a play room with a TV and comfy seating, all complimentary. A limited selection of baby items is available for sale.

Transportation to/from the Park

All transportation to Animal Kingdom from Disney resorts is via bus.

Park Touring Strategies

Disney veterans often call this a half-day park because there aren't as many big-draw rides and attractions compared to the others. In reality, there are about the same number of attractions as at Hollywood Studios, but many pass on the animal-viewing opportunities, like the Pangani Forest Exploration Trails. These trails are some of the best parts of the parks, regardless of your age. The animals are impressive, your access and view of them are excellent, and the theme around the trails makes the experience feel like you have been sent halfway around the world. So try not to miss these, if you have the time. Other strategies include:

- Use the FASTPASS system wisely. Get a pass for the Kilimanjaro Safaris or Expedition Everest early. The first is the signature ride of the park, and the other is the hottest new thrill ride; both fill up rather quickly. Use your time waiting for the pass to be valid by viewing the aforementioned Pangani Forest Exploration Trails or the Maharajah Jungle Trek.

- Make sure you get to the *Festival of the Lion King* and/or *Finding Nemo—The Musical* at least 30 minutes before show time to get a seat. On busy park days, consider a full hour, to be sure. These two stage shows are often-overlooked treasures of the park.

- This park can be a great place to bring your food budget back under control. Take advantage of the mostly counter-service food options to dine on a cheaper (than usual) lunch.

- Save Kali River Rapids for a time of day when either the warm afternoon weather will help you dry off or you're about to head back to your hotel and can dry off there. This is a *soaker!*

- Plan to visit this park on a day when you know you'll want a pool or napping afternoon for the kids. You can see a lot of what you want to see and still get in some good time at the resort.

DID YOU KNOW? FP

Animal Kingdom FASTPASS attractions include:

- DINOSAUR
- Expedition Everest
- *It's Tough to Be a Bug!*
- Kali River Rapids
- Kilimanjaro Safaris
- Primeval Whirl

The Oasis

The Oasis is, simply enough, the entrance to Animal Kingdom. You'll feel like you're walking into a jungle as you enter one of the many winding paths that lead to the rest of the park. The Oasis is also home to guest relations services, where you can rent a stroller or a wheelchair, find an ATM and lockers, or visit the information desk.

The Oasis Exhibits

Attraction Type: Experience area/playground

As you rush through this area to get into the park, you may not notice the variety of exotic animals residing here, tucked away in very natural-looking habitats. Make the time, perhaps when leaving for the day, to idle in this area and appreciate the variety and uniqueness of the animals.

Tots	Young Children	Teens	Young Adults	Mature Adults
+ + +	+ + +	+ + +	+ + +	+ + +

Discovery Island

Discovery Island features a village that has grown up around the massive Tree of Life. It has shopping and dining, as well as a show within the tree and some animals on display in trails behind it. The village buildings that house the shopping and dining are vividly colored, with inviting open doors that spit out air-conditioning that can lure you in during the hot central Florida summers.

The Tree of Life

Attraction Type: Experience area/playground

The Tree of Life is not so much an attraction as it is a landmark; kids enjoy wandering around it, studying the hundreds of animal shapes carved into the trunk. Play with kids by challenging them to find different hidden animals carved into the trunk and roots of the tree, especially during long waits to see *It's Tough to Be a Bug!*

Do not, however, use this as a meeting place for your family; it is so large that it is not really a good spot to meet.

Tots	Young Children	Teens	Young Adults	Mature Adults
+ + + ⬜ ⬜	+ + + ⬜ ⬜	+ ⬜ ⬜ ⬜ ⬜	+ ⬜ ⬜ ⬜ ⬜	+ ⬜ ⬜ ⬜ ⬜

It's Tough to Be a Bug! 🔲 FP AC oo

Attraction Type: Theater/movie/show

Flik and his friends put on a show, complete with a stink bug, fluttering butterflies, and acid-spitting creepy crawlers. This is one of my favorite 3-D movie shows in all of Walt Disney World, and it's easy to overlook warnings that it can frighten smaller children. Certainly, the tie-in to the movie makes you expect that anyone could attend, but dark periods and some scary off-screen effects and characters can send the younger set into a craze. Otherwise, the effects are great, the storyline is fun, and the show rates as a *Must Do!* attraction.

Tots	Young Children	Teens	Young Adults	Mature Adults
+ ⬜ ⬜ ⬜ ⬜	+ + + + ⬜	+ + + + ⬜	+ + + + ⬜	+ + + ⬜ ⬜

Discovery Island Trails

Attraction Type: Experience area/playground

The least scenic and interesting of the four animal walks, it still has some worthwhile animals and photo opportunities. In particular, the underwater viewing areas can be nice.

Tots	Young Children	Teens	Young Adults	Mature Adults
+ ⬜ ⬜ ⬜ ⬜	+ + ⬜ ⬜ ⬜	+ ⬜ ⬜ ⬜ ⬜	+ + ⬜ ⬜ ⬜	+ + ⬜ ⬜ ⬜

Mickey's Jammin' Jungle Parade

Attraction Type: Parade/fireworks

Winding through Africa, Asia, and Discovery Island, this daytime parade features many of the typical characters clad in safari gear. Not the most compelling parade in all of Walt Disney World, but it's still a lot of fun. If you've had enough of parades, this gives you a great opportunity to hop onto shorter ride lines elsewhere in the park, as the parade draws many guests to its parade route.

Tots	Young Children	Teens	Young Adults	Mature Adults

Camp Minnie-Mickey

Camp Minnie-Mickey has been reputed to be the locale for the next big attraction, but to date it's home only to a show and a character greeting area. This land is very popular with families with younger children, but guests of all ages should come by to see the *Festival of the Lion King*, so be prepared for some larger crowds just before show time.

Festival of the Lion King

Attraction Type: Theater/movie/show

This vivid live-action stage show really doesn't retell the movie, but it does include many of the popular songs from the same. It looks like it has taken many of its costumes and cues from the Broadway staging of the tale. It's performed in a now-enclosed theater in the round. Music, singing, dancing, acrobatics, and a little audience participation combine to create a lively atmosphere that guests of all ages—even a stubborn teen—will find themselves tapping their toes to.

Tots	Young Children	Teens	Young Adults	Mature Adults

Camp Minnie-Mickey Greeting Trails

Attraction Type: Character encounter

Let your kids meet many of their favorite characters clad in safari gear, as well as those from many of the different animal-themed Disney movies.

Tots	Young Children	Teens	Young Adults	Mature Adults

DID YOU KNOW?

The Animal Kingdom is physically larger than the Magic Kingdom and Epcot combined. So get out those walking shoes—you're going to need them!

Africa

Despite having only two attractions listed under this land, this is a busy and popular area of the park. The fictional town of Harambe, a rural outpost near the savannahs of Africa, is so detailed in its construction that it's easy to imagine yourself on the Dark Continent. Live entertainment is frequently found here, particularly African musicians who have kids help along with the performance, banging away on provided drums. It's also home to one of the larger restaurants, a bar, some shopping, the rail connection to Rafiki's Planet Watch, and the signature ride for the park, Kilimanjaro Safaris. Don't ask me why, but I like to linger in the area to just take it all in.

Kilimanjaro Safaris 🏃 FP

Attraction Type: Theme ride

Climb aboard long, open-air SUVs for a safari expedition through the plains of Africa. Wind through the habitats of lions, rhinos, elephants, giraffes, and hippopotamuses. It's truly impressive how Disney makes you feel like you're really riding through the savannah, while keeping the animals and you separated without you ever knowing how. A small plot twist at the end of the ride provides some little excitement, but not enough to scare any of your expedition party. Visiting Animal Kingdom and not riding on this attraction is like visiting Paris and never seeing the Eiffel Tower. Unthinkable.

Tots	Young Children	Teens	Young Adults	Mature Adults
+++++	+++++	+++++	+++++	+++++

HIDDEN MAGIC!

If you're a concierge-floor guest at the Animal Kingdom Lodge, you can get exclusive access to a morning safari through this ride, followed by breakfast with your guide. Check with the hotel for prices and availability.

Zebras and giraffes on the Kilamanjaro Safaris.
Photo © Disney.

Pangani Forest Exploration Trail 🔲

Attraction Type: Experience area/playground

A broad array of African wildlife in scenic habitat settings makes for an enjoyable and eye-opening stroll. The gorillas are the highlight, but the underwater viewing areas are also worth the time. Other animals include meerkats, colobus monkeys, and a building filled with rodents and bugs!

Tots	Young Children	Teens	Young Adults	Mature Adults
+++	++++	+++	++++	++++

Rafiki's Planet Watch

This land can be reached only by taking the Wildlife Express Train from Africa. This area is less a land than a complex of buildings that provides guests with an insight into what it takes to run a large animal facility such as Animal Kingdom. Exhibits on conservation, animal care, environmental issues, and endangered species make this an educational area, but it can bore some quite easily. It's well done, so don't necessarily overlook it, but be prepared to leave if you're losing your kids' attention. Also be aware that this area requires a short 10-minute walk to reach the facilities.

Wildlife Express Train

Attraction Type: Theme ride

It's just a train ride, but the trip is scenic and it can be a nice rest for your feet. The ride takes five minutes each way and has an audio track telling you about the care of the animals. The ride to Rafiki's Planet Watch goes by the animal-care centers, while the ride back features some authentic Asian huts.

Tots	Young Children	Teens	Young Adults	Mature Adults
+ +	+			+

Habitat Habit!

Attraction Type: Experience area/playground

Learn about the care of endangered animals and how to get more interaction at home with the animal world as you make the trek from the train depot to the other attractions in the area. The cotton-top tamarinds are of particular interest.

Tots	Young Children	Teens	Young Adults	Mature Adults
+	+			

Conservation Station 🄰🄲

Attraction Type: Experience area/playground

This is really the core area of Rafiki's Planet Watch. It has a variety of different exhibits that teach guests about the challenges of animal protection, environmental concerns, and planet conservation. The more fun areas are the windows that look into the working areas of the animal-care center, especially the feeding area that allows for some hands-on interaction with staff members and the foods they feed the animals.

Tots	Young Children	Teens	Young Adults	Mature Adults
+ + +	+ + +	+ + +	+ +	+ +

Affection Section

Attraction Type: Experience area/playground

This petting zoo has more variety than your local farm, but only a little bit. Mostly it has the same animals you could pet at home, along with the occasional llama or other exotic creature.

Tots	Young Children	Teens	Young Adults	Mature Adults

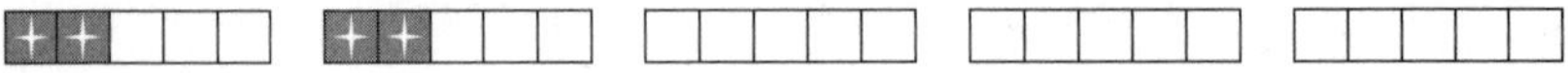

Asia

Although this land does not place you in a village like Harambe in Africa, your visit to the jungle outskirts of the fictional Asian Kingdom of Anandapur really does make you feel as if you are somewhere in southeast Asia. New and popular attractions, along with a table- and counter-service restaurant, have made this area much busier in the last few years.

Maharajah Jungle Trek

Attraction Type: Experience area/playground

Another of the animal trails, this one has Bengal tigers as its highlight act. But the Komodo dragon, bat room (that can be skipped around if you are squeamish), and ancient temple ruins that serve as the setting for the entire trail make it even more of a sight that you don't want to miss.

Tots	Young Children	Teens	Young Adults	Mature Adults

Flights of Wonder

Attraction Type: Theater/movie/show

The cozy, partially covered outdoor theater is the setting for animal handlers who put their feathered friends through their paces, including stunts, swooping, and soaring. All the animal actions are natural behaviors, so no silly birds on tricycles here. It's not quite a *Must Do!* attraction, but this lively and entertaining show can be fun for all ages. Volunteers, particularly adults with cameras, will be rewarded with a rare video keepsake, so volunteer if you're not too timid. Sit in the center, close to the front, to enjoy the show as much as possible.

Kali River Rapids 🅵🄿 👭

Attraction Type: Thrill ride

With the storyline of environmental catastrophes, raging fires, and soil erosion causing the fictional Chakranadi River to flow out of control, your 12-person boat careens and plunges down the waterway. The soaking on this short water ride is complete—far more so than on a traditional flume ride. Ponchos can help some, but ultimately you're going to get wet. There's a storage area in the middle of the boat that all have to share, but don't expect it to be waterproof; it keeps your backpack just somewhat dry. Guests must be 38 inches or taller to enjoy this ride.

Water ride down the Kali River Rapids.
Photo © Disney.

Expedition Everest 🟦 FP ∞ 👥

Attraction Type: Thrill ride

Riding on rickety old tea train cars around the tallest mountain on the planet is suspect enough. Knowing that the peak is protected by a mythical Yeti really makes for double trouble as your car careens in and out of the icy setting. Your encounter with the beast is fleeting but memorable, and thrill seekers will welcome this recent addition to the park. Waiting areas are mostly air-conditioned, and the trinkets and displays as you wait in line are really well done. It's an entertaining distraction if you have to wait a while. Guests must be 44 inches or taller to enjoy this ride.

Tots	Young Children	Teens	Young Adults	Mature Adults
	+++	+++++	+++++	+++++

DinoLand, U.S.A.

Think dinosaurs living in the '50s. This land brings the child-popular dinosaur craze to its own land, but plants it in a kitschy retro American town to "fun it up" a bit. Some think it's cute; others just get confused. Either way, there are a few good attractions and shows here, as well as some play areas that will keep kids of many ages occupied.

DINOSAUR FP AC ∞ 👥

Attraction Type: Thrill ride

You and your crew time-warp back to the era of the dinosaurs to bring a docile, plant-eating dinosaur back to the present in jeeps that simulate a bumpy ride. Of course, something goes awry, and soon you're not so much chasing a peaceful, plant-eating dinosaur as you are being chased by a nasty T-rex who thinks you look yummy. This ride is amazingly scary for little ones, even the most hardy of them. Guests must be 40 inches or taller to enjoy this ride.

Tots	Young Children	Teens	Young Adults	Mature Adults
	+	+++++++	+++++	++++

Ride through time in DINOSAUR.
Photo © Disney.

Dino-Sue

Attraction Type: Experience area/playground

This is a perfect replica of Sue, the recently discovered skeleton that is the largest intact T-Rex ever found. This is a fun stop for that dino-crazy kid, but otherwise it's just an interesting diversion if you're walking in that area.

Tots	Young Children	Teens	Young Adults	Mature Adults
+	+	+	+ +	+ +

The Boneyard

Attraction Type: Experience area/playground

A two-part playground, the first a large, well-built, and safe jungle gym complex that will keep the little ones running and climbing for some time as you relax nearby. The second part is what's really different: a sand pit that is continually reset and allows children to excavate a dinosaur skeleton underneath. Very cool! Note that there are some smaller pits to the side if you have a smaller child who needs some space.

Tots	Young Children	Teens	Young Adults	Mature Adults
+ + + + + +	+ + + + + +	+ +		

Finding Nemo—The Musical 🔳 AC

Attraction Type: Theater/movie/show

This live show is set in a now-enclosed theater setting. Based on the *Finding Nemo* movie, it features innovative puppetry with performers who sing and talk in full view while manipulating their characters. At first glance, it seems like it would be confusing, but this captivating, Broadway-quality show is an essential *Must Do!* for pretty much everyone.

Tots	Young Children	Teens	Young Adults	Mature Adults
+ + + +	+ + + +	+ + + +	+ + +	+ + +

TriceraTop Spin

Attraction Type: Carnival attraction

A dinosaur variation of the classic Dumbo ride, this is worth doing if one of your little ones demands it. Otherwise, it's the same thing you can do elsewhere at Walt Disney World.

Tots	Young Children	Teens	Young Adults	Mature Adults
+ + + +	+ + + +	+	+ +	+ +

Primeval Whirl FP 🔳

Attraction Type: Thrill ride

This one won't make you scream for your life, but it's fun, and different than most of the current roller coasters you'll ride. It isn't full of gigantic drops or corkscrew turns, but it spins you around in your car while going forward on the rails of the coaster track. Whimsical

moving decorations that cover the track structure fall into that
DinoLand, U.S.A., theme with vivid, albeit annoying, regularity.
Guests must be 48 inches or taller to enjoy this ride.

Tots	Young Children	Teens	Young Adults	Mature Adults
	+ + +	+ + + +	+ + + +	+ + +

Fossil Fun Games

Attraction Type: Experience area/playground

The selection of carnival games barely serves as a useful distraction
for people waiting for their FASTPASS times to come up for either
Primeval Whirl or DINOSAUR. On the other hand, the area is
completely devoid of creepy carnies, so it might have some redeem-
ing qualities.

Tots	Young Children	Teens	Young Adults	Mature Adults
+ +	+ + +	+ +		

Cretaceous Trail

Attraction Type: Experience area/playground

This is nothing but a quiet path through the woods with a couple of
dinosaur statues that you can climb around on. Boring, and not even
all that educational.

Tots	Young Children	Teens	Young Adults	Mature Adults
+	+			

Summary

Well, that's Animal Kingdom in a nutshell. Hopefully you'll agree
that it's not a glorified zoo, but a theme park with animals from
around the world to provide some unique and innovative attractions
to go along with some of the more traditional entertainment that
other parks provide. It may not be the first park you visit, but it's still
worth your time when you're at Walt Disney World.

The Rest of the Kingdom and Beyond

Walt Disney World has more than just the four big theme parks to occupy your time. Water parks, nightclub districts, racetracks, golf courses, spas—you name it, they seem to have it! The Orlando area adds even more attractions, including yet more theme parks, dolphin encounters, and fabulous dining. While you probably won't sample them all, you may find that perfect diversion that breaks up your week of theme-park days and really makes your vacation special. Have fun!

Disney Water Parks

In This Chapter

- Discover the secrets of Typhoon Lagoon
- Prepare for the chilly thrills of Blizzard Beach
- Find out what water fun is available for different ages
- Learn the important strategies for enjoying the water parks, even on hot and busy days

Walt Disney World has two separate water parks, Typhoon Lagoon and Blizzard Beach. Typhoon Lagoon is a windswept landscape littered with the remains of a typhoon-struck shoreline. Everywhere you turn, you see the impact of the mythical typhoon. The centerpiece of the park is the *Miss Tilly* fishing trawler that has landed squarely on the top of Mount Mayday. In the case of Blizzard Beach, a freak snowstorm has hit central Florida, and from it sprang a ski resort. But as with all good things, it had to come to an end. The tropical sun has begun to melt the snow, creating a series of water slides all around Mount Gushmore.

In both parks there are slides, wave pools, exploration zones, and kids' areas that create different but equally appealing water park destinations. The mix of slides and attractions are certainly not identical, but both offer fun and relaxation for all ages.

General Park Information

What provisions will you need when you visit the windswept waters of Typhoon Lagoon or the cool slopes of Blizzard Beach? Let's look at the park basics.

Park Layout

In both parks as you enter you are in an entry promenade that has stores, lockers, changing areas, and counter-service dining. From there, you move forward to the center of the parks. Here is how they differ.

Typhoon Lagoon

The center of the park is dominated by the Surf Pool that occupies a great deal of the overall park real estate. Surrounding the pool is the lazy river ride, Castaway Creek. The rest of the park is then basically all behind the wave pool and surrounding creek, with large Mount Mayday located dead center. The children's water play area is more to the rear left, while the reef is to the rear right; the slides are in the rear center.

Blizzard Beach

To the right as you enter the park are two kids' water park areas. The main attractions are primarily grouped around Mount Gushmore, which is located in the center and to the back of the park. Surrounding all of these rides is Cross Country Creek. The park's wave pool is to the left of the park.

HIDDEN MAGIC!

With the choice of two water parks the question is: Which park is best for me? Really, either park will work for just about any group, but if you have the choice, here are my suggestions:

- **Groups with small children:** Typhoon Lagoon, for the beach and surf pool, as well as the kids' area.
- **Groups with preteens:** Blizzard Beach, for Tike's Peak.
- **Groups with teens:** Blizzard Beach, for the larger number of thrill slides. The only exception is if you are taking surfing lessons at Typhoon Lagoon.
- **Adult-only groups:** It's a tie. Blizzard Beach for the thrill seekers, or Typhoon Lagoon if you're looking to calm things down a bit.

Park Operating Hours

The parks traditionally are open from 10 A.M. to 5 P.M., though the hours change seasonally. Be sure to check the calendars ahead of time at www.disneyworld.com. Just highlight the *Plan* at the top of the site, and select the park you will visit. Next from the left menu, you can pick the calendar. Then, you simply select the month you are visiting, and the monthly calendar will show the park's operating hours.

Park Tickets

You can buy tickets at the gate for $49 for adults (ages 10 and over) or $41 for children (ages 3 to 9). Children under 3 are free. You can also add the Water Park Fun and More option to your Magic Your Way ticket for $55. This is the total cost, regardless of the number of days on your tickets.

The basic rule of thumb is, buy the Water Park Fun option if you plan more than one day at the water parks, otherwise just buy a one-day ticket.

Dining Summary

Dining establishments at Typhoon Lagoon and Blizzard Beach provides the necessary basics and not much more. Basic fast-food lunchtime dining with some range of options is augmented by snack and sweets selections located around the park. These destinations are where you should consider packing a lunch to save some money.

There are some adult beverage options at these parks, including basic beer and wine, as well as a full bar, so you can get the umbrella drink that every holiday by the pool demands.

Shopping at the Parks

Shopping consists of the basic needs for a day at the beach: magazines, sun block, underwater cameras, and all the usual items. You can also rent towels and lockers here.

Child Care at the Park

Restrooms provide changing tables, and some baby supplies are for sale in the park stores. There are no formal child care facilities here, as in the theme parks.

Transportation to/from the Park

All transportation to Typhoon Lagoon and Blizzard Beach from the resorts is via bus.

Park Touring Strategies

As with real estate, there are three basic rules to your strategy: location, location, location! Make staking out your permanent "base of operations" (lounge chairs, shade, and maybe a small table) the first, most important thing you do. Here are the plans:

At Typhoon Lagoon

- The centerpiece of the park is the large surf pool with adjacent beach. This is your immediate destination when you enter the park, especially if it looks to be a busy day at the park. Seating is in an arc around the entry to the pool.

- Consider where the sun will move during the day. As you face the wave pool, you're facing west and slightly north.

- If you have a 2- to 6-year-old, try sitting either in the limited seating in Ketchakiddee Creek or to the left side of the arc around the entry to the surf pool to keep your tots from being bumped by enthusiastic older guests.

At Blizzard Beach

- Upon entering the park, you need to stake out your seating area. Find chairs in the part of the park where you will be most active.

- Ensure your seating is in a shaded area. You can always drag your chair out into the sun, but when the shaded areas are taken, that's it.

- Try to set up your base camp near the most age-appropriate child zone area. For kids 48 inches and shorter, that's Tike's Peak, for older preteens it would be by the Ski Patrol Training Camp.

At Both Parks

- After establishing your base camp, go to the restrooms to change and get your lockers, towel rentals, and whatever else you need.

- Be careful to not leave valuables out. They can disappear here as easily as anywhere else, and often kids will mistakenly pick up things without realizing they're not theirs. Consider renting a locker.

Typhoon Lagoon Attractions

A nice mix of both relaxing and exhilarating attractions makes for a good family time. Make sure that you try a blend of them to get the most of your visit. Here are a few of the more notable attractions.

Crush 'n' Gusher

Attraction Type: Thrill ride

This open and closed tube ride sends you down chutes and turns on a one- or two-seater inner tube. The ride is not a scary thrill, but it's ideal if you have a young teen you can ride with.

Humunga Kowabunga

Attraction Type: Thrill ride

From the highest point in the water park, you zoom straight down the biggest thrill ride in this park. It's a great way to get a wedgie and lots of fun for teens who like to race. Guests must be 48 inches or taller to enjoy this ride.

> **DISNEY DON'T**
>
> Don't let your feet pay the price of a day at the pool. Wear some kind of protective water shoes. The pavement here can get unbearably hot and can burn your feet. Select rides will make you hold the shoes in your hands, but that's worth it to save your tootsies!

Shark Reef

Attraction Type: Experience area/playground

Guests snorkel through this reef area that has a variety of colorful fish, themed decor, and passive sharks. The sharks stay toward the floor of the pool, so they rarely scare off younger visitors. So what about someone who isn't willing to swim in the reef area? The sunken hull of an overturned boat serves as a dry land viewing area into the reef. A series of portholes look into the reef so that you can watch not only the sea life, but also your family swimming by.

Swimming through the Shark Reef.
Photo © Disney.

Storm Slides

Attraction Type: Thrill ride

Although it's not as fast as the Humunga Kowabunga, this exciting ride has lots of turns and twists. Guests must be 60 inches or taller to enjoy this ride.

Surf Pool

Attraction Type: Experience area/playground

The Surf Pool dwarfs in both size and realism to its counterpart at Blizzard Beach, so if you're looking for the most ocean-like experience, Typhoon Lagoon is your better destination. The waves are not too wild, but remain pretty realistic.

HIDDEN MAGIC!

Before the park opens to guests, they hold surfing classes. Really! The surf pool can create a perfect wave every two minutes or so, and they use it to teach surfing. There's an extra charge to attend, but if you have teens, this could be a once-in-a-lifetime opportunity and a great experience to show them that the vacation is for them, too. Call 407-WDW-PLAY (939-7529) to make a reservation.

Blizzard Beach Attractions

The attractions are definitely targeted primarily at teens and young adults who want to push the envelope. That being said, there are a bunch of rides for everyone else, from the slowest of river rides to slaloms that will have you zigging and zagging like crazy. Here are a few fan favorites.

HIDDEN MAGIC!

What are the *Must Do!* rides at Typhoon Lagoon and Blizzard Beach? Let's take a look!

- Shark Reef (Typhoon Lagoon)
- Storm Slides (Typhoon Lagoon)
- Crush 'n' Gusher (Typhoon Lagoon)
- Summit Plummet (Blizzard Beach)
- Snow Stormers (Blizzard Beach)
- Runoff Rapids (Blizzard Beach)
- Chairlift (Blizzard Beach)

Summit Plummet 🏂 👓 🚹

Attraction Type: Thrill ride

This is the biggest of the thrill rides in all of Blizzard Beach. Climb the stairs, and when you think you're done, climb some more. Basically, you start from the very top of Mount Gushmore on the ski-jump course. You go straight down a 120-foot vertical slide at an amazing speed. The course is straight, and the velocity will have you enjoying the fastest ride of your life. A must ride for thrill seekers. Guests must be 48 inches or taller to enjoy this ride.

Summit Plummet is a fast start to your day!
Photo © Disney.

Melt-Away Bay

Attraction Type: Experience area/playground

This wave pool simulates the beach experience for those who wish they were a few hours east or west of Orlando. The waves are moderately sized, and the sandy beach seating areas make for a nice imitation of the real thing. Again, it's not exciting here, but it's not supposed to be, is it?

Chairlift

Attraction Type: Theme ride

Perhaps this is my favorite ride in the whole park because I'm lazy. You can take the chairlift (three to a chair) to a point almost at the top of Mount Gushmore. When you get off, you're only a climb away from many of the thrill rides, and right at the entrance to Teamboat Springs. I pick it as a *Must Do!* not only for the energy savings, but for the great view of Blizzard Beach and well beyond. Guests must be 32 inches or taller to enjoy this ride.

Runoff Rapids

Attraction Type: Thrill ride

Ride on one- or two-person inner tubes down open or enclosed slides.

Snow Stormers

Attraction Type: Thrill ride

Ride mats down slalom course slides that emphasize left-to-right movement more than overall velocity.

Kids Areas

Typhoon Lagoon has one large kids area, where Blizzard Beach has two, designed for different ages.

Ketchakiddee Creek (at Typhoon Lagoon)

Attraction Type: Experience area/playground

Little kids deserve some fun of their own at Typhoon Lagoon. Two- to six-year-olds have Ketchakiddee Creek, exclusively designed for them. They can ride down age-appropriate slides, build sand castles, and explore in the area's playground. Water cannons and other fountains in the playground provide for fun while keeping them cool on hot summer days. Guests must be 48 inches or shorter to enjoy this area.

DID YOU KNOW?

Most parents consider Blizzard Beach the best water park choice for families with children. Two different areas reserved for different age groups of kids mean that the fun is custom tailored to their needs.

Tike's Peak (at Blizzard Beach)

Attraction Type: Exploration area/playground

Reserved for ski bunnies 48 inches and shorter, this area is a great area for young children. The slides are built for them and include a wading area with a waterfall, lots of shaded seating (both with and without sand), kid-size chairs, sandboxes, and several different slides for just the wee ones. The staffing here is good, too, with plenty of lifeguards to help the kids so that while you want to attend to your child, you have a helper at the other end of the slide. This is a well-done area and is a blessing for families with the younger set.

Ski Patrol Training Camp (at Blizzard Beach)

Attraction Type: Exploration area/playground

This area is like Tike's Peak but is designed for the preteen set. You'll find lots of fun slides, basically tamed-down versions of the regular ones in the park. But Disney has made a lot of other specialized fun, including a hanging T-bar drop and an ice walk (a lattice-work net the kids can hold onto strung over a series of anchored floats in the pool—a kind of water obstacle course). This is also a great place for kids who aren't quite ready for the faster rides, although the older ones may be fighting to go on the big-kid rides after a while.

Summary

Typhoon Lagoon and Blizzard Beach are both a great distraction from the rush of your Disney vacation. Enjoy a day at the beach without the two-hour drive to the Florida coast. Use these parks as a great break from the theme parks sometime in the midst of your trip, and you'll find yourself energized and ready for more.

Downtown Disney and the BoardWalk

22

In This Chapter

- Prepare for your shopping and dining sprees at Downtown Disney
- Take an evening stroll on the planks of the BoardWalk
- Plan your nights out at Walt Disney World

Downtown Disney and the BoardWalk offer up some great night-time diversions for those looking to get outside the theme parks. Shopping, dining, and entertainment are staples, offering both families and adult-only groups some places to go and things to do.

Downtown Disney is a large complex, built in three different zones. There is the Marketplace—primarily a shopping district. Then there is the Hyperion Wharf area (formerly known as Pleasure Island), which is a space under transition. This former night club area is now being morphed into a recreation and entertainment zone that is still focused on nightlife, but of a more family friendly variety. Then there is the West End, which is anchored by a permanent Cirque du Soleil theater and has a broad array of table-service dining.

The BoardWalk is Disney's homage to the Atlantic Seaboard resorts of the late 1930s. This crescent-shaped wooden promenade hugs a lagoon that is also home to the Yacht and Beach Club resorts, as well as the BoardWalk Inn and Villas. Turn-of-the-twentieth-century buildings covered with bright lights line the promenade. Stores, nightclubs, and restaurants provide guests with just some of the fun that this family friendly night spot has to offer.

Are either of these worth your time? Which would be best for your group? Let's take a look!

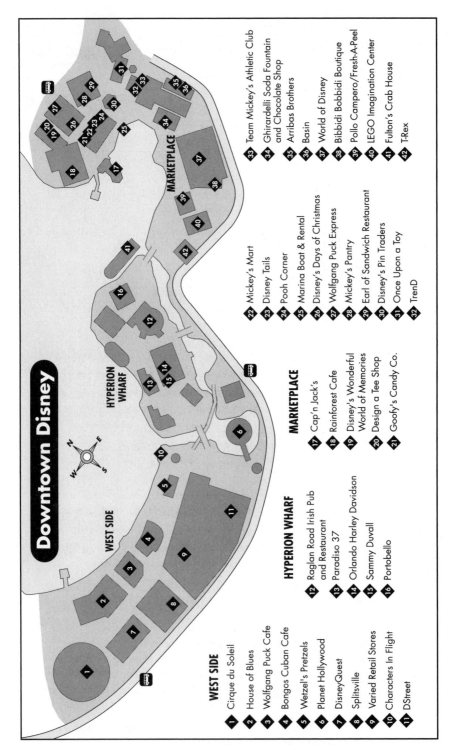

Downtown Disney

WEST SIDE

1. Cirque du Soleil
2. House of Blues
3. Wolfgang Puck Cafe
4. Bongos Cuban Cafe
5. Wetzel's Pretzels
6. Planet Hollywood
7. DisneyQuest
8. Splitsville
9. Varied Retail Stores
10. Characters In Flight
11. DStreet

HYPERION WHARF

12. Raglan Road Irish Pub and Restaurant
13. Paradiso 37
14. Orlando Harley Davidson
15. Sammy Duvall
16. Portobello

MARKETPLACE

17. Cap'n Jack's
18. Rainforest Cafe
19. Disney's Wonderful World of Memories
20. Design a Tee Shop
21. Goofy's Candy Co.
22. Mickey's Mart
23. Disney Tails
24. Pooh Corner
25. Marina Boat & Rental
26. Disney's Days of Christmas
27. Wolfgang Puck Express
28. Mickey's Pantry
29. Earl of Sandwich Restaurant
30. Disney's Pin Traders
31. Once Upon a Toy
32. TrenD
33. Team Mickey's Athletic Club
34. Ghirardelli Soda Fountain and Chocolate Shop
35. Arribas Brothers
36. Basin
37. World of Disney
38. Bibbidi Bobbidi Boutique
39. Pollo Campero/Fresh-A-Peel
40. LEGO Imagination Center
41. Fulton's Crab House
42. T-Rex

The layout of Downtown Disney.

HIDDEN MAGIC!

What are the *Must Do!* sights at Downtown Disney and BoardWalk? Let's explore:

Downtown Disney:

- Cirque du Soleil
- World of Disney

BoardWalk:

- Surrey Rentals
- Jellyrolls

General Downtown Disney Information

Downtown Disney Layout

Downtown Disney is separated into three distinct areas: the Marketplace, a middle area under development known as Hyperion Wharf, and the West Side. As you move from east to west, which is the same direction the resort buses move, you go from the Marketplace, to Hyperion Wharf, then onto the West Side. I have organized all the shopping, entertainment, and dining options by type, and tell you which of these areas they are in as we go along.

Open Hours

Although technically there's no opening time for Downtown Disney, you'll find that few of the restaurants are open for lunch, making this more of a dinner destination. Most of the stores are open during the day, opening anywhere from 10 A.M. to noon.

DID YOU KNOW?

A great way to help your kids enjoy the trip and prepare them for dealing with all the great items for sale at the parks is to plan ahead. One such plan is to give them a budget for gifts. A good idea is to give them a "one shirt, one toy" budget. They can buy one of each, but once they've done so, that's it. To make it more fun, you can give them homemade vouchers, or IOUs, that you (or they) make ahead of time.

Put the power in their hands, and you'll find that they become smarter consumers and enjoy the experience!

Transportation to/from Downtown Disney

As the transfer hub of Walt Disney World, you'll find that just about every point in the resort sends a bus this way. Just pick up the bus you need at either of the two stops, located at the east end of the Marketplace and between Hyperion Wharf and the West Side.

Boats are also available to select resorts, like Saratoga Springs and Port Orleans. Catch these at the dock in the marketplace over by Cap'n Jack's Restaurant.

Dining at Downtown Disney

I said early on in this chapter that many Walt Disney World guests should consider a visit to Downtown Disney. If you are staying at a Moderate or Value resort, where dining options are less plentiful, Downtown Disney becomes even more important. Here you can quickly open up your dining options from fast food to high-end cuisine. Now that most all Downtown Disney restaurants are on the Disney Dining Plan, that makes this an even more evening destination!

Dining at the Marketplace

The Marketplace has quite a few restaurants, which you can read more about in Chapter 15. You have several table-service choices, starting with the kid-friendly Rainforest Café. Other options include the more upscale Italian Portobello, the fun but expensive dining on the steamboat at Fulton's Crab House, and the quieter nautical setting of Cap'n Jack's Restaurant. Each has its own appeal, so read up on what is right for your budget and traveling party.

Counter-service restaurants are numerous, too. A new food court includes Pollo Campero, serving wonderful fried chicken; Fresh A-Peel, featuring fresh produce, and a NYC Babycakes cupcake store featuring vegan and gluten-free sweets. There is also a great sandwich place in the Earl of Sandwich, a Wolfgang Puck Express, and a Ghirardelli Soda Fountain & Chocolate Shop for snacks.

Dining at Hyperion Wharf

As this area develops, it is sure to add many great new dining options to the existing ones. What you have now includes a personal favorite, the Raglan Road Irish Pub and Restaurant, as well as the kid-friendly T-REX Café and the Latin flavors at Paradiso 37.

Dining at the West Side

The West Side provides a nice assortment of table-service dining options, certainly more than one might expect. There's the uniquely Southern cuisine at the House of Blues, the Cuban fare at Bongos Cuban Café, and the wonderfully contemporary fare at Wolfgang Puck's. Finally, the popular Planet Hollywood chain has American foods and gobs of movie set scenery. Fast food is not so plentiful, although Wolfgang Puck has an express window and there is a Wetzel's Pretzels. Go to Chapter 15 for more on these establishments.

Entertainment at Downtown Disney

Downtown Disney has some unique and evolving entertainment to offer. There are a few bar scenes that run the gamut from Irish pub to Miami chic. You'll also find an open-air theater for seasonal performances in the Marketplace, and, of course, the marquee destination of the Cirque du Soleil theater.

Entertainment at the Marketplace

There's a great deal of fun to be had at the Marketplace, mostly for kids. Disney has increased the level of public entertainment here, and the stores all try to get into the game as well. Consider this a place where you can walk around with kids and have enough distractions so they won't be bored.

A covered lakeside platform in the middle of the Marketplace is the stage for fairly regular entertainment performances. These Disney-themed events offer pleasant, G-rated entertainment for kids.

If you're looking for some more peppy fun, why not rent a boat at the marina? This is a great diversion for members of your party who aren't that into shopping. They can have fun while the professional shoppers browse to their hearts' content.

Entertainment at Hyperion Wharf

As this area is redeveloped, expect that new entertainment options will pop up rather regularly. A movie theater with in-theater dining is planned, as are some nightclubs.

Entertainment at the West Side

Not all the entertainment at Downtown Disney is nightclubs and bars. The West Side has more family friendly entertainment and some wonderful stage performances.

AMC Pleasure Island Movie Theaters

With 24 theaters, even a rainy-day crowd of theme park refugees won't feel too crowded. Entrances are across from the entrance of the Virgin Megastore and at the Hyperion Wharf end of the West Side. Many theaters have been equipped with the newest HD and 3-D technologies.

Cirque du Soleil's *La Nouba* 🔲

Any fan of this troupe's high-flying, new-age theatrics should be sure to visit this show. Anyone not familiar with Cirque du Soleil can find out more about this troupe, whose performances are a fusion of circus acrobatics, theater, art, and music, at www.cirquedusoleil.com. Certainly unique, they've made a name for themselves by creating esoteric and exotic performances that combine some impressive and innovative physical feats of skill. Prices range from $70 to $122 for adults, and $56 to $96 for kids 3 to 9. For tickets, you can buy online or call 407-939-1298.

The Cirque du Soleil theater at the West Side of Downtown Disney.
Photo © Disney.

DisneyQuest Indoor Interactive Theme Park

Disney created DisneyQuest as a way to bring the fun of a theme park to cities where the weather did not want to cooperate. Most of these indoor parks, like the one in downtown Chicago, have closed. Although this one is still open at the time of this writing, rumors abound that it will be replaced with an ESPN Zone restaurant and entertainment complex.

Assuming that it survives, this is a great place to go on a rainy day or in the evening with kids. This multifloor entertainment venue combines advanced computer technologies to guide guests through a variety of "rides," including one in which you build your own roller coaster and then ride it via a virtual-reality simulator. The park also includes a fast-food restaurant. Prices are $42 for adults and $36 for kids 3 to 9. When purchasing tickets for the theme parks, consider adding the Water Park Fun and More option (see Chapter 4). DisneyQuest is usually open from 11:30 A.M. until 11 P.M.

Characters in Flight

This new entertainment option, added in 2009, gives you the chance to go up in a hot air balloon and scan the Orlando and Walt Disney World landscape. Rising to 400 feet, the tethered balloon takes guests up at a somewhat affordable hit to your pocket book, at under $20 per person.

House of Blues

Although this is a restaurant, it also has live entertainment Thursday through Sunday. The R&B, rock 'n' roll, and other musical performances are constantly changing and worth checking out. The Gospel Brunch entertainment is always fantastic as well.

Splitsville

Added in late 2012, this 50,000-square foot entertainment center has dining, nightclubs with music and dancing, and recreational sporting like bowling and billiards. This is a great destination for families, but also adult-only groups looking to break away a bit from the park scene for a night.

Shopping at Downtown Disney

This is the mecca of Disney shopping. From the flagship World of Disney store that seems to have everything Mickey oriented, to the unique boutiques, you will find more than just your average suburban mall's selection of standard goodies. We also look at what things cost.

Shopping at the Marketplace

This is what the Marketplace is all about. If there's something made with a Disney icon sewn, printed, embossed, or ironed on it, it's probably for sale here. There's a lot more for sale here than just Mickey ears, so have some fun watching that credit card heat up! Let's look at a few of the highlights in order, as you move from the bus depot to the Hyperion Wharf side of the Marketplace.

Design-A-Tee Shop

This new store is the first you will encounter as you enter from the Marketplace bus stop. It lets you design a personalized Disney T-shirt, which can come in handy on your trip if you want that coordinated family look, or to get that special present for someone back home.

Disney's Wonderful World of Memories

This store is a scrapbooker's dream! It offers up an interesting array of scrapbook supplies, Disney-themed books, journals, DVDs, stickers, picture frames, and even high-end digital cameras. If you're planning to turn your vacation pictures into a photo keepsake, you'll find some great supplies here to spice it up a bit. This store is connected to the Art of Disney shop.

The Art of Disney

This higher-end art store has a great array of frame-ready art and sculptures, all with a Disney theme. Occasionally, a Disney illustrator is working here, so you can watch him or her create. Most of the art here is on the more expensive side, but some affordable alternatives might be perfect for your kid's room, including movie posters.

Disney's Days of Christmas

It's the holiday season 365 days a year here. Ornaments, toys, and other holiday-themed items are for sale here year-round. Although there's an obvious tilt toward Christmas, other items are available themed to Hanukkah, Thanksgiving, Halloween, and other seasonal festivities.

There's also an embroidery station here, so if you forgot to get a pair of ears at the Magic Kingdom, you can get them here. They're a bit more expensive and the lettering is not the same, but it may keep you out of trouble!

Disney Tails

With Pluto as his pet and Goofy as his best friend, it's no surprise that Mickey has a store dedicated just to goodies for dogs. Items for cats and other pets are available as well, ranging from collars, food bowls, treats, clothes, and beds.

Goofy's Candy Co.

As if your kids aren't on enough of a sugar high already, here's a store that can raise it just a bit more. At a select time of day, you can even watch some sweets being made. The selection is pretty wide, and there are a lot of stations where kids can make their own selections.

This store also now has a party room that can be rented. They do some pretty fun candy-making activities, and you are sure to have all young guests hopped up on sugar by the time they leave. They can handle parties of up to 12 for around $350. Call 407-WDW-BDAY (939-2329) for pricing and reservations.

Mickey's Pantry

This kitchen-themed store has Disney cookware, table settings, and some food items. While I have no need for a Mickey toaster, it's a great place to pick up some cookie cutters shaped like Disney characters, as well as some great kitchen tools.

> **HIDDEN MAGIC!**
>
> For a fun treat when you get home, pick up one of the larger Mickey ear-shaped cookie cutters at Mickey's Pantry. I use them as a pancake or egg mold when making breakfast for my nieces and nephews. Simple, cheap fun!

Once Upon a Toy

This gigantic toy store is a great place to visit, but know that it's hard to leave without buying something. There's everything from build-your-own Mr. Potato Head and My Little Pony stations to a working monorail model. Toy sections are dedicated to many different themes, including *Star Wars, Pirates of the Caribbean,* and Disney Princesses. This is also the best place in the Marketplace to get Disney DVDs, especially those older movies. A newer feature is a Build Your Own Lightsaber area. Build a *Star Wars* weapon to your own specifications for about $20, and get a *pin* based on whether you made a Jedi or Sith variety.

> **MICKEY-SPEAK**
>
> **Pin trading** at Walt Disney World is a big deal. Pin-trading clubs have popped up throughout the country, and rare ones have started to fetch some real bucks. The small pins are often given as a perk for select vacation packages and are also sold in many locations. Cast members have gotten into the fun. They're encouraged to trade with guests, so if you see a pin you like on a cast member, make an offer. Just make it a fair one, okay?

Team Mickey Athletic Club

Golf, football, baseball, NASCAR, ESPN clothing—you name it, they've got it. This store offers some great clothing options, particularly for adults who didn't find that just-right item at the World of Disney store.

> **DID YOU KNOW?**
>
> Located between the Summer Sands, Team Mickey, and Arribas Brothers stores is a customized T-shirt shop. The automated airbrush system can personalize a shirt for you and has tons of Disney art already programmed in that you can add.

World of Disney

This is easily the centerpiece store of Downtown Disney. The multi-roomed store is packed to the rafters with Disney clothing, toys, jewelry, and knick-knacks. There are several departments, organized by age, for everyone from Mom and Dad down to the little tikes. There's also a jewelry and watch room with more expensive baubles, but also a nice array of earrings that might be a great gift for a young princess.

Speaking of princesses, an entire room is dedicated to Princess paraphernalia, with the great new addition of the Bibbidi Bobbidi Boutique. While the second one placed in the castle at the Magic Kingdom may seem like a more magical setting, this original location can give the rest of your group a shopping outlet while your princess is getting her makeover.

This store has almost anything with a Disney imprint on it that you might be looking for, unless they've moved it to one of the nearby stores, like The Art of Disney, Disney's Days of Christmas, Once Upon a Toy, or Team Mickey Athletic Club.

Bibbidi Bobbidi Boutique

This child-focused salon is a wonderful new addition to the World of Disney store. This area in the back of the store is a beauty shop designed just for young girls. Complete with bright red salon chairs built to their size and other decor touches that make it a very magical experience, this store helps little princesses-in-training feel extra special. The menu of services starts with a simpler makeover that includes hair styling and makeup for around $50. You can add on other services until you end up with the over $200 Castle Makeover that also includes a princess costume, accessories, and a photo shoot. While the costs are certainly high, the experience is really a wonderful way to make a princess feel special. If you have it within your means, you might consider it. Reservations are highly recommended and can be made at 407-WDW-STYLE (407-939-7895).

> **HIDDEN MAGIC!**
>
> Here are my favorite stops in Downtown Disney:
>
> - **Nightlife Destination:** Raglan Road Irish Pub
>   The bar brings an authentic pub experience that barely edges out the boisterous bar fun of House of Blues and the *Miami Vice*–like vibe at Bongos.
>
> - **Full-Service Restaurant:** Raglan Road Irish Pub and Restaurant
>   The entertainment, cuisine, and atmosphere are all top notch and are ideal for both a family and an all-adult group.
>
> - **Fast Food:** Earl of Sandwich
>   Real sandwiches, with piles of meat and fresh breads, make this a cut above traditional fast foods.
>
> - **Shopping:** World of Disney
>   Everything Disney for everyone. If they don't have it or can't tell you where to get it, it probably doesn't exist.
>
> - **Honorable Mention:** Shopping at The Art of Disney/Disney's Wonderful World of Memories
>   The store has some great books, drawing tools, and other creative purchases, even for the artistically untalented!
>
> - **Uniquely Memorable Experience:** Gospel Brunch at the House of Blues
>   Powerful singing and great food—enough said!

LEGO Imagination Center

The inside of this LEGO store is actually a bit stark and boring, and the selection is not all that great, but the outdoor playing area is fantastic. They've made for a fun children's playground, complete with buckets of LEGO parts that kids can play with to their heart's content.

As part of a recent rehab of the area, they've also added a number of giant LEGO sculptures. A vacationing family, a shark, and a few others have been added to the older ones, which include a dragon that's actually in the nearby lake. You'll find a lot of good photo opportunities, and this is a good place to let the kids loose to play.

Look also for even more evolution of this area as it expands with the Hyperion Wharf expansion, and as LEGO opens a nearby theme park.

Shopping at Hyperion Wharf

Many of the stores in Pleasure Island were closed during the reconstruction here, but one that is sure to remain a popular stop is the Harley store. Other apparel and trinket stores will come and go, especially as this area evolves. In addition to the ones listed here, there are plans for a design-your-own-T-shirt store by Hanes.

Orlando Harley-Davidson

The popularity of the orange-and-black motorcycle gear is not just an American thing; the store is a popular stop for international guests as well. The real draw here is the clothing line, as the quality and selection are quite good.

Fuego Cigars by Sosa

This is an extension of the original cigar shop, but converted into a clubby bar atmosphere for the smoking crowd. Serving drinks and smokes, this may seem like a more logical destination as the area fills in.

Curl by Sammy Duvall

This surf shop focuses on apparel that certainly might be ideal when you are visiting during the scorching Orlando summer months.

Shopping at the West Side

Shopping at the West Side takes a less Mickey Mouse approach to things, with high-end art all the way down to penny candy.

D Street

The collection craze of pins is, to a smaller degree, being replaced by Vinylmation. These small vinyl statues of Mickey Mouse are painted in an ever-increasing variety of fashions. Other trendy Disney-themed clothes and products are available here as well.

Starabilias

The array of movie, television, and other autographed memorabilia is pretty impressive. The collection of actual costumes, vintage photographs, movie posters, sports gear, and more, usually autographed, would give any collector a great distraction for at least 15 minutes. And, of course, it's all for sale—at a price.

Pop Gallery

This newer store is on a side alley of the West End but is worth a quick stroll over, even if you just look through the window. The art sold inside is vividly colorful, and although the prices are above most travel budgets, this is a nice gallery.

General BoardWalk Information

What do you need to know before taking a stroll along the BoardWalk? Let's take a look at some of the basic information about this seaside treat!

The BoardWalk Promenade.
Photo © Disney.

BoardWalk Layout

As mentioned, the BoardWalk is a crescent-shaped promenade that lines the lagoon. As you face the center of the BoardWalk from the lagoon (facing south), walkways to the left lead to Epcot and the Yacht and Beach Clubs. To the right, walkways lead to Hollywood Studios, as well as the Swan and Dolphin resorts.

Boats also run from a dock in the center of the BoardWalk to Epcot's International Gateway, the Yacht and Beach Clubs, the Dolphin and Swan resorts, and Hollywood Studios.

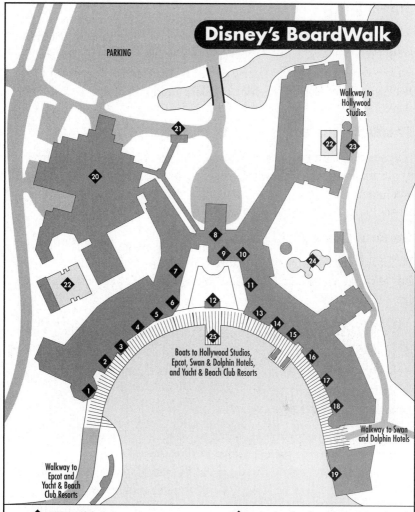

Disney's BoardWalk

PARKING

Walkway to Hollywood Studios

Boats to Hollywood Studios, Epcot, Swan & Dolphin Hotels, and Yacht & Beach Club Resorts

Walkway to Swan and Dolphin Hotels

Walkway to Epcot and Yacht & Beach Club Resorts

1. ESPN Club & Store
2. ESPN The Yard–Sports Arcade
3. Boardwalk Bakery
4. Kouzzina
5. Seashore Sweets'
6. Flying Fish Restaurant
7. Belle Vue Room
8. Lobby
9. Disney's Harbor Club
10. Health Club
11. Wyland Galleries
12. Surrey Rental
13. Screen Door General Store
14. Boardwalk Character Carnival
15. Thimbles and Threads
16. Big River Grille & Brewing Works
17. DVC Sales Center
18. Jellyrolls–Piano Bar
19. Atlantic Dance Club
20. Conference Center
21. Bus Stop
22. Quiet Pools
23. Community Hall
24. Luna Park Pool
25. Transportation Dock

BoardWalk map.

Open Hours

The BoardWalk does not technically open or close, as it is just an open promenade with stands, stores, nightclubs, and restaurants. Most of these open in the early evening, around 4 or 5 p.m., with select restaurants opening for breakfast and lunch.

Transportation to/from the BoardWalk

If you're staying at a Disney resort hotel, you can take a boat or bus to get to the BoardWalk, with select resorts located within walking distance.

By foot or boat:

- BoardWalk Inn and Villas
- Yacht and Beach Club resorts
- Swan and Dolphin resorts
- Epcot
- Hollywood Studios

If you're staying at another Disney resort hotel, you can take a bus to get to the BoardWalk, but via a connection at Downtown Disney. Or you can just take a bus to the BoardWalk Inn from a theme park.

Dining Summary

Dining here has a surprising range of options within only a few restaurants. Starting on the higher end of the scale, you can get top-notch seafood at the Flying Fish. The middle-range cost options include family dining at Kouzzina, as well as family friendly pub foods at both the ESPN Club and the Big River Grille & Brewing Works. Finally, you can go really simple with a pizza from the Spoodles Pizza Window or a small snack from the BoardWalk Bakery.

But the real dining treat here is dessert. Ice cream, candy, elephant ears, and more sweets are available throughout the area. Many guests eat elsewhere in Walt Disney World and then come here for dessert and entertainment. Good decision on their part.

DISNEY DON'T

If you're in the BoardWalk area around mealtime and have a Park Hopper ticket, don't forget about the proximity of Epcot for meal options. A short five-minute boat ride away is the International Gateway, which will plunk you down right in the middle of an 11-nation feast. Even if you just want a fast-food meal to carry around with you, you can come here for fish and chips, crepes, gyros, and so much more.

Entertainment at the BoardWalk

There's a nice mix of entertainment at the BoardWalk, with something for every age group. The options of the BoardWalk are listed here in order as you walk from the Atlantic Dance Hall at the west end to the ESPN Club at the east end.

Atlantic Dance Hall

Anchoring one end of the BoardWalk, this large dance hall is hard to miss, especially with the story-high lettering along the roof. The hall has a main room with tiered seating surrounding a large dance floor and a bar along the lagoon-side wall. An upper floor offers more seating and a good view of the dance floor as well. Building-long outdoor porches run alongside the lagoon side of both floors, giving you a great view of the lagoon, as well as Epcot fireworks. They also provide a quick escape from the music inside, or perhaps to have a more private romantic moment.

The music spans generations, but it's always lively and energetic. They quite seamlessly mix big-band hits with disco and other genres.

The hall can often be reserved for private functions, so don't count on its availability. It has occasional cover charges, but only for special events.

Jellyrolls

Do you like your music from a live person, not a CD player? Jellyrolls is the liveliest joint on the BoardWalk. This dueling piano bar gets jumping with a duo of piano players going at it, with you singing along. If you want a lively time, this is the BoardWalk place to go.

The social bar atmosphere can get noisy, understandably. There's usually a cover charge, and you have to be 21 to get in, so don't plan on visiting with the kids.

Surrey Rental

A great diversion for a group visiting the BoardWalk is to rent a surrey bike. These four- or six-seat bikes can be picked up at the rental stand located in the courtyard at the center of the BoardWalk. They have awnings for that rare evening Orlando sprinkle and a bell for clearing out the crowd in your way. There are plenty of places to ride them, so don't worry about running out of real estate. Families with smaller children may just go up and down the BoardWalk, while those with teens may take the path all the way around the lagoon or back by the Swan and Dolphin resorts.

If you're here with a group of four or more, this is a must. Every fun moment together doesn't have to be on a roller coaster. This is a pleasant way to enjoy some time together, recap the day's events, and get into the spirit of the BoardWalk.

> **HIDDEN MAGIC!**
>
> The activity level may be high throughout Walt Disney World, but the BoardWalk is a throwback to a quieter, slower time. That makes it a perfect place to relax a little. What can you do to take a break? Here are some great relaxing distractions:
>
> - Rent a surrey bike and ride around the lagoon to see the sights.
> - Join one of the crowds enjoying a street magician, musician, or juggler.
> - Sit outside and enjoy a craft-brewed beer at the Big River Grille & Brewing Works.
> - Visit the fortune teller, carnival games, or caricaturist on the BoardWalk.
> - Grab something sweet from Seashore Sweets or the BoardWalk Bakery, and have a seat outside and watch the crowd pass by.

ESPN the Yard

This video game arcade keeps all the fun sports themes, as you might expect. Connected to the ESPN Club via the ESPN Club Store, this is a great place to play while you wait for a table at the Club.

Stands and Entertainment Along the BoardWalk

To really build on the atmosphere, the BoardWalk is lined with food and drink stands, carnival attractions, fortune tellers, and caricaturists. This is part of the fun, although you do have to pay to play for a few of the activities, so check the prices first. The entertainers are usually free and are especially fun, particularly the jugglers and magicians.

Shopping Summary

Shopping at the BoardWalk is pretty anemic, but there are a few highlights. The shopping on the west side of the BoardWalk is little more than traditional Disney resort hotel convenience shopping. But in the center courtyard is a Wyland Gallery, and to the west is the store in the ESPN Club that provides for some great ESPN and sports-themed merchandise.

Screen Door General Store

Basically, you have three stores in this area, all connected inside and matching three different sets of shopping needs.

The first of these is the Thimbles and Threads Clothing and Swimwear store. It has a range of clothes that includes mostly Disney-imprinted merchandise. It also sells swimwear and related clothing.

The second part of the store is the BoardWalk Character Carnival. Here you'll find more character attire and toys, with little of note that you can't find elsewhere. Drawings of the BoardWalk done in a style reminiscent of that earlier era can be a great keepsake from your vacation, especially if you're staying at one of the area resorts.

The final store is the actual Screen Door General Store. This is a basic amenities store for hotel guests, including some pricey foodstuffs. But if you're in one of the suites with a kitchenette in the BoardWalk or Beach Club Villas, this worthwhile convenience store could be a lifesaver, especially if you forgot to pack your toothpaste or shampoo.

Wyland Galleries

The gallery displays sculptures and paintings with a nautical theme by renowned artist Robert Wyland.

ESPN Club Store

This small store has a variety of ESPN-themed merchandise, which is found only in a few other stores throughout Walt Disney World. This is yet another good place to idle away any time you may have waiting for a table or if you're minding kids playing in the Yard.

> **DID YOU KNOW?**
>
> A small outdoor pavilion is perched on the path that surrounds the lagoon. Located past the ESPN Club on the walk toward Epcot and the Yacht and Beach Club resorts, this picturesque spot can be a nice place to snap a picture of the BoardWalk or to just share a private moment. It's frequently used for smaller weddings and other important events.

Summary

So there it is in a nutshell. Downtown Disney is a large complex, complete with shopping, dining, and entertainment. The BoardWalk is a wonderfully lower-key evening diversion. Whether you're traveling in an adult-only pack or taking your family, there's plenty to do to keep you busy. Good food, some wonderful atmospheres, and some fun clubs make for a unique environment that should occupy at least one of your nights at Walt Disney World.

Other Activities at Walt Disney World

In This Chapter

- Discover how to get some outdoor fun
- Learn how to plan a wedding at the number one U.S. honeymoon destination
- Consider the fun of adding a cruise to your vacation

After all the excitement of the four theme parks, two water parks, and two nightlife districts Disney has thrown your way, what else could you possibly want to do at Walt Disney World? Well, if you're not yet filled up with fun, there are still a few more options at your fingertips. Disney wants to make sure that if you want to do it, they can provide it. Let's look at some of the other activities on property.

Sporting Activities

Just as you enter the Walt Disney World property, you might see the gigantic sports facility that is the ESPN Wide World of Sports Complex. This is just the tip of the iceberg of the different sporting and outdoor activities that they have cooked up for you. Whether you want to sit back and watch a Major League Baseball game, watch preseason NFL practices, drive a race car, or play on a PGA golf course, they probably have you covered.

ESPN Wide World of Sports Complex

This multi-venued sports facility brings together well-maintained sports fields and other facilities to support a variety of sporting events. They play hosts to a wide array of youth sport contests, both on court (volleyball, cheerleading, and basketball) as well as on field (softball, baseball, soccer), including the annual Pop Warner youth football championships. They also serve as the home base for a growing roster of endurance races, including 5K, 10K, and half- and full-marathons as well. Perhaps the best-known use of these impressive sports facilities is as the spring training home of the Atlanta Braves. Call 407-839-3900 or Ticketmaster for Braves tickets, or check the Disney site for other complex events.

Walt Disney World Motor Speedway

You can actually drive a NASCAR or IndyCar race car at the Walt Disney World Speedway, located near the entrance of the Magic Kingdom. Several experiences can place you either behind the wheel or in the passenger seat on this 1-mile track. Added in 2012 are also a line of luxury cars, including a Ferrari, a Lamborghini, and a Porsche.

All of these can include you as the driver or the passenger for a variety of prices and time durations.

You can learn more about these different options, their costs, and their time duration, as well as make reservations, at 1-800-237-3889 (Richard Petty), 1-888-357-5002 (IndyCar), or 855-822-0149 (Exotic Cars).

Make sure you plan ahead so you don't miss out on this high-octane fun.

Walt Disney World Golf Courses

Lots of families taking a Florida vacation consider hitting the links a required luxury of the trip. With 81 holes of golf around Walt Disney World, there are a lot of high-quality options for the duffers in the crowd.

DID YOU KNOW?

Twilight special pricing is available, so visit www.disneyworld.com for more information on getting your golf on for less!

The Palm and Magnolia are probably the highest-end courses, and they host an annual PGA tournament. The Magnolia is more suited to long ball hitters, where the Palm has more hazard challenges. Both get residual noise from the nearby Magic Kingdom and Motor Speedway, but it isn't too bad. If you are looking for a photo-op, the Magnolia has the oft-photographed Mouse Ears sand trap.

Lake Buena Vista is more like a typical suburban country club course. Osprey Ridge is more rustic in its design (by Tom Fazio), and the Audubon Preserve certification means you will get a great view of nature while you golf.

All four of the 18-hole courses have GPS-equipped carts, which are required (translation: No walking) to keep up the pace of play.

Oak Trail is a 9-hole walking course, and is ideally designed for family golfing with shorter distances and well-groomed fairways.

Resort guests can make reservations 90 days in advance; all others can call 60 days out. If you stay at a Disney resort, you get complimentary club rental, and they even pick you up and drop you off at your resort!

Palm, Magnolia, Osprey Ridge, and Lake Buena Vista Rates:

- Resort guests: $109–$139
  (Twilight Rate: $55–$59)

- Nonresort guests: $124–$164
  (Twilight Rate: $59–$70)

Oak Trail (All Guests):

- Adult: $38

- 17-and-under: $20

To reserve golf tee times, call 407-938-GOLF (938-4653).

HIDDEN MAGIC!

Where are the *Must Do!* activities? Well, none of these may be labeled as *Must Do!* experiences because everyone has their own flavor of fun when it comes to the great outdoors. But if you are an avid golfer, NASCAR fan, or an outdoor enthusiast, the fun here is certainly on target. Make sure you work activities like these into your schedule, as they can be an ideal break from the fast-paced theme park action.

Outdoor Activities at Walt Disney World

Disney has always had the facilities to enjoy some of Florida's natural beauty. Whether you are inclined to boating, fishing, or the high art of miniature golf, you have much of that available here as well. For more information about most of the activities listed here, such as boating, horseback riding, tennis, and others, visit www. waltdisneyworld.com or make reservations at 407-WDW-PLAY (939-7529).

Boating

Marinas abound at Walt Disney World. Many resorts have a marina where you can rent an array of watercraft, both powered and not. Many of these marinas also offer other water sports, including water-skiing and parasailing.

Some of the more notable marinas can be found at the following locations:

- Contemporary Resort
- Polynesian Resort
- Grand Floridian Resort
- Yacht and Beach Club resorts
- Old Key West Resort
- Wilderness Lodge Resort
- Fort Wilderness Resort
- Caribbean Beach Resort
- Coronado Springs Resort
- Port Orleans Resorts
- Downtown Disney

Some special boat rentals are also available that can make for an even better time. Here are some of the noteworthy ones. Times and rates vary, so call for details.

- *Grand1:* This 45-foot yacht can be the setting for a romantic catered twilight dinner or for a larger group.
- **Celebration Cruises:** Groups of up to 10 can be driven around as they celebrate whatever their hearts' desire.

- **Sea Rays and Sea Raycers:** Single and two-person rental boats, both powered and not, can make for a fun afternoon for both adult-only groups, as well as for an older child who may feel that everything on the trip had been focused on younger siblings.

Fishing

Fishing is strictly catch and release here and can be done at most any of the resort marinas. You can go out solo, or with larger groups. Supplies—even the use of a rod and reel—are included.

Tennis

Tennis is available at several resorts:

- Yacht and Beach Club resorts
- Grand Floridian Resort (clay)
- BoardWalk Inn
- Saratoga Springs Resort (clay)
- Old Key West Resort

DISNEY DON'T

You may not need to bring your fishing tackle with you when you are hitting the lakes, but don't come here hoping to borrow a racket for a couple of sets of tennis. Tennis equipment is not available for rental or usage, so pack your own, including balls.

Jogging

Jogging tracks are available at most of the Disney resorts, so you should be able to get in that morning workout. Take a few precautions, however. First, make sure you account for the Orlando-area climate—not only for the temperature, but also for the heavy humidity—and prepare accordingly. Second, consider that most Disney vacations involve a great deal of walking, so a jog on top of that may be adding insult to injury.

Horseback Riding

The Tri-Circle D Ranch set in the Fort Wilderness Resort and Campground offers horseback riding, pony rides for smaller guests, and horse-drawn wagon rides. These can offer yet another great way to relax on your vacation and possibly get a breather from the high-paced action of the theme parks. Call 407-939-7529 for pricing and availability.

Miniature Golf

You'll find two miniature golf courses at Walt Disney World, and both offer a nice diversion for families. Fantasia Gardens Miniature Golf Course, located near Downtown Disney, is the better of the two, with more magical decor and a generally better maintained facility. Disney's Winter Summerland Miniature Golf Course, which shares a parking lot with the Blizzard Beach water park, is nice as well, themed to a yard of snow sculptures.

Other Outdoor Activities

Other fun available throughout Walt Disney World includes bike and surrey bike rentals, carriage and wagon rides, volleyball, basketball, and even Segway rides through the wooded areas of Fort Wilderness. Call 407-WDW-PLAY for information on most of these activities.

Special Events and Adult Fun at Walt Disney World

Not everything at Walt Disney World is about kids. Romance and more adult-focused fun like spas are in growing abundance. Check these out to see if you'd like to add that special touch of fun.

Weddings and Honeymoons

Walt Disney World is reputedly the number one destination in the United States for honeymoons, far surpassing Las Vegas and even Niagara Falls. When you see all the guests going around in top hats and veil mouse ears, you'll start to believe it.

As it happens, weddings have become more than a cottage industry here as well. With wedding pavilions popping up throughout the Walt Disney World property, the locales for tying the knot have become numerous—and busy.

Chief among these is the Wedding Pavilion located next to the Grand Floridian Resort. It has not only the pavilion itself, but also the planning and reception facility, to boot. Other locales include the intimate but somewhat public pavilion located near the BoardWalk, the gazebo at the Yacht Club, and a special terrace at the Wilderness Lodge. You can even arrange a wedding in the Magic Kingdom or Epcot.

There's a website for planning a wedding, vow renewal, or honeymoon: www.disneyweddings.com. They even have a full staff of wedding planners, whose work has been featured on some wedding-planning shows on television.

Spas at Walt Disney World

Three resorts offer major spas, while six others offer limited spa services. Here's a list of the full-service spas:

- Grand Floridian Spa and Health Club (call 407-824-2332 for reservations)
- The Spa at Disney's Saratoga Springs (call 407-827-4455 for reservations)
- The Mandara Spa at the Disney Dolphin Resort (call 407-934-4772 for reservations)

Select spa services are also offered at these locations:

• Animal Kingdom Lodge	• Coronado Springs Resort
• BoardWalk Inn	• Wilderness Lodge Resort
• Contemporary Resort	• Yacht Club Resort

There are advantages to each spa. Personally, I prefer the Mandara for the cool Asian-inspired ambiance. However, when it comes to choosing one from the three major spas, I think you should pick based on which one is easiest for you to get to.

Disney Cruise Line

Disney operates four cruise ships, including the original *Disney Wonder* and *Disney Magic*. In 2011 and 2012, the *Disney Dream* and *Disney Fantasy* were added. Most are based out of Port Canaveral, Florida, just a quick bus ride from Walt Disney World. Disney even operates its own island retreat, Castaway Cay, which is filled with activities for all ages. Cruises now include Pacific and European destinations as well.

These ships offer great entertainment and fantastic kids' activity zones that mean parents can get some alone time, too. While they don't have casinos like other ships, they do include larger than average staterooms, good dining, and lots of family oriented activities.

The Disney Magic *cruise ship.*
Photo © Disney.

Child Services

So what do you do with your kids if you want some adult-alone time on the cruise? Most cruise experts will tell you that the Disney ships have more structured children's activities than any other cruise line. Here are just a few of the bigger ones:

- For kids age 3–12, there are two age-separated club programs. Trained staff can keep these kids occupied for the better part of the day.

- Some areas are reserved exclusively for teens, so they can enjoy the fun of a cruise ship and can get away from their parents as well. These clubs do not allow parents in but are monitored, so you can be comfortable letting your teens have some supervised fun away from you.

- For those under the age of 3, baby-sitting services are available. Note, however, that you can use this service only for a cumulative total of 10 hours on your cruise, and you do have to pay an extra fee.

DID YOU KNOW?

The Disney Cruise Line is often applauded for its civic and ecological efforts. In the 2008 World Savers awards from *Condé Nast Traveler* magazine, it was given honorable mentions for volunteer work in Caribbean port cities, for the use of special hull coatings to save fuel, for educational programs in the Caymans, and for sea-life conservation projects.

Dining

The dining on the ships offers the traditional cruise experience, with the addition of child-oriented meal options as well as some decor-related fun. I am not saying that everyone has to eat mac and cheese, but the kids will easily find something that they like.

The rotational dining system ensures that you get to try all of the standard dining options with your family, each of which offers a different style of entertainment sure to mesmerize child and adult alike.

Adults-only restaurants, Palo and Remy, provide elegant and tasty escapes from the child-rich decks of the boat. Extra charges apply, but they can add a nice touch to the voyage.

To find out more about current itineraries and prices, visit www. disneycruise.com.

Summary

Disney has a great deal to offer outside of theme parks. If your stay allows you the time to try some of these other diversions, you may find that you'll be better relaxed. They can provide the perfect break from a day-in, day-out theme park schedule. Consider them, and consider yourself fortunate that they're available!

Other Orlando-Area Attractions

In This Chapter

- Explore the Orlando area for other great vacation ideas
- Learn how you can break out of the Disney zone for a while
- See what Harry Potter has done to mix things up in Orlando

No doubt, the Orlando area was put on the map when Walt Disney World was created. Certainly, it continues to be the 400-pound gorilla of the area, employing more people than any other company, as well as having the greatest impact on the local economy.

But it's certainly not the only thing to do in Orlando. Other parks have sprung up in the area. Hotels grow like weeds, helping house many of the area visitors. Restaurants and other diversions have followed as well. While you're down here, you might want to sample some of these other options. Let's take a look at the Orlando area and what it has to offer.

Theme Parks

The Orlando area is home to many attractions that vie with Walt Disney World for your time. Certainly, you can consider Universal Studios/Islands of Adventure as the lead challenger, but others are worth mentioning as well. Some offer very relaxed, unique marine experiences; others are roller coaster havens. Take a look and see if any might be worth your time.

Universal Studios Theme Parks

Universal Studios is the lead competitor to Walt Disney World in the Orlando area, and if your group is up for more thrill rides, this might be a good side trip on your vacation.

> **HIDDEN MAGIC!**
>
> Most people who come to Universal Studios are heading for the parks. But the CityWalk has a lot of great nightlife and dining that can help make it a great evening experience. Dining and nightlife can be had at a great variety of venues, including a Pat O'Brien's (like the famed New Orleans bar), a Hard Rock Cafe, and an Emeril's Restaurant.

Universal Studios is actually two theme park areas paired with a nightlife district. The parks, Universal Studios Florida and Islands of Adventure, are accessed after passing by the Universal CityWalk. A one-day ticket to the two parks starts at $112 ($104 for children age 3–9), but you can always find specials that also give you access to other parks, like Wet 'n Wild. Make sure you check the website (www.universalorlando.com) for current prices and these special discount packages.

What's the appeal of these parks? Let's take a look.

Universal Studios Florida

Universal Studios Florida is the original Universal park in the Florida area, and it has a lot of good thrill rides. Designed to look like the backlot of a movie production facility, the park has strong movie tie-ins for all its rides. The lands within the park are not so easily defined but, as you go clockwise from the entrance, are divided into Production Central, New York, San Francisco/Amity, World Expo, Kid Zone, and Hollywood. Universal definitely aims for a slightly older crowd than the Magic Kingdom. Most of the thrills are ride simulators, but there are also some kid rides to be found.

Islands of Adventure

This park kicks up the excitement with more roller coasters than in Universal Studios. Five lands surround the lagoon in the center of the park (clockwise from the entrance): Marvel Super Hero Island, Toon Lagoon, Jurassic Park, The Lost Continent, and Seuss Landing.

But the real draw now is the Wizarding World of Harry Potter. This new land has been well-themed to the Hogwart's school grounds and nearby Hogsmeade, even down to serving butterbeer. The main attraction here is Harry Potter and the Forbidden Journey, which walks you through the castle, then sends you soaring around the castle through some innovative technology. A more tame roller coaster, Flight of the Hippogriff, gives younger fans something to ride. And for those thrill enthusiasts there's the Dragon Challenge, a full-bore roller coaster that was re-themed to this exciting new world.

Be aware that lines into this land are still very robust, so waiting is a requirement. But if you are a fan of the book and movies series, you will likely find it worth the wait. One note, however: The lead ride has been plagued with complaints surrounding the ride vehicles. If you are larger in size you might find that you have to skip this attraction due to tighter seating. Adjustments have been made, but at times there have been restrictions for riders if they were 6', 3" tall or taller, or had chests of 46" or larger.

If you have older teens who you think might yearn for some more up-tempo thrills, or especially if you have an all-adult group similarly inclined, you should consider at least a day at Universal Studios Florida and Islands of Adventure, with an emphasis on the latter park.

Sea World Parks

Sea World has grown into a multiple-park venue, with a water park, an aquatic life experience park, and the long-popular Sea World main park. Tickets can be ordered in advance at www.seaworld.com or 1-800-4ADVENTURE (423-8368). Ticket combinations with other parks such as Busch Gardens are also available, so look into those, too.

Sea World Adventure Park

This aquatic theme park gives visitors up-close and entertaining access to the wonders of the ocean. Long-popular shows with the famed killer whale Shamu, as well as manatees, dolphins, and other displays of sea life from around the world, are entertaining and educational all at once. There are also a few rides, such as the Kraken roller coaster and the Journey to Atlantis log flume. One day tickets are $80 for adults ($72 for children), with package combinations with Busch Gardens in Tampa Bay and Aquatica available.

Discovery Cove

This attraction is not a theme park at all. Discovery Cove is a relatively new addition to the Orlando area that offers you a chance to swim with the dolphins. One of the Anheuser-Busch properties (like Sea World and Busch Gardens), it's located next to Sea World. Reservations are required, as only 1,000 guests are allowed in at a time. Inside, guests can have a 30-minute session with dolphins, swim among rays in their own lagoon, or snorkel in a coral reef and along a lazy tropical river. Also inside are an aviary and a resort pool, all in a lush jungle setting that provides a very rare and relaxing experience. Tickets range from $229 to $289, depending on the time of year. Less expensive tickets without the dolphin experience are available. Reservations can be made at www.discoverycove.com or 1-877-4-DISCOVERY (1-877-434-7268).

Aquatica, Sea World's Water Park

This water park often has ticket packages that combine with Sea World and Busch Gardens. This fairly new park has many of the standards that you would expect from a water park, like a wave pool, a lazy river, and lots of extreme water slides. One-day tickets start at $42 ($36 for children age 3–9), and are, as with all others parks listed here, available as part of several multi-park ticket options.

Wet 'n Wild

The Wet 'n Wild water park takes what you get at the two Disney water parks and thrills it up a bit. Some of the better attractions range from the thrill rides like Blue Niagara to multi-person rides such as the Black Hole and Disco H_2O, that are very inventive and fun for a group. The kids' areas are toned-down safe zones. Single-day tickets run $48 (adult) and $42 (child).

LEGOLAND Florida

Located on the historic Cypress Gardens property, this LEGO-inspired park is growing quickly, and already has enough attractions to warrant a day's time. If you want to get away, but think your kids might be a bit too young for Universal Studios, this could be a great destination.

International Drive

There's no nice way to put it: International Drive is a crazed, over-developed avenue of stores, hotels, restaurants, and attractions. It's a great place to go if you're ready to get away from the theme park haze or if you're looking for something different for dinner. It is also likely where you will stay if your reason for visiting is a convention at the Orange County Convention Center. Just make sure that you plan enough time to get there, as the traffic congestion is significant, especially in the evening.

Summary

Now you have an idea about what lies outside the Disney enclave. Don't feel like you have to stay on Disney property all the time. As long as you're prepared, there's no reason why this shouldn't be a great addition to your vacation experience.

Itineraries

The itineraries included here are tools to help you navigate the parks. Each provides a general path through the parks, based on different kinds of travel groups. How do you use them?

> Step 1: Put a check in the boxes of attractions that you want to try.

> Step 2: Put an X in the boxes of attractions you want to avoid.

> Step 3: When you enter the park, go down the checklist, visiting each land in order, and hitting those attractions checked.

> Step 4: When you've hit all the rides you want to visit in a specific land, if you still have time, you can try some of the other attractions that remain on the card.

Those rides that I suggest you hit are numbered in parentheses. I also show the other options, by wherever you are in the park. Fireworks and parades are listed but not put into the itinerary order because they are scheduled events, and you may have to jump out of your plan at a certain time to watch. When you're done making your plans, simply cut them out and take them with you!

LEGEND

Must Do!	🔲
FASTPASS	FP
Air Conditioned Area	AC
Height Requirement	👫
Significant Darkness	👀

Magic Kingdom with Children Itinerary

☐ Make your way through Main Street, U.S.A., to the park's center hub.

☐ Pick up FASTPASS vouchers for any of the rides that most appeal to you. Redeem them whenever they become valid, then seek out your next FASTPASS.

ADVENTURELAND

☐ (1) Pirates of the Caribbean **AC**

☐ (2) The Magic Carpets of Aladdin

☐ (3) Jungle Cruise **FP**

☐ (4) *The Enchanted Tiki Room* **AC** **∞**

Other Choices

☐ Swiss Family Treehouse

FRONTIERLAND

☐ (5) *Country Bear Jamboree* **AC**

Other Choices

☐ Splash Mountain **FP** **♿** -40"

☐ Big Thunder Mountain Railroad **FP** **♿** -40"

☐ Frontierland Shootin' Arcade

☐ Tom Sawyer Island

LIBERTY SQUARE

Other Choices

☐ *The Hall of Presidents* **AC**

☐ The Haunted Mansion **FP** **AC**

☐ Liberty Square Riverboat

FANTASYLAND

☐ (6) *Mickey's PhilharMagic* **♪** **FP** **AC**

☐ (7) "it's a small world" **♪** **AC**

☐ (8) Cinderella Castle **♪**

☐ (9) Dumbo the Flying Elephant

FANTASYLAND *continued*

☐ (10) Peter Pan's Flight **♪** **FP** **AC** **∞**

☐ (11) The Many Adventures of Winnie the Pooh **FP** **AC** **∞**

☐ (12) The Barnstormer **♿** -35"

Other Choices

☐ *Dream Along with Mickey*

☐ Mad Tea Party

☐ Prince Charming Regal Carrousel

TOMORROWLAND

☐ (13) Buzz Lightyear's Space Ranger Spin **♪** **FP** **AC**

☐ (14) *Monsters, Inc. Comedy Club* **AC**

☐ (15) Tomorrowland Speedway **♿** -54" (alone)

Other Choices

☐ Stitch's Great Escape! **FP** **AC** **∞** **♿** -40"

☐ Space Mountain **♪** **FP** **AC** **∞** **♿** -44"

☐ TTA People Mover

☐ Astro Orbiter

☐ Walt Disney's Carousel of Progress **AC**

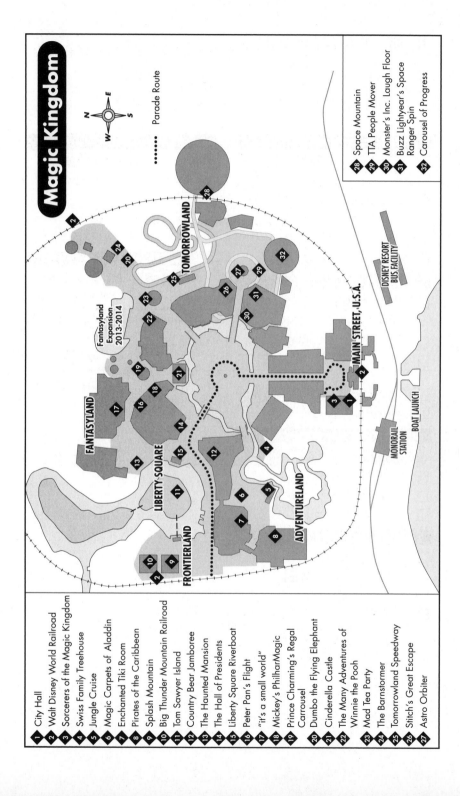

Magic Kingdom

N W E S

•••••• Parade Route

1. City Hall
2. Walt Disney World Railroad
3. Sorcerers of the Magic Kingdom
4. Swiss Family Treehouse
5. Jungle Cruise
6. Magic Carpets of Aladdin
7. Enchanted Tiki Room
8. Pirates of the Caribbean
9. Splash Mountain
10. Big Thunder Mountain Railroad
11. Tom Sawyer Island
12. Country Bear Jamboree
13. The Haunted Mansion
14. The Hall of Presidents
15. Liberty Square Riverboat
16. Peter Pan's Flight
17. "it's a small world"
18. Mickey's PhilharMagic
19. Prince Charming's Regal Carrousel
20. Dumbo the Flying Elephant
21. Cinderella Castle
22. The Many Adventures of Winnie the Pooh
23. Mad Tea Party
24. The Barnstormer
25. Tomorrowland Speedway
26. Stitch's Great Escape
27. Astro Orbiter
28. Space Mountain
29. TTA People Mover
30. Monster's Inc. Laugh Floor
31. Buzz Lightyear's Space Ranger Spin
32. Carousel of Progress

FANTASYLAND

TOMORROWLAND

LIBERTY SQUARE

FRONTIERLAND

ADVENTURELAND

MAIN STREET, U.S.A.

Fantasyland Expansion 2013-2014

DISNEY RESORT BUS FACILITY

MONORAIL STATION

BOAT LAUNCH

Magic Kingdom with Adults and Teens Itinerary

☐ Make your way through Main Street, U.S.A., to the park's center hub.

☐ Pick up FASTPASS vouchers for any of the rides that most appeal to you. Redeem them whenever they become valid, then seek out your next FASTPASS.

TOMORROWLAND

☐ (1) Space Mountain 🔵 FP AC ∞ 👫 -44"

☐ (2) Buzz Lightyear's Space Ranger Spin 🔵 FP AC

☐ (3) *Monsters, Inc. Comedy Club* AC

☐ (4) Stitch's Great Escape! FP AC ∞ 👫 -40"

Other Choices

☐ Tomorrowland Speedway 👫 -54" (alone)

☐ TTA People Mover

☐ Astro Orbiter

☐ Walt Disney's Carousel of Progress AC

ADVENTURELAND

☐ (5) Pirates of the Caribbean AC

☐ (6) Jungle Cruise FP

☐ (7) *The Enchanted Tiki Room* AC ∞

Other Choices

☐ The Magic Carpets of Aladdin

☐ Swiss Family Treehouse

FRONTIERLAND

☐ (8) Big Thunder Mountain Railroad FP 👫 -40"

☐ (9) Splash Mountain FP 👫 -40"

Other Choices

☐ Frontierland Shootin' Arcade

☐ Tom Sawyer Island

☐ *Country Bear Jamboree* AC

LIBERTY SQUARE

☐ (10) The Haunted Mansion FP AC

☐ (11) *The Hall of Presidents* AC

Other Choices

☐ Liberty Square Riverboat

FANTASYLAND

☐ (12) *Mickey's PhilharMagic* 🔵 FP AC

☐ (13) "it's a small world" 🔵 AC

Other Choices

☐ Dumbo the Flying Elephant

☐ Peter Pan's Flight 🔵 FP AC ∞

☐ Cinderella Castle 🔵

☐ *Dream Along with Mickey*

☐ Mad Tea Party

☐ The Many Adventures of Winnie the Pooh FP AC ∞

☐ Prince Charming Regal Carrousel

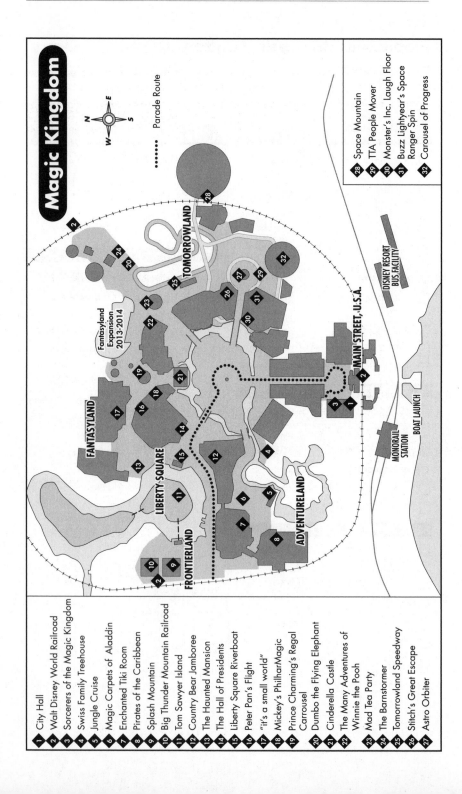

Magic Kingdom

Parade Route

1. City Hall
2. Walt Disney World Railroad
3. Sorcerers of the Magic Kingdom
4. Swiss Family Treehouse
5. Jungle Cruise
6. Magic Carpets of Aladdin
7. Enchanted Tiki Room
8. Pirates of the Caribbean
9. Splash Mountain
10. Big Thunder Mountain Railroad
11. Tom Sawyer Island
12. Country Bear Jamboree
13. The Haunted Mansion
14. The Hall of Presidents
15. Liberty Square Riverboat
16. Peter Pan's Flight
17. "it's a small world"
18. Mickey's PhilharMagic
19. Prince Charming's Regal Carrousel
20. Dumbo the Flying Elephant
21. Cinderella Castle
22. The Many Adventures of Winnie the Pooh
23. Mad Tea Party
24. The Barnstormer
25. Tomorrowland Speedway
26. Stitch's Great Escape
27. Astro Orbiter
28. Space Mountain
29. TTA People Mover
30. Monster's Inc. Laugh Floor
31. Buzz Lightyear's Space Ranger Spin
32. Carousel of Progress

FANTASYLAND

LIBERTY SQUARE

FRONTIERLAND

ADVENTURELAND

TOMORROWLAND

MAIN STREET, U.S.A.

Fantasyland Expansion 2013-2014

MONORAIL STATION

BOAT LAUNCH

DISNEY RESORT BUS FACILITY

Epcot with Children Itinerary

☐ Pick up FASTPASS vouchers for any Future World attraction that most appeals to you. Redeem them whenever they become valid, then seek out your next FASTPASS.

FUTURE WORLD PAVILIONS & ATTRACTIONS

☐ (1) The Seas with Nemo & Friends **AC**

☐ (2) The Seas with Nemo & Friends Pavilion **AC**

☐ (3) *Turtle Talk with Crush* **AC**

☐ (4) Living with the Land **FP** **AC**

☐ (5) Innoventions East & West **AC**

☐ (6) Spaceship Earth **AC** **OO**

☐ (7) Ellen's Energy Adventure **AC**

☐ (8) Mission: SPACE Advanced Training Labs **AC**

Other Choices

☐ Mission: SPACE **FP** **AC** **fi** -44"

☐ Test Track **FP** **AC** **fi** -40"

☐ Soarin' **FP** **AC** **fi** -40"

☐ *The Circle of Life* **AC**

☐ *Honey, I Shrunk the Audience* **FP** **AC**

☐ Journey into Imagination with Figment **AC**

☐ Imageworks **AC**

WORLD SHOWCASE PAVILIONS & ATTRACTIONS

☐ (9) Agent P's World Showcase Adventure **▨**

☐ (10) KidCot Fun Stop at Mexico Pavilion

☐ (11) KidCot Fun Stop at Norway Pavilion

☐ (12) KidCot Fun Stop at China Pavilion

☐ (13) *Reflections of China* **AC**

☐ (14) KidCot Fun Stop at Germany Pavilion

☐ (15) KidCot Fun Stop at Italy Pavilion

☐ (16) KidCot Fun Stop at American Adventure Pavilion

☐ (17) *The American Adventure* **AC**

☐ (18) KidCot Fun Stop at Japan Pavilion

☐ (19) KidCot Fun Stop at Morocco Pavilion

☐ (20) KidCot Fun Stop at France Pavilion

☐ (21) *Impressions de France* **AC**

☐ (22) KidCot Fun Stop at United Kingdom Pavilion

☐ (23) KidCot Fun Stop at Canada Pavilion

☐ (24) *O Canada!* **AC**

Other Choices

☐ *IllumiNations*

☐ Gran Fiesta Tour **AC**

☐ Maelstrom **FP** **AC**

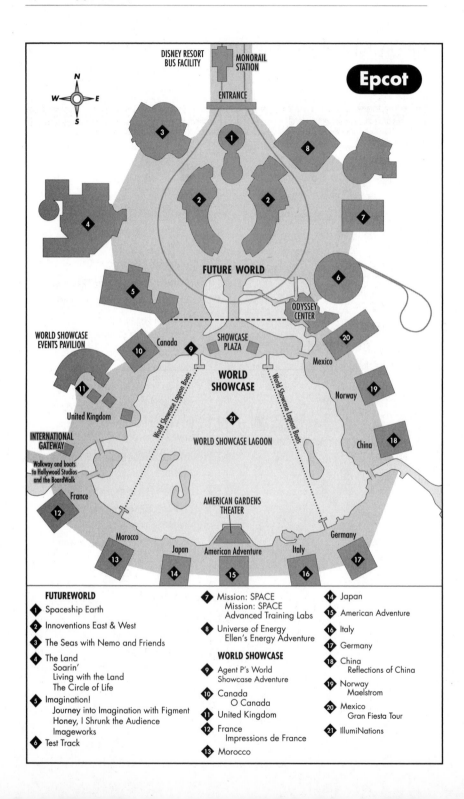

Epcot

DISNEY RESORT
BUS FACILITY

MONORAIL
STATION

ENTRANCE

N
W · E
S

FUTURE WORLD

ODYSSEY
CENTER

WORLD SHOWCASE
EVENTS PAVILION

SHOWCASE
PLAZA

Canada

WORLD
SHOWCASE

Mexico

World Showcase Lagoon Boats

World Showcase Lagoon Boats

Norway

United Kingdom

INTERNATIONAL
GATEWAY

Walkway and boats
to Hollywood Studios
and the BoardWalk

WORLD SHOWCASE LAGOON

China

France

AMERICAN GARDENS
THEATER

Morocco

Germany

Japan

American Adventure

Italy

FUTUREWORLD

1. Spaceship Earth
2. Innoventions East & West
3. The Seas with Nemo and Friends
4. The Land
   Soarin'
   Living with the Land
   The Circle of Life
5. Imagination!
   Journey into Imagination with Figment
   Honey, I Shrunk the Audience
   Imageworks
6. Test Track

7. Mission: SPACE
   Mission: SPACE
   Advanced Training Labs
8. Universe of Energy
   Ellen's Energy Adventure

WORLD SHOWCASE

9. Agent P's World
   Showcase Adventure
10. Canada
    O Canada
11. United Kingdom
12. France
    Impressions de France
13. Morocco

14. Japan
15. American Adventure
16. Italy
17. Germany
18. China
    Reflections of China
19. Norway
    Maelstrom
20. Mexico
    Gran Fiesta Tour
21. IllumiNations

Epcot with Adults and Teens Itinerary

☐ Pick up FASTPASS vouchers for any Future World attraction that most appeals to you. Redeem them whenever they become valid, then seek out your next FASTPASS.

FUTURE WORLD PAVILIONS & ATTRACTIONS

☐ (1) Mission: SPACE **FP** **AC** **ft** -44"

☐ (2) Test Track **FP** **AC** **ft** -40"

☐ (3) Soarin' **FP** **AC** **ft** -40"

☐ (4) Living with the Land **FP** **AC**

☐ (5) The Seas with Nemo & Friends Pavilion **AC**

☐ (6) Spaceship Earth **AC** **OO**

☐ (7) Ellen's Energy Adventure **AC**

Other Choices

☐ Innoventions East & West **AC**

☐ *Turtle Talk with Crush* **AC**

☐ Mission: SPACE Advanced Training Labs **AC**

☐ The Seas with Nemo & Friends **AC**

☐ *The Circle of Life* **AC**

☐ *Honey, I Shrunk the Audience* **FP** **AC**

☐ Journey into Imagination with Figment **AC**

☐ Imageworks **AC**

WORLD SHOWCASE PAVILIONS & ATTRACTIONS

☐ (8) Agent P's World Showcase Adventure 🔲

☐ (9) Mexico Pavilion

☐ (10) Norway Pavilion

☐ (11) China Pavilion

☐ (12) *Reflections of China* **AC**

☐ (13) Germany Pavilion

☐ (14) Italy Pavilion

☐ (15) American Adventure Pavilion

☐ (16) *The American Adventure* **AC**

☐ (17) Japan Pavilion

☐ (18) Morocco Pavilion

☐ (19) France Pavilion

☐ (20) United Kingdom Pavilion

☐ (21) Canada Pavilion

Other Choices

☐ *Impressions de France* **AC**

☐ *O Canada!* **AC**

☐ *IllumiNations*

☐ Gran Fiesta Tour **AC**

☐ Maelstrom **FP** **AC**

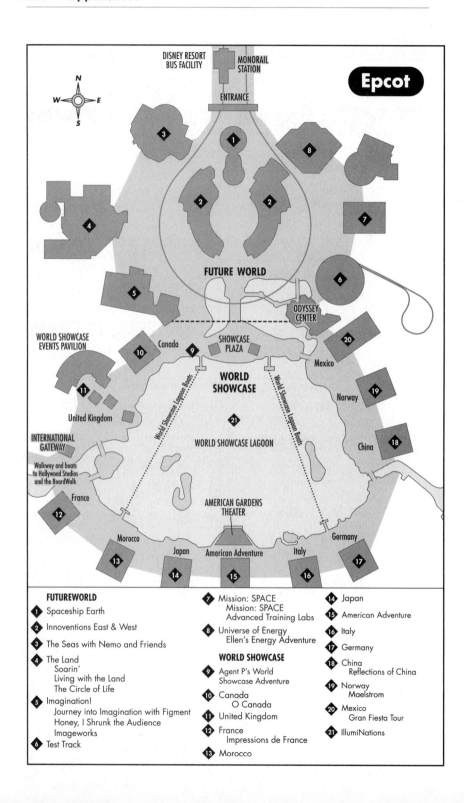

Epcot

DISNEY RESORT
BUS FACILITY

MONORAIL
STATION

ENTRANCE

N
W   E
S

FUTURE WORLD

ODYSSEY
CENTER

WORLD SHOWCASE
EVENTS PAVILION

Canada

SHOWCASE
PLAZA

Mexico

WORLD
SHOWCASE

Norway

World Showcase Lagoon Boats

World Showcase Lagoon Boats

United Kingdom

China

INTERNATIONAL
GATEWAY

WORLD SHOWCASE LAGOON

Walkway and boats
to Hollywood Studios
and the BoardWalk

France

AMERICAN GARDENS
THEATER

Morocco

Japan

American Adventure

Italy

Germany

FUTUREWORLD

1 Spaceship Earth

2 Innoventions East & West

3 The Seas with Nemo and Friends

4 The Land
Soarin'
Living with the Land
The Circle of Life

5 Imagination!
Journey into Imagination with Figment
Honey, I Shrunk the Audience
Imageworks

6 Test Track

7 Mission: SPACE
Mission: SPACE
Advanced Training Labs

8 Universe of Energy
Ellen's Energy Adventure

WORLD SHOWCASE

9 Agent P's World
Showcase Adventure

10 Canada
O Canada

11 United Kingdom

12 France
Impressions de France

13 Morocco

14 Japan

15 American Adventure

16 Italy

17 Germany

18 China
Reflections of China

19 Norway
Maelstrom

20 Mexico
Gran Fiesta Tour

21 IllumiNations

Hollywood Studios with Children Itinerary

☐ Pick up FASTPASS vouchers for any attraction that most appeals to you. Redeem them whenever they become valid, then seek out your next FASTPASS.

MICKEY AVENUE/ PIXAR PLACE

☐ (1) Toy Story Mania! **AC** **FP**

☐ (2) *Voyage of the Little Mermaid* **FP** **AC**

☐ (3) *Disney Junior—Live on Stage* **AC**

☐ (4) The Magic of Disney Imagination **AC**

Other Choices

☐ Hollywood Studios Backlot Tour

☐ The American Film Institute Showcase **AC**

☐ Walt Disney: One Man's Dream **AC**

STREETS OF AMERICA

☐ (5) *Lights, Motors, Action! Extreme Stunt Show* **FP**

☐ (6) *Jim Henson's Muppet Vision 3-D* **AC**

☐ (7) *Honey, I Shrunk the Kids* Movie Set Adventure

ECHO LAKE

☐ (8) *The American Idol Experience* **⚡** **AC**

VINE STREET

☐ (9) *Indiana Jones Epic Stunt Spectacular* **FP**

Other Choices

☐ Star Tours **FP** **AC** **👫** -40"

☐ *Sounds Dangerous—Starring Drew Carey* **AC** **oo**

HOLLYWOOD BOULEVARD

☐ (10) The Great Movie Ride **AC**

Other Choices

☐ *Pixar Pals Countdown to Fun*

SUNSET BOULEVARD

☐ (11) *Beauty and the Beast—Live on Stage*

Other Choices

☐ Rock 'n' Roller Coaster Starring Aerosmith **FP** **AC** **oo** **👫** -48"

☐ The Twilight Zone Tower of Terror **FP** **AC** **oo** **👫** -40"

☐ *Fantasmic!*

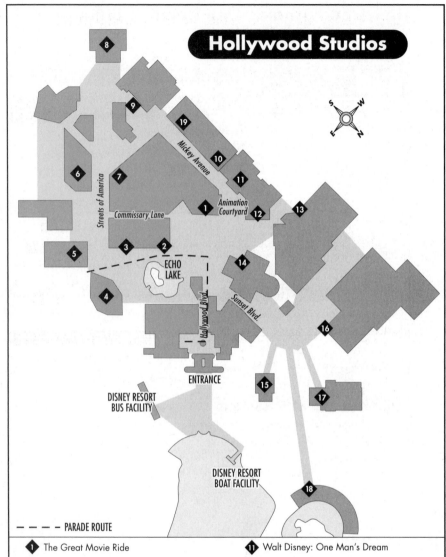

Hollywood Studios

— — — — **PARADE ROUTE**

1. The Great Movie Ride
2. American Idol Experience
3. Sounds Dangerous - Starring Drew Carey
4. Indiana Jones™ Epic Stunt Spectacular
5. Star Tours
6. Jim Henson's Muppet Vision 3-D
7. Honey, I Shrunk the Kids Movie Set Adventure
8. Lights, Motors, Action!™ Extreme Stunt Show
9. The Hollywood Studio Backlot Tour
10. Legend of Captain Jack Sparrow
11. Walt Disney: One Man's Dream
12. Voyage of The Little Mermaid
13. The Magic of Disney Animation
14. Disney Junior–Live on Stage!
15. Beauty and the Beast–Live on Stage
16. Rock 'n' Roller Coaster Starring Aerosmith
17. The Twilight Zone™ Tower of Terror
18. Fantasmic!
19. Toy Story Mania!

Hollywood Studios with Adults and Teens Itinerary

☐ Pick up FASTPASS vouchers for any attraction that most appeals to you. Redeem them whenever they become valid, then seek out your next FASTPASS.

SUNSET BOULEVARD

☐ (1) Rock 'n' Roller Coaster Starring Aerosmith **FP** **AC** **∞** **†** -48"

☐ (2) The Twilight Zone Tower of Terror **FP** **AC** **∞** **†** -40"

Other Choices

☐ Beauty and the Beast—Live on Stage

☐ Fantasmic!

HOLLYWOOD BOULEVARD

☐ (3) The Great Movie Ride **AC**

Other Choices

☐ Pixar Pals Countdown to Fun

VINE STREET

☐ (4) Indiana Jones Epic Stunt Spectacular **FP**

☐ (5) Star Tours **FP** **AC** **†** -40"

Other Choices

☐ Sounds Dangerous—Starring Drew Carey **AC** **∞**

STREETS OF AMERICA

☐ (6) Jim Henson's Muppet Vision 3-D **AC**

☐ (7) Lights, Motors, Action! Extreme Stunt Show **FP**

Other Choices

☐ Honey, I Shrunk the Kids Movie Set Adventure

MICKEY AVENUE/ PIXAR PLACE

☐ (8) Hollywood Studios Backlot Tour

☐ (9) The Magic of Disney Imagination **AC**

☐ (10) Toy Story Mania! **AC** **FP**

Other Choices

☐ Disney Junior—Live on Stage **AC**

☐ Voyage of the Little Mermaid **FP** **AC**

☐ The American Film Institute Showcase **AC**

☐ Walt Disney: One Man's Dream **AC**

ECHO LAKE

☐ (11) The American Idol Experience **◩** **AC**

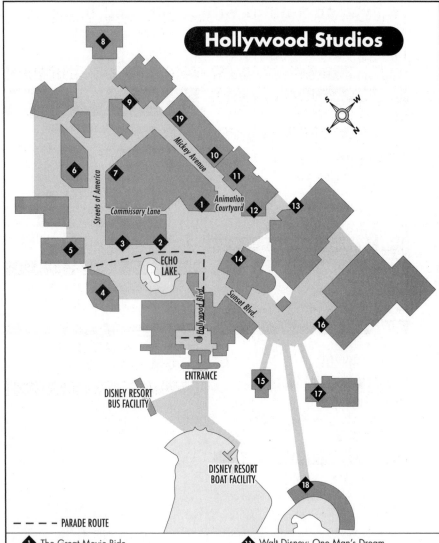

Hollywood Studios

— — — PARADE ROUTE

1. The Great Movie Ride
2. American Idol Experience
3. Sounds Dangerous - Starring Drew Carey
4. Indiana Jones™ Epic Stunt Spectacular
5. Star Tours
6. Jim Henson's Muppet Vision 3-D
7. Honey, I Shrunk the Kids Movie Set Adventure
8. Lights, Motors, Action!™ Extreme Stunt Show
9. The Hollywood Studio Backlot Tour
10. Legend of Captain Jack Sparrow
11. Walt Disney: One Man's Dream
12. Voyage of The Little Mermaid
13. The Magic of Disney Animation
14. Disney Junior–Live on Stage!
15. Beauty and the Beast–Live on Stage
16. Rock 'n' Roller Coaster Starring Aerosmith
17. The Twilight Zone™ Tower of Terror
18. Fantasmic!
19. Toy Story Mania!

Animal Kingdom with Children Itinerary

☐ Pick up FASTPASS vouchers for any attraction that most appeals to you. Redeem them whenever they become valid, then seek out your next FASTPASS.

☐ Pass through the Oasis and Discovery Island to Africa.

AFRICA

☐ (1) Kilimanjaro Safaris **FP**

☐ (2) Pangani Forest Exploration Trail

RAFIKI'S PLANET WATCH

Other Choices

☐ Wildlife Express Train

☐ Habitat Habit!

☐ Conservation Station **AC**

☐ Affection Section

CAMP MINNIE-MICKEY

☐ (3) *Festival of the Lion King* **AC**

☐ (4) Camp Minnie-Mickey Greeting Trails

DISCOVERY ISLAND

☐ (5) *It's Tough to Be a Bug!* **FP AC**

Other Choices

☐ Tree of Life

☐ Discovery Island Trails

☐ *Mickey's Jammin' Jungle Parade*

DINOLAND U.S.A.

☐ (6) The Boneyard

☐ (7) *Finding Nemo—The Musical* **AC**

Other Choices

☐ DINOSAUR **FP AC ∞ ⋔** -40"

☐ Dino-Sue

☐ TriceraTop Spin

☐ Primeval Whirl **FP ⋔** -48"

☐ Fossil Fun Games

☐ Cretaceous Trail

ASIA

☐ (8) *Flights of Wonder*

☐ (9) Maharajah Jungle Trek

Other Choices

☐ Kali River Rapids **FP ⋔** -38"

☐ Expedition Everest **FP ⋔** -44"

THE OASIS

☐ (10) The Oasis Paths

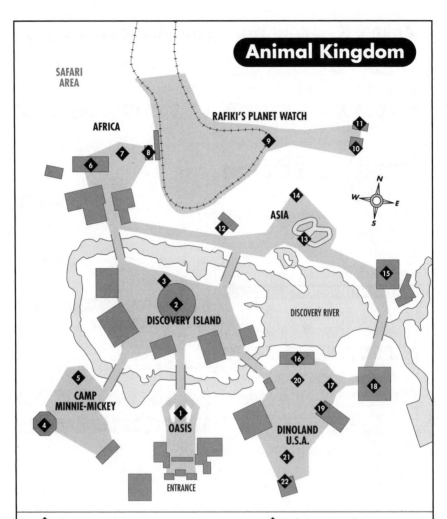

Animal Kingdom

SAFARI AREA

RAFIKI'S PLANET WATCH

AFRICA

ASIA

DISCOVERY ISLAND

DISCOVERY RIVER

CAMP MINNIE-MICKEY

OASIS

DINOLAND U.S.A.

ENTRANCE

1. The Oasis Exhibits
2. It's Tough to Be a Bug!
3. Discovery Island Trails
4. Festival of the Lion King
5. Greeting Trails
6. Kilimanjaro Safaris
7. Pangani Forest Exploration Trail
8. Wildlife Express Train
9. Habitat Habit!
10. Conservation Station
11. Affection Station
12. Flights of Wonder
13. Kali River Rapids
14. Maharajah Jungle Trek
15. Expedition Everest–Legend of the Forbidden Mountain
16. The Boneyard
17. Fossil Fun Games
18. Finding Nemo–The Musical
19. Primeval Whirl
20. TriceraTop Spin
21. Dino–Sue
22. DINOSAUR

Animal Kingdom with Adults and Teens Itinerary

☐ Pick up FASTPASS vouchers for any attraction that most appeals to you. Redeem them whenever they become valid, then seek out your next FASTPASS.

☐ Walk through the Oasis and Discovery Island to Asia.

ASIA

☐ (1) Expedition Everest **FP** -44"

☐ (2) Kali River Rapids **FP** **fi** -38"

☐ (3) Maharajah Jungle Trek

☐ (4) *Flights of Wonder*

AFRICA

☐ (5) Kilimanjaro Safaris **FP**

☐ (6) Pangani Forest Exploration Trail

RAFIKI'S PLANET WATCH

Other Choices

☐ Wildlife Express Train

☐ Habitat Habit!

☐ Conservation Station **AC**

☐ Affection Section

DISCOVERY ISLAND

☐ (7) *It's Tough to Be a Bug!* **FP** **AC**

Other Choices

☐ Tree of Life

☐ Discovery Island Trails

☐ *Mickey's Jammin' Jungle Parade*

CAMP MINNIE-MICKEY

☐ (8) *Festival of the Lion King* **AC**

Other Choices

☐ Camp Minnie-Mickey Greeting Trails

DINOLAND, U.S.A.

☐ (9) DINOSAUR **FP** **AC** **OO** **fi** -40"

☐ (10) Primeval Whirl **FP** **fi** -48"

☐ (11) *Finding Nemo—The Musical* **AC**

Other Choices

☐ Dino-Sue

☐ The Boneyard

☐ TriceraTop Spin

☐ Fossil Fun Games

☐ Cretaceous Trail

THE OASIS

☐ (12) The Oasis Paths

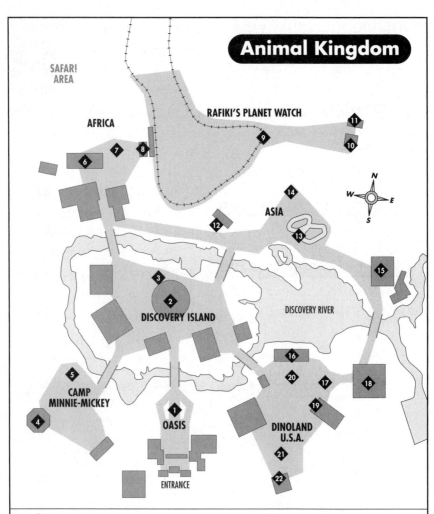

Animal Kingdom

SAFARI AREA

RAFIKI'S PLANET WATCH

AFRICA

ASIA

DISCOVERY ISLAND

DISCOVERY RIVER

CAMP MINNIE-MICKEY

OASIS

DINOLAND U.S.A.

ENTRANCE

1. The Oasis Exhibits
2. It's Tough to Be a Bug!
3. Discovery Island Trails
4. Festival of the Lion King
5. Greeting Trails
6. Kilimanjaro Safaris
7. Pangani Forest Exploration Trail
8. Wildlife Express Train
9. Habitat Habit!
10. Conservation Station
11. Affection Station
12. Flights of Wonder
13. Kali River Rapids
14. Maharajah Jungle Trek
15. Expedition Everest–Legend of the Forbidden Mountain
16. The Boneyard
17. Fossil Fun Games
18. Finding Nemo–The Musical
19. Primeval Whirl
20. TriceraTop Spin
21. Dino–Sue
22. DINOSAUR

Cards

Use these cards as you plan your vacation to Walt Disney World. You can record vital information, such as travel information, resort transportation options, meal-reservation confirmation numbers, and your daily schedule.

You will also want to put a check next to those attractions you want to visit and put an X next to the ones you want to avoid.

When you're done, simply cut them out and take them with you!

LEGEND

Must Do!	🗲
FASTPASS	**FP**
Air Conditioned Area	**AC**
Height Requirement	👪
Significant Darkness	👓

Phone Numbers

Advance Reservations: 1-407-WDW-DINE (1-407-939-3463)

Special Activities: 1-407-WDW-TOUR (1-407-939-8687)

Hotel Name: _____

Hotel Phone Number: _____

Meal Reservations

Restaurant:_____

Date: _____ Time: _____

Confirmation #:_____

Restaurant:_____

Date: _____ Time: _____

Confirmation #:_____

Restaurant:_____

Date: _____ Time: _____

Confirmation #:_____

Restaurant:_____

Date: _____ Time: _____

Confirmation #:_____

Restaurant:_____

Date: _____ Time: _____

Confirmation #:_____

Restaurant:_____

Date: _____ Time: _____

Confirmation #:_____

Daily Schedule

Write down what park or restaurant you will be visiting.

	Day 1	Day 2	Day 3	Day 4	Day 5	Day 6	Day 7
Breakfast Time Confirm. # **Morning** Park/ Activity							
Lunch Time Confirm. # **Afternoon** Park/ Activity							
Dinner Time Confirm. # **Evening** Park/ Activity							

Park/Extra Magic Hours

Write down the opening and closing times of each park and circle whether the park has morning or afternoon Extra Magic Hours.

Magic Kingdom Extra Magic Hours?	- A.M. / P.M.	- A.M. / P.M.	- A.M. / P.M.	- A.M. / P.M.	- A.M. / P.M.	- A.M. / P.M.	- A.M. / P.M.
Epcot Extra Magic Hours?	- A.M. / P.M.	- A.M. / P.M.	- A.M. / P.M.	- A.M. / P.M.	- A.M. / P.M.	- A.M. / P.M.	- A.M. / P.M.
Hollywood Studios Extra Magic Hours?	- A.M. / P.M.	- A.M. / P.M.	- A.M. / P.M.	- A.M. / P.M.	- A.M. / P.M.	- A.M. / P.M.	- A.M. / P.M.
Animal Kingdom Extra Magic Hours?	- A.M. / P.M.	- A.M. / P.M.	- A.M. / P.M.	- A.M. / P.M.	- A.M. / P.M.	- A.M. / P.M.	- A.M. / P.M.

Magic Kingdom
MAIN STREET, U.S.A.

- [ ] Main Street Vehicles
- [ ] *SpectroMagic Parade*
- [ ] *Wishes Nighttime Spectacular*
- [ ] Walt Disney World Railroad
- [ ] *Share a Dream Come True Parade*

Magic Kingdom
FANTASYLAND

- [ ] Cinderella Castle 🗲
- [ ] *Dream Along with Mickey*
- [ ] Mad Tea Party
- [ ] Adventures of Winnie the Pooh **FP AC ∞**
- [ ] The Barnstormer 📏 -35"

Magic Kingdom
ADVENTURELAND

- [ ] Pirates of the Caribbean **AC**
- [ ] The Magic Carpets of Aladdin
- [ ] *The Enchanted Tiki Room* **AC ∞**
- [ ] Jungle Cruise **FP**
- [ ] Swiss Family Treehouse

Magic Kingdom
FRONTIERLAND

- [ ] Big Thunder Mountain Railroad **FP** 📏 -40"
- [ ] Splash Mountain **FP** 📏 -40"
- [ ] *Country Bear Jamboree* **AC**
- [ ] Frontierland Shootin' Arcade
- [ ] Tom Sawyer Island

Epcot
FUTURE WORLD

- [ ] Spaceship Earth **AC ∞**
- [ ] Innoventions **AC**
- [ ] Ellen's Energy Adventure **AC**
- [ ] Mission: SPACE 🗲 **FP AC** 📏 -44"
- [ ] Mission: SPACE Advanced Training Labs **AC**
- [ ] Test Track 🗲 **FP AC** 📏 -40"

Epcot
FUTURE WORLD

- [ ] The Seas with Nemo & Friends **AC**
- [ ] The Seas with Nemo & Friends Pavilion **AC**
- [ ] *Turtle Talk with Crush* 🗲 **AC**
- [ ] Soarin' 🗲 **FP AC** 📏 -40"
- [ ] Living with the Land **FP AC**
- [ ] *The Circle of Life* **AC**
- [ ] *Honey, I Shrunk the Audience* **FP AC**
- [ ] Journey into Imagination with Figment **AC**
- [ ] ImageWorks **AC**

Magic Kingdom
FANTASYLAND

- [ ] "it's a small world" 🖊 AC
- [ ] Dumbo the Flying Elephant
- [ ] Prince Charming Regal Carrousel
- [ ] *Mickey's PhilharMagic* 🖊 FP AC
- [ ] Peter Pan's Flight 🖊 FP AC ∞

Magic Kingdom
LIBERTY SQUARE

- [ ] Liberty Square Riverboat
- [ ] *The Hall of Presidents* AC
- [ ] The Haunted Mansion FP AC

Magic Kingdom
TOMORROWLAND

- [ ] Tomorrowland Speedway 🚻-52"
- [ ] Stitch's Great Escape! FP AC ∞ 🖊 -40"
- [ ] Space Mountain 🖊 FP AC ∞ 🖊 -44"
- [ ] B. Lightyear's Space Ranger Spin 🖊 FP AC
- [ ] TTA People Mover
- [ ] Astro Orbiter
- [ ] Walt Disney's Carousel of Progress AC
- [ ] *Monsters, Inc. Comedy Club* AC

Magic Kingdom
TOURING NOTES

_____

_____

_____

_____

_____

_____

_____

Epcot
WORLD SHOWCASE

- [ ] Mexico Pavilion
- [ ] Gran Fiesta Tour AC
- [ ] Norway Pavilion
- [ ] Maelstrom FP AC
- [ ] China Pavilion
- [ ] *Reflections of China* AC
- [ ] Germany Pavilion
- [ ] Italy Pavilion
- [ ] American Adventure Pavilion
- [ ] *The American Adventure* 🖊 AC

Epcot
WORLD SHOWCASE

- [ ] Japan Pavilion
- [ ] Morocco Pavilion
- [ ] France Pavilion
- [ ] *Impressions de France* AC
- [ ] United Kingdom Pavilion
- [ ] Canada Pavilion
- [ ] *O Canada!* AC
- [ ] *IllumiNations* 🖊
- [ ] KidCot Fun Stops
- [ ] Agent P's World Showcase Adventure 🖊

Hollywood Studios

HOLLYWOOD BOULEVARD

- [ ] The Great Movie Ride 🎬 **AC**
- [ ] *Pixar Pals Countdown to Fun*

VINE STREET

- [ ] *Indiana Jones Epic Stunt Spectacular* 🎬 **FP**
- [ ] Star Tours 🎬 **FP AC** 🛗 -40"
- [ ] *Sounds Dangerous* **AC** ∞

Hollywood Studios

STREETS OF AMERICA

- [ ] *Jim Henson's Muppet Vision 3-D* **AC**
- [ ] *Honey, I Shrunk the Kids* Set Adventure
- [ ] *Lights, Motors, Action! Stunt Show* 🎬 **FP**

ECHO LAKE

- [ ] *The American Idol Experience* 🎬 **AC**

Animal Kingdom

THE OASIS

- [ ] The Oasis Exhibits

DISCOVERY ISLAND

- [ ] Tree of Life
- [ ] *It's Tough to Be a Bug!* 🎬 **FP AC**
- [ ] Discovery Island Trails
- [ ] *Mickey's Jammin' Jungle Parade*

Animal Kingdom

CAMP MINNIE-MICKEY

- [ ] *Festival of the Lion King* 🎬 **AC**
- [ ] Camp Minnie-Mickey Greeting Trails

RAFIKI'S PLANET WATCH

- [ ] Wildlife Express Train
- [ ] Habitat Habit!
- [ ] Conservation Station **AC**
- [ ] Affection Section

LOST CHILD

My Name is: _____

My Parents are: _____

My Hotel: _____

My Phone: _____

LOST CHILD

My Name is: _____

My Parents are: _____

My Hotel: _____

My Phone: _____

Hollywood Studios

MICKEY AVENUE/ PIXAR PLACE

- [ ] *Disney Junior—Live on Stage* `AC`
- [ ] *Voyage of the Little Mermaid* `FP` `AC`
- [ ] Hollywood Studios Backlot Tour
- [ ] The American Film Institute Showcase `AC`
- [ ] The Magic of Disney Imagination `AC`
- [ ] Walt Disney: One Man's Dream `AC`
- [ ] Toy Story Mania! `AC` `FP`

Hollywood Studios

SUNSET BOULEVARD

- [ ] Rock 'n' Roller Coaster Starring Aerosmith `FP` `AC` `OO` -48"
- [ ] The Twilight Zone Tower of Terror `FP` `AC` `OO` -40"
- [ ] *Beauty and the Beast—Live on Stage*
- [ ] *Fantasmic!*

Animal Kingdom

AFRICA

- [ ] Kilimanjaro Safaris `FP`
- [ ] Pangani Forest Exploration Trail

ASIA

- [ ] Maharajah Jungle Trek
- [ ] *Flights of Wonder*
- [ ] Kali River Rapids `FP` -38"
- [ ] Expedition Everest `FP` -44"

Animal Kingdom

DINOLAND U.S.A.

- [ ] DINOSAUR `FP` `AC` `OO` -40"
- [ ] Dino-Sue
- [ ] The Boneyard
- [ ] *Finding Nemo—The Musical* `AC`
- [ ] TriceraTop Spin
- [ ] Primeval Whirl `FP` -48"
- [ ] Fossil Fun Games
- [ ] Cretaceous Trail

LOST CHILD

Can you please help me? I have been separated from my parents. Please contact a Disney Cast Member and ask them to contact my parents. My hotel and phone number are on the other side of this card.

Thank you!

LOST CHILD

Can you please help me? I have been separated from my parents. Please contact a Disney Cast Member and ask them to contact my parents. My hotel and phone number are on the other side of this card.

Thank you!

Walt Disney World Resort Accomodations

Deluxe Resorts

Guest room at Disney's Contemporary Resort.
Photo © Disney.

Guest room at Disney's Polynesian Resort.
Photo © Disney.

Deluxe Villas

Living room and kitchenette in guest room at Saratoga Springs Resort.
Photo © Disney.

Treehouse Villa at Saratoga Springs Resort.
Photo © Disney.

Moderate Resorts

Guest room at Disney's Port Orleans Resort.
Photo © Disney.

Pirate-themed guest room at Disney's Caribbean Beach Resort.
Photo © Disney.

Value Resorts

A Value Resort guest room.
Photo © Disney.

The living room of Value Resort Family Suite.
Photo © Disney.

Cabins

Bedroom of Wilderness Cabins at Fort Wilderness.
Photo © Disney.

Kitchen and living room of Wilderness Cabins at Fort Wilderness.
Photo © Disney.

Index

L

M

Q

quick service dining plan, 125-126
Quicksilver Tours, 25

R

Rafiki's Planet Watch
  Affection Section, 306
  Animal Kingdom, 304
  Conservation Station, 305
  Habitat Habit!, 305
  Wildlife Express Train, 305
Raglan Road Irish Pub and
  Restaurant, 195
rainfall, 5-7
Rainforest Café, 186, 196
rate seasons, 6, 60-61
Reflections of China, 264
rental cars, 25
reservations
  contact information, 10
  dining, 122-124
  what to buy, 12
  where to buy, 10-12
resorts
  deluxe resorts, 67-82
  deluxe villa resorts, 100-107
  dining options, 137
  Disney rooms, 63
  Disney Vacation Club, 66
  Hilton Orlando Bonnet Creek,
    115-116
  hotel comparison chart, 63
  Hotel Plaza Boulevard, 109-112
  moderate resorts, 83-90
  on property hotels, 53-63
  rates, 6
  Shades of Green, 116
  value resorts, 91, 93-97

Waldorf Astoria Orlando,
    114-115
  Walt Disney World Dolphin,
    112-113
  Walt Disney World Swan,
    113-114
Restaurant Akershus, 170
Restaurant Marrakesh, 174
Restaurantosaurus, 189
Rider Switch pass (FASTPASS
  ticket system), 208-209
rides
  Animal Kingdom, 303-310
  Blizzard Beach, 322-323
  Epcot, 251-258, 263
  Hollywood Studios, 277-280,
    283-284, 289-290
  Magic Kingdom, 218-220,
    225-228, 231, 233-239
  Typhoon Lagoon, 319-320
River Roost Lounge, 48
Rock 'n' Roller Coaster Starring
  Aerosmith, 289
romantic dinner locations, 48
rooms, deluxe resorts, 68
Rose & Crown Dining Room, 176
Royal Plaza, 111
rules, reservations, 123
Runoff Rapids, 323

S

San Angel Inn, 177
Sanaa, 140
Saratoga Springs Resort, dining
  options, 157-158
Saratoga Springs Resort & Spa,
  105-106
Sci-Fi Dine-In Theater, 184
Scootarama, 212

Y-Z

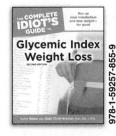
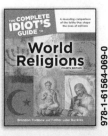

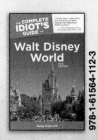